Advance Praise

"In *The Parts of Him I Kept*, Natasha Williams crafts a lyrical and deeply moving memoir about love, loss, and resilience in the face of her father's schizophrenia. Through tender prose and raw honesty, Williams explores the enduring bonds that tether us, even amid chaos and ultimately healing."

— Jai Chakrabarti, author of *A Small Sacrifice for an Enormous Happiness*

"Natasha Williams has written an extraordinary memoir of growing up with a schizophrenic father and frequently dysfunctional mother. It is as emotionally wrenching (and occasionally terrifying) as you would expect, but it is also funny, wise, beautifully observed and astonishingly tender."

— James Lasdun, author of *Afternoon of a Faun, Victory*, and other titles

"'Is there a word for what gets said without language, how we carry the weight of the lives that come before us?' This is one of the questions of this profound meditation on love and family. Natasha Williams offers us a portrait of America at a time when everything was in flux, when people searched for new ways to live, and (if they were lucky) ended up simply loving each other."

— Nick Flynn, author of *This Is the Night Our House Will Catch Fire, Low* and *Another Bullshit Night in Suck City*

"Read the first thirty pages of *The Parts of Him I Kept*, and I bet you would cancel your own wedding to read the rest of it. Natasha Williams has a hell of a story to tell, and she writes like an angel."

— Abigail Thomas, author of *Still Life at Eighty*

"What elevates *The Parts of Him I Kept* to a timeless memoir is William's ability to draw the reader into the vivid and lyrically rendered world of a father and daughter's deep, abiding love for each other despite her father's schizophrenia. She takes us on a journey that is poignant, hilarious, and yes, at times dangerous, even deadly. But in the end, Williams asks us to rethink the limit of what love can endure."

— Daisy Foote, author of *Bhutan* and *Horton Foote: The Road to Home*

"This book is somehow heart-breaking and funny at the same time. It's stunning and frightening and yet strangely uplifting when you realize just how much strength and courage it took to write it. I could not put this book down once I started it, and I know it will stay with me for the rest of my life."

— Steve Hamilton, two-time Edgar Award-winning, *New York Times* bestselling author of *An Honorable Assassin*

"A gifted work of graceful eloquence, this memoir is an homage to the universal power of tenderness."

— Lisa St. John, author of *Swallowing Stones*

"Natasha Williams achingly exquisite memoir takes us on a journey through complex trauma and unexpected tenderness, illuminating her path of self-discovery and providing real hope for those who long to heal."

— John Sibley Williams, winner of the Cider Press Review Poetry Award for *Scale Model of a Country at Dawn*

"In *The Parts of Him I Kept*, Natasha Williams balances compassion for her charismatic, schizophrenic father, and her own need for boundaries with a man who thought he could read minds. What is remarkable about the author's vivid, elegantly crafted prose, is that even at her father's most heinous moments, Williams never tips into pity—for him or for herself."

— Tina Barry, author of *I Tell Henrietta*

"With tenderness and understanding, Williams manages to retrieve what love she shared with her deeply disturbed father to create a riveting book."

— Laura Shaine Cunningham, author of *Sleeping Arrangements*

"This memoir is a testament to the strength of the human spirit, capturing the struggles, complexities, and transformative moments of living in a family deeply affected by mental illness."

— Emily Metheny

The Parts of Him I Kept

The Parts of Him I Kept

The Gifts of My Father's Madness

Natasha Williams

Apprentice House Press
Loyola University Maryland

Copyright © 2025 by Natasha Williams

All rights reserved. No part of this book may be reproduced or transmitted in any form or by any means, electronic or mechanical, including photocopy, recording, or any information storage and retrieval system, without prior permission from the publisher (except by reviewers who may quote brief passages).

First Edition

Casebound ISBN: 978-1-62720-599-3
Paperback ISBN: 978-1-62720-597-9
Ebook ISBN: 978-1-62720-601-3

Library of Congress Control Number: 2025932636

Cover Art by Christoph Hitz
Author Photo by Jim Smith
Interior Design by Molly Clement
Editorial Development by Natalie Misyak
Promotional Development by Emily Metheny

Published by Apprentice House Press

Loyola University Maryland
4501 N. Charles Street, Baltimore, MD 21210
410.617.5265
www.ApprenticeHouse.com
Info@ApprenticeHouse.com

Credits

Excerpted versions of chapters have appeared in the following publications:

FRAGMENTED WORLDS, *Post Road Magazine*, Spring 2023, Vol. 41

DROWNING, *South Dakota Review*, 2023/2024 Vol. 57 #4

A LOVE SUPREME, *LIT Magazine*, Issue 35, Fall 2023

OUR IMPERFECT WORLD, *Open Minds*, Issue 35, Fall 2023

WHY I BRING THEM, *Bread Loaf Journal*, Vol. VIII

CALMING THE BEAST, *Change Seven*, Oct. 2022

Dedication

This book is dedicated to my father who maintained the best sense of humor despite unspeakable loss. To my husband, who is funny in the morning and the most generous man I know. And to our daughters, Cora and Cali, who posed the questions I hadn't dared to ask and who are everything to me.

I wrote this memoir as a testament to my father's life but I've come to understand that our story is one of many needed to fill in the archives of lives lived on the margins; to make visible the heroic effort it takes to live with mental illness and to care for family members who do.

In honor of those living with mental illness, I will donate 20% of profits annually from the sale of this book to The Ride for Mental Health, one of the first rides in the country to benefit McLean Hospitals' research and treatment of mental illness. And to Family of Woodstock which provides shelters, court advocates, counseling and case management services for Ulster County's after hours Mental Health and Social Services.

What Binds Us—

And when two people have loved each other
see how it is like a
scar between their bodies,
stronger, darker, and proud;
how the black cord makes of them a single fabric
that nothing can tear or mend-

—Jane Hirshfield, *Of Gravity & Angels*

Author's Note: *As a memoir that spans a lifetime and includes memories from three generations of family, I want to acknowledge that the dialogue with quotations are not verbatim but rather my best attempt to capture the memories and voice of the members of our family. Everything that happens in this writing is true to my memory and much of it has been vetted with family members- that said, at times I have represented an amalgam of a character or a scene out of time when it made more sense to the story.*

PREFACE

I have a picture from *Life Magazine* of a young man at Pilgrim State Hospital, where my father was frequently committed. The man looks very much like Dad: young, dark-haired, trapped. His hands are strapped around his waist, and he looks directly into the camera with a defiant stare that says, *I dare you to look.*

My father, Francis, had his first breakdown on the day of his college graduation. He was diagnosed with paranoid schizophrenia long before he met my mother, nearly ten years before I was conceived. It turns out she had a predilection for insane men. His first hospitalization was one of a lifetime of civil commitments, the term still used for hospitalizing a person against their will. As a child, I would try to convince my father to go voluntarily because I knew he would be let out sooner; he once took this as a sign that I was in cahoots with the devil. That was the last time I tried that.

Mental health care in the United States in the early 1960s, when my father was first hospitalized, ran the gamut of physical restraints, insulin shock, electroconvulsive therapy, lobotomies, and, finally, psychotropic medication. What that care never offered was a comprehensive approach to the social isolation regularly shouldered by the mentally ill and their families. It also failed to recognize the far-reaching nature of many schizophrenic delusions and insights—the significance of feeling called by God. So much about life with my father was like an unheard prayer: imagining a higher purpose, listening for voices that promised he was the Messiah but repeatedly failed to deliver the apostles.

I thought of my father when the New York Mental Hygiene Law was recently enacted in New York City. The bill allows the police to commit people for emergency assessment if they appear mentally ill, or display an inability to meet basic living needs, or are thought to be a harm to themselves or others. So much ambiguity, so much need. I pictured Dad when he was on a mission from God. His long wool coat open, flapping like a cape, as he marched down 6th Avenue to see the children in the playground. Sitting on a bench with fall leaves spiraling to the ground, listening to the children play. "It's as close as you can get to God," he would tell the officer before being asked to leave, a vagrant who made mothers uncomfortable. If then were now and the officer decided to get him off the street and mandate psychiatric care, would they have called us before they sent him to the hospital? When they asked if he had family, would he have told them *my grandmother was under the influence of the devil but they could telephone her if they wanted to*? He had our number; many mentally ill people lose contact with family.

When Dad returned to us manic from roaming the streets or overmedicated after being hospitalized, the forever question was how to protect him? When you have a loved one with mental illness, you're perpetually on the seesaw of caring for them or knowing they need more care than you can give. The support of social services was like hurricane relief after countless storms. If my father were still alive, if I didn't know where he was, if he were roaming the cold city streets in need of psychiatric care, I might be grateful for an imperfect law in our imperfect world.

In the midst of today's unprecedented mental health crisis, *The Parts of Him I Kept* is the story of the burden and privilege of caring for those who fall far from the tree. It offers another outlook on our humanity, a record of lives lived on the margins. This is one family's story that explores the limits of our medical and cultural understanding of schizophrenia, and illuminates how families find hope, and even thrive in the face of the extraordinary challenge of mental illness.

Part 1

UNDERTOW

1986

My father, Francis, took his two-year-old daughter, a half sister I barely knew, for a drive to the piers overlooking the bay of Stapleton, Staten Island. The quiet island harbor was just two blocks from where I grew up, with a clear view of the Twin Towers rising up from the tip of Lower Manhattan like beacons of civilization. I'd been gone for years, even though I was only twenty-one, trying to find my own way as far as possible from the chaos of my father's life.

"She wouldn't go to sleep, so I drove her around in the car and then headed out to the piers to see the city lights while Jackie finally slept," he told me later, desperate to explain. He told me he didn't see the yellow caution tape that warned the pier had been demolished—although later, he would claim there was none. With reflexes made slow by years of medication for his schizophrenia, he didn't brake in time, and the car plunged into the freezing cold New York Bay with Jackie in the back seat.

They sank devastatingly fast. Somehow my father managed to get out through the driver's side window. He swam up to breathe but couldn't get his buoyant body back down to reach Jackie. She was fighting for air, trapped in the car in the freezing water.

In the news report of the accident, witnesses said he smashed through the driver's window to escape. This is virtually impossible, but my father was uncommonly strong. They said he repeatedly tried to reach her. I cried when I read that. Once the emergency workers arrived, they pulled my father from the frigid bay. I imagine they would have needed hoists to get his three-hundred-pound body out and over the breakwater. Critically hypothermic, he was taken to the hospital while divers continued their attempts to retrieve Jackie. They found her body floating face down in the darkened car. I can picture her: thin hair looking airborne in the water, her back against the car's roof. She had been underwater for forty minutes.

Preserved by the cold, she was miraculously resuscitated. The *Daily News* front page read: *Back from a Watery Grave*. "It's like she was brought back from the dead," one of the EMTs was cited as saying. Her brain and vital systems had been suspended by the cold. It seemed impossible but she wasn't the first or the last to come back from death. The BBC reported on a group of Danish students also "temporarily" drowned in the Praesto Fjord. By the time the paramedics got there, two hours later, the students were pronounced dead. But cold can suspend life and put the body into metabolic slow motion, taking the moment of death and "smearing it out." Machines were used to circulate the blood and slowly increase their body temperature. Six hours after the incident, all seven teenagers had come back to life. Similarly preserved by the cold water, Jackie was alive when she reached the hospital, but her prognosis remained to be seen.

A friend of the family who still lived on Staten Island called to tell me. I was living in the Berkshires at the time, training to be a masseuse. My journals that year toggle between prayer-like efforts at self-discovery and a record of my dreams. In my journal there's no mention of the accident.

I called the hospital, stepping reluctantly into the role of my father's closest relative, the only adult child he was in contact with. He answered the phone in slow motion, like he was still underwater. "He-l-lo?"

"Dad, it's Tash. What happened? They said you tried to kill yourself."

"That's ridiculous. I tried to get to her, Tash, but... I just couldn't." He paused, as if reliving his failed attempts. "Have you seen the papers? I look like a bum," he said of the front-page story. "But she's alive. It's a miracle, baby! You gotta come get me." By this point, they knew Jackie had significant brain damage and would remain in intensive care.

When I arrived to take Dad home, there was a throng of reporters at the main entrance who bombarded him with questions.

"Mr. Williams, can you tell us why you drove off the pier?"

"Is it true you wanted to take your own life?"

We held our heads down as we made our way to the car. I kept my eyes to the ground to hide my shame in a father made notorious for *not* saving his baby girl. Mostly, though, I wanted to avoid their questions and keep under wraps my identity as the half sister who believed Jackie would be better off dead than alive.

"Why did you bring your daughter in the car with you?" they asked, microphones extended, swarming with a reckless appetite for a story.

"Mr. Williams, what do you have to say?" they demanded.

He said nothing. If they had known him, they would have known better than to expect answers from a man who never had them, a man whose silence was like an invocation.

* * *

When we got to their dirty, smoke-filled Staten Island home, Jackie's mother, Barbara, was sitting in the dark, an overfull ashtray next to her seat. She met my father at Pilgrim State Psychiatric Hospital when I was ten years old, both of them diagnosed with schizophrenia. My father's Messiah complex, and his profound ability to make you feel seen, made him a charismatic figure in their group therapy and Barbara was an enthusiastic believer. She suffered a particularly feminine manifestation of schizophrenia called a Mary Magdalene complex. Even as a child, I understood this was a match made in heaven. They were the love of each other's lives, but their life together had been hard. This wasn't the first child they had lost. I wondered if she had been to the hospital to see her baby since they had no car and she had no license. I didn't ask.

She sat smoking and talking as if Jackie were in the room. "You're going to be all right, my little angel. God is watching over you, and everything is going to be fine. Isn't that right, Frankie?" she pleaded, looking to him for reassurance.

My father looked up at her from the old armchair across the room where he sat in wordless agony, his head in his hands. I was used to the way he couldn't say what was on his mind. The unspoken inheritance of the child of a schizophrenic is a story without words, a world without boundaries, a fable without a moral.

It was all too much, this dark room with no air to breathe. I had to get out, away from the undertow of his life, away from the father who couldn't safeguard his daughter, away from the feeling my father was an anchor pulling me down. I never went to see Jackie.

JELLYFISH BEACH

1972

There was a time my father cleared the ocean of jellyfish for me. Jones Beach was our favorite place when I was a child. I remember one particular day, when I was seven years old, the tide was just right for hundreds of jellyfish to drift toward land. They floated thick in the water, consorting at the shore, amorphous spheres with feelers that stung to the touch. Viscous bodies were scattered on the sand by retreating waves, their tentacles still dangerous, naked and vulnerable to the sun, like insides laid bare.

"Dad, what can we do?" I asked, looking at the jellyfish littering the beach. It was captivating to see nature out of balance, the way it exposes the instinct to survive, a drive made grotesquely beautiful in its physicality. I felt that way—my drive to survive had a ruthless quality that only my father understood in me.

Undeterred by the stinging jellies, Dad marched to the shoreline and swiped at his thick dark hair. "Come on, I'll protect you," he promised, holding his arms out. At five foot eleven and 180 pounds, Dad could easily lift my undersized frame past the smack of jellyfish into the deeper swells.

"But they'll sting us. Look at them all! We have to clear out an area to swim."

Dad looked at the horizon, as if contemplating a Zeus-like effort, where he opens the sea with his mind. My father was primordial; something brewing inside him might come to life, if you didn't mind waiting—but we didn't have time for his big ideas.

"We'll bury them in holes!" I directed, pulling on his hand to look for a stick. Galvanized by my call for action, he smiled, swiped his hair again and an unspoken plan was hatched. He found a stick and headed to the water. I dug the first hole in the sand with driftwood while he pulled the transparent moon disks out of the ocean and dragged them blindly, his wet hair in his eyes, along the sand to where I was hunched digging. Like a dog flicking sand out of a hole, I dug a deep grave, and Dad dropped the jelly into its sandy dark burial ground. I had the thought that I should kill it rather than burying it alive. I decided to pulverize its body with the stick. I was powerful as I smashed its perfect roundness into something resembling sandy brains. I covered the creature with sand and marked the grave while Dad stood and watched. Then, on to the next. Two older ladies walked past, as my father dragged our next victim to shore. They looked at Dad fishing the jellies out of the water. They stopped talking, paused, and looked up at me on the beach, then looked down. I was used to people minding their own business and I was glad for it, but also, we seemed invisible, as if our life was of no consequence to anyone but us.

It was afternoon and the sun burned my shoulders, but my hot face felt important. Dad's hair was wet and his head glistened with sweat. I dug another pit and watched as my father dragged multiple stinging jellies for me to mutilate like a ritual sacrifice. It was a sort of carnage, but my father's calm participation made it feel like we were making things right. Together we were ridding the world of one of God's mistakes.

It did seem like God made mistakes.

After we killed maybe twenty jellyfish—each creature covered with sand, marked with an X so we could identify the grave—we found relief from the heat, dipping calmly in the roiling waves. I bobbed up and down in Dad's arms, in the ocean's push and pull.

If my mother had been there, she would have told me to figure it out, or she might have taken pictures of me while I slaughtered the animals. But she wasn't there. She wasn't one to stick by family and she had no interest in my father anymore. Although there was no one to document my childhood alone with my father, no iconic pictures of a father and daughter at the beach, I remember him holding me securely above the undercurrent.

We lay on the beach till our skin burned red and the sun started to set. "Can we eat?" I asked, and we gathered up our towels. I followed his steady step through the sand and over the burning pavement. Dad's sandals slapped like fins out of water, and I leaned into his hand to keep up. Our steps cut a consistent, comforting rhythm: *flap, flap,* and my catch-up *skip*, as if together we made a heartbeat.

A MOTHER'S LOVE

1968

I have an eight-by-ten black and white photo on my dresser of my mother and me together. I am three years old; my young mother is bent on her knees holding me to her. Her long, straight brown hair and horn-rimmed glasses highlight her smile, as if she loved being a mother. I look content in her arms.

I don't have memories of the three years my parents were together except ones imagined from the few pictures we saved—pictures preserved by my grandmother when my mother, done being a photographer, threw out all the photos she took of my childhood. In one image, I'm a toddler standing with bare legs in a diaper, wearing only a shirt vest, with arms outstretched facing my father, who is gazing at me, as if I held the key to something he was searching for. I'm looking wistfully from large wet eyes that appear to have been crying at the figure behind the camera, as if it is my mother I want.

Instead of nurturing, my mother was fiercely independent. She let go of relationships like she discarded the archives of our childhood. As an adult, I would mine for her memories. Her usual response: "I don't know if I can give you what you want, but you can ask."

"What made you break up with Frank?"

"I decided it was over on my birthday."

He had been out all day, she told me, and she had been left to care for a two-year-old toddler she hadn't wanted in the first place.

Despite all his promises that this would be the best thing that ever happened to them, he had no idea what it took to parent a child, and she was ready to give him a piece of her mind.

When he pulled up outside their Lower East Side tenement, she ran out to the hall to confront him. She raged at him from the apartment door as he climbed up the five flights of stairs.

"You haven't even wished me happy birthday, Frank! I can't do this anymore. We're done! You need to move out!" she screamed at him as he reached the door, unaware he had spent the day searching for a ring imbued with magical powers. He handed her the jewelry box when he reached the landing.

"Happy Birthday, Judith. A token of love. I spent the day commandeering for you, my dear," he said theatrically. Inside the box was an impressive Mexican turquoise ring with inlaid coral and onyx. The thoughtfulness of the gift brought her eyes to his, in search of forgiveness and even the love she had been ready to throw away minutes before.

The gift was "perfect" for her, she exclaimed and went on about how their neighbors were going to New Mexico and when would they be able to take that trip he was always promising would change their life? She said nothing more about his leaving and felt badly that she hadn't realized how much he did care for her after all.

But the reconciliation didn't last long. She wanted to join a couples encounter group; he refused. She went anyway and came home with the realization that he would never have the capacity to share his feelings, might not even fully comprehend them himself. She went straight to find him in the bedroom. Standing rigid by the bed, her stomach anxious with her revelation, she blurted out, "I don't want to be in this relationship anymore, Frank. I don't think we are going to make this work."

To her surprise, he didn't put up a fight. "Okay, if that's what you want," he said and left. I can imagine, in the face of her hard certainty, it seemed better to give up than to battle.

* * *

That summer, Mom and I lived in the upstairs apartment of a twin house in New Dorp, Staten Island. Our brown-carpeted living room was heavy with her cigarette smoke and disillusion.

She was twenty-eight, and I was a precocious three-year-old to whom my mother gave free rein. During the week, she ran a preschool program, which I attended. Weekends, she was possessed by sleep as if by one of the Fates attempting to knit a link between her circumstances and the fairy tale my father had promised. Mainly, I remember her sleeping on a mattress on the floor of her bedroom.

Years later, my mother and I found a picture taken in that apartment. I'm standing at a low-lying shelf with a guinea pig in a cage. My hair is uncombed, the tangles backlit like a beehive. My mouth is open, and my hands are animated by a conversation lost on film.

"Do you remember the time you went to get food for the guinea pig while I was asleep?" my mother asked. "You were only three but you were independent even then. You went downstairs and down the block to the local market where they knew us to ask for discarded lettuce. I woke up and didn't know where you were. I panicked and ran down the block and found you at the market. I yelled at you for not telling me when you left."

She wished she hadn't yelled—not that she would have stopped me if I had asked.

A LOVE SUPREME

1972

Once my mother figured out that living with a schizophrenic wasn't as interesting as she expected, she left me—from the age of six—to navigate weekends with him unsupervised. It was a particularly Montessori approach to parenting on her part; only I knew how, and if, I wanted to spend time with my father. Dad, on the other hand, was more of a traditionalist. When he was sane, he regularly drove across the Verrazano Bridge to bring me home for the weekend. With delusions of being the Messiah, he felt a duty of noblesse oblige to sire children and found purpose in his role as father.

The trip was an adventure, surrounded by other commuters headed home or to the beach for the weekend, part of that great exodus from the boroughs to Long Island. "Everyone and their mother are on the expressway tonight," I said triumphantly, always happy to be with him even in dense weekend traffic, our windows open to the smell of the ocean and car exhaust.

"Yeah, baby," he said and smiled, his dark blue eyes shining.

We were headed to Hempstead, Long Island, to the house where my father grew up. A quiet, working-class neighborhood where newspapers were tossed on the driveway and stray grass grew long in the uneven sidewalk. It was a small white Cape-style four-bedroom with clapboard siding and a front porch Grandpa closed in years before, an unremarkable house improved with hopes for better prospects. My father's siblings, four total, each five years apart, had worn a pathway into the green linoleum floors with their unsupervised play over the decades. Now Grandma lived next door, worked the night shift at the hospital, and helped Dad with his affairs.

Late into the night, I found companionship in the magic of television while Dad sat wordlessly smoking at the kitchen table. With a liverwurst sandwich on a small Melmac plate on my lap, I watched *Pillow Talk* like a how to. Doris Day sang with her honey sweet voice to Rock Hudson. My father resembled a leading man in his dark handsome features and his schemes for success, but he never could hold down a job; his sole steady income was from social security disability. With his degree in history and teacher certification, he had occasional substitute "gigs," as he called them, in a social studies classroom, usually in schools with the toughest of tough students. But they never lasted.

Dad slept well into the afternoon like a lion in his sun-drenched bed, his snores rumbling from the back room. I roamed the house in a realm of my own making, singing songs about a princess with many names, Christina Maria Antoinette. I imagined myself in each name as different types of princesses: the Maria one more fiery, the Christina one more beautiful, and Antoinette more important. My dress-up clothes heaped like personas on the floor.

I knew Dad was finally up when I heard his concert of yawns from the back room like a melodic roar. He sat on the edge of the bed with his feet planted in front of him like two legs of a tripod. "Come on, Dad," I said, sitting on the bed next to him, the warm afternoon light streaming in through the wooden Venetian blinds. "We need to go the store," I said, leaning into his side. The smell of coffee mingled in the air with Dad's Irish Spring soap.

"Okay, baby. Let me have a cup of coffee first." I wasn't a patient child by nature, but my father's slow responses, the lethargy brought on from the pills meant to still the voices in his head, were a physical reminder of his illness. I had been schooled early on by my grandmother to understand what he was up against. My impatience filtered through his illness like hot metal is forged into shape by heat, his illness the crucible.

By late afternoon with his disability check cashed, we headed to the supermarket. Dad took the big cart and pushed it through the aisles like a monarch whose fortune was determined by a small jar of caviar plopped in the cart with a flourish of his hand. I picked sugared cereals and popsicles—food my mother didn't allow.

"Get what you want. We're having a party!" he announced, and when I found the taller-than-me stuffed giraffe I fell in love with in the toy aisle, he said, "Yeah, put it in! We'll see if we can swing it."

At the register, we unloaded our packed cart: family-size packets of meat and leafy greens, milk, coffee, and snacks for late-night TV watching was what we could afford. Counting out his last dollars and the change in his pocket in nickels and dimes, we strutted out with the prize giraffe in my arms and bags of groceries in Dad's.

When we were having a "party," that meant he would usually invite Freddie, who usually didn't come. "Come on over, man. I've got a steak. Bring me a 5-dollar bag and we'll smoke a joint," he'd say. Sometimes Freddie would come and make a sale, but mostly we were a party of two.

Dad cooked collard greens with garlic and sizzled steak in a cast iron pan and served us with the gusto reserved for feeding the ones he loved. It was at my father's that I understood that home was a place you just had to show up to be fed.

"Some steak, huh, Tash?"

"It's so good, Dad."

"Too bad we don't have cheesecake for dessert."

"We could get some."

"Yeah, maybe, baby," he said. The cake was yet another thing he would have to forgo in life.

Dad was overjoyed when Freddie actually showed up. With a mix of altruism and righteousness, Dad wanted to save the world, but at the very least he wanted to share what he had. "Sit down, man. Let me get you some steak!" he insisted, moving the piles of mail, including the UNICEF donation cards, with those less fortunate children of God. The twenty-dollar check he would eventually write was the least and most he could do.

"You see those starving children, man?" he shouted at Freddie from the kitchen. "We throw away garbage bags of food while children are dying of starvation. When I was on the street, I lived on what I found in the dumpster," he complained, putting a plate of food in front of Freddie. "We could feed the poor if the government did its job instead of wasting its time with me. I could perform miracles if they weren't thwarting me at every turn!" He was shouting now, walking to the window and looking out for the spies who were as real as the starvation to him. The idea that we were being watched made me feel seen in our invisible world.

"Hey, man, I feel you," Freddie said, pushing the plate away. "I gots to go pick up my girl now. You still want that bag?" he said, getting up to leave. Dad gave Freddie money and he let himself out.

Dad put on a pot of coffee, turned on music, rolled a joint to light up. He inhaled deeply and exhaled dragon-like. The room was thick with smoke and disappointment and Coltrane's chaotic incantation. "A love supreme, a love supreme, a love supreme" reverberated behind the saxophone's howls. Bebop resounded on our walls like a muffled call to prayer. Dressed in scarves wrapped around my undersized torso, one tied gypsy-like around my head, I danced in the middle of the room. Dime store clip earrings dangled at my neck. I twirled to his lap, where he sat slumped over his coffee, listening for his holy calling in the music. He seemed so alone with his thoughts and sometimes that silence felt like a form of care.

At Harvard's anechoic chamber, designed to be the quietest room on the continent, the musician John Cage took a seat in the womb-like absorbent walled chamber. For years he had been trying to find perfect silence, looking for understanding in the absence of noise. He expected the sound of nothing but instead heard two tones: one high and one low. The engineer explained, "The high one was your nervous system and the dull roar was your blood in circulation." After all, the sound of our life is so much more than what is said, so much more than what makes sense.

I pulled on his hand to join me and he chuckled, anchored to his chair by something weightier than our life could contain. I returned to spinning on the linoleum in the small living room where the beige walls were sticky and darkened to a golden yellow from generations of chain smokers. The cymbal gonged, the drums rumbled, the saxophone wailed, Dad exhaled, and I tried dervish-like to call him to me. "You know I'm the Son of God? My princess, I have a message to impart!" he said in that formal tone he used when he felt important. I only knew something weighed on him. Maybe I was to blame because I didn't understand what he had to do and I felt impatient with the waiting.

In the hours before the drive back to my mother's, we watched Sunday night opera on TV and I cried because the arias were so sad and beautiful and because I was going to leave him soon. "What's wrong, baby?" he asked and called me over to his lap with an open arm.

"I'm just going to miss you," I said, tears streaming down my face.

LIKE PIRATES

1973

Shortly after my mother left my father, she found an apartment in a building with a group of beatnik friends who came from Manhattan to form an artist community in Stapleton, Staten Island. They made sculptures out of cat shit, painted the harbor with smelly oil paints, and danced on the pinions of the docks on the Staten Island side of the New York Bay. Cheap rents, a view of Lower Manhattan, and a shared yard made it an ideal location.

Our apartment was on the third floor of the four-story brick tenement with rusty fire escapes that crisscrossed the front and back like an Escher puzzle. There were nine families in nine apartments: a poet, a filmmaker, several painters, dancers, authors, a journalist, a peace activist, an academic, a lawyer, and a sex worker's family.

Bob and Nannette's apartment on the top floor of the building was where we gathered for parties and potlucks. Bob was an effeminate man, a painter of harbor scenes and still life frames. He introduced Eva, his daughter, and me to the Andrew Sisters. "Listen to this, girls," he cackled as he swooned into the living room, his hands flared out at his sides. His partner, Nannette, was a dancer with a southern-bred grace about her. Her absent-minded, gentle care was quintessentially maternal, the way I thought a mother should be.

There were five children in our building, one biracial whose parents sent him to private school in Manhattan, the rest of us white and schooled closer to home. The neighborhood was a combination of poor black families who lived in the projects, white working-class Irish cops, and Italian mafiosi who lived in the twin- and single-family homes. We lived on the outskirts of both communities.

The front door was green metal and creaked like a ship under its industrial weight, noisily announcing our comings and goings to no one in particular. The backyard with ocean breezes and shared garden space had an abandoned Volkswagen van, a tire swing, and a small mimosa tree I associate with urban backyards. Seemingly at random, it would fleetingly flower feathered blooms, a ruined promise, coagulated on the ground.

Across the gravel street where we parked our cars was a lot overgrown with weeds and littered with bottles, used condoms, and candy wrappers. Sometimes we used sticks to pick up the condoms, flicking them at each other to see how fast the other reacted.

The library, Woolworths, the pizzeria, and candy store were all a block away. They surrounded a central town green where the methadone addicts slept and waited for the clinic to open. Mr. Ruben's poultry was at the end of our block, and when we were flush or Mom's welfare check had just come, I'd pick out a live chicken for slaughter from the stacked cages. I always picked the one that made eye contact, feeling guilty but looking forward to chicken for dinner.

Our real backyard was the uninhabited piers in Stapleton's now abandoned port of embarkment during the Second World War. The long slabs of concrete jutted into the water across the gravel road that went along the bay. We roamed the piers where boxes of old slips sat in piles in the corners of the empty warehouses where we played. We were traders roaming the docks, using forms as collateral for trading bricks and rocks and the occasional pile of found pornographic magazines we wanted to look at but were afraid to touch.

One day, two friends from the building and I decided to clean up the polluted lot. We were budding young gentrifiers who wanted to improve the real estate, to get out of our cars without broken glass and hypodermic needles underfoot. In the face of our parents' non-conformity, we yearned for control. We ventured out with garbage bags and a vision of what the neighborhood could be, should be. We found broken glass and metal bits stuck in the ground from years of being driven over, dog shit calcified on the ground, and weeds taller than us growing everywhere. The work was more than we bargained for. So, we broke more bottles instead.

"You want litter? Take this!" Eva said, angrily smashing a bottle on the ground. Greg and I started throwing what we could heave in the bushes while the adults weren't watching.

We jumped off the roof of our abandoned VW van. Sometimes we placed pennies on the tracks to see the sparks the commuter trains made headed to the ferry bound for Manhattan. Usually, we saved our pennies for candy from the corner store where the owner stood behind the counter and asked, "What do you want, doll?"

"I'm no doll," I sassed, because women weren't dolls, and I knew better than to let adults tell me who I was.

"Whatever you say, doll," he said, collecting my money. After which, I made it a point to steal a Starburst whenever I could.

Because I was no doll.

In the afternoons, like pirates, we claimed antique bottles buried from older days when an active brewery functioned on the hill above the town. We dug them from the mountains of dirt that sat on the Bay Road, unearthed from recent septic work. Our parents sat on top of the dirt piles, smoking joints, drinking beer, and registering our finds with half attention, more concerned with the

Vietnam War or the next art opening coming up.

Our apartment was quiet and empty except for the occasional unfitting love interest, like someone else's husband or our neighbor's adult son. I remember sitting on the couch of our downstairs neighbor Marva, an Iranian filmmaker, whose apartment was furnished like a nomadic tent with Persian tapestries. I waited for a cup of borrowed sugar, imagining that this draped calm was how one lived without random men, and I wondered if Marva had children or if she wanted them.

* * *

Some nights meals would be prepared at our house and other times not. My mother felt if I were hungry, I would eat. When I was eight, I fell off the growth curve. In an old medical record years later, I found a note from the doctor: "The child called me a bastard for keeping her waiting so long. The mother, who didn't say anything, seems to condone this behavior." A series of tests showed at eight years old my bones resembled a six-year-old, but ruled out growth disorders. I remember a group of residents in white coats gathered in the hospital room to discuss my case. I felt important in my exceptional smallness as my mother explained that we were mostly vegetarian.

"Your daughter needs iron and calcium to grow. Does she drink milk? Where does she get her protein?" the doctor questioned my mother.

"I eat meat at my father's," I said.

"Here are some guidelines for you to follow," the doctor offered. Maybe this was why she started plying me with fish oil and disgusting yeast drinks?

"Natasha knows better than I do if she's hungry and what she wants to eat!" Mom complained about the doctor's orders to friends later, over a dinner I was not eating.

Emboldened to do and say what I wanted, I told my preschool Montessori teachers to be quiet and friends to shut up, but privately I felt beast-like in my uncivilized childhood.

When Dad showed up to bring me home for the weekend, tromping to the car, my hand in his thick tar-stained palm, I felt rescued. I relished our weekends of late-night TV and as-needed shoplifting. I felt a profound bond with my broken father. We were united as outsiders in a world that prized success and well-behaved children.

PERFECT FIT

1963

My mother, Judith Bertha Brink, was born into a working-class family in the Steel and Snow Belt of Buffalo, New York. An only child, she was raised by a nearly deaf mother who didn't have access to a hearing aid until my mother was four. I could feel my mother's alienation: a daughter given Bertha for a middle name—almost imagine what it may have been like to have a mother you had to yell at to be heard.

She says she and her family were a bad fit; she could never conform to their expectations of her, didn't behave the way a young lady should, and didn't fit in with other kids. When they insisted she go to school, she threw up every morning, which reinforced her feelings that something was wrong with her and now everyone knew it. She resented being forced to socialize, and on some level, she believed her parents didn't really love her because they didn't accept her for who she was. She was a good student once she adapted to school. She got good grades but wasn't popular. She went to Ohio Wesleyan and joined a sorority where she eventually made friends.

When she finished college, my mother moved to New York City with her college roommate in search of the beatnik artists she had read about in Alan Ginsberg's and Jack Kerouac's books. It was at a party on the Lower East Side, within weeks of moving to the city, that she met my father. Beatnik culture and its flavor of social rebellion fit my mother like a pair of comfortably worn Frye boots, and she was ready to join the movement and kick some conventional ass.

She teased her dark brown hair into the beehive style of the day. She had sexy thick lips and black horn-rimmed glasses that set off her high cheekbones. She wore a straight waist dress, one that my grandmother had sewn. It was part of an entire wardrobe Grandma had sewn her fashioned on trendy magazines my mother had chosen before she left for college. My mother tells me this without a hint of gratitude—to her, the clothes were simply a convenient by-product of a mother who cared too much what people thought.

* * *

The Lower East Side of Manhattan in 1963 was one of many New York neighborhoods where warehouses were being repurposed for living. They became affordable homes for artists to make art and still live in Manhattan. The party was an open house event—access via a commercial gated elevator which opened into an industrial-size loft. Tree-size jade plants stood in front of the large windows open to the night air. Beat poets, painters, and dancers mingled easily in the populist gathering. Red Gallo wine and joints were shared in the spirit of a collective counterculture. A few children wandered on the sidelines of the party, taking sips of wine from the remains in the glasses left around the room. Some years later, I would be one of them.

My father walked into the room, handsome and vibrant, a man in the prime of his life. Five foot eleven with thick dark hair he slicked back with water, strong features, and animated dark blue eyes that lit up in another's company. A picture of him from this era shows him sitting forward on a chair. He's slender and wears a white, short-sleeved shirt, his forearm bent on his knee, with a canary on the tip of his finger. He's gazing at the bird, apparently charmed by its weightless beauty. He had an uncommon ability to make you feel seen, no matter how unsubstantial a person felt— which was just what my mother was after— being seen and heard.

As the evening progressed, my mother watched him intently talking with other people. He spoke passionately and easily about big ideas, more interested in understanding than taking a position on an idea. He was boundless in a way that instantly attracted my mother. She asked her friend Nancy about him. There were stories—something about a mental breakdown but a brilliant thinker and musician. She tells me they didn't speak to each other at the party. When I asked my father what he remembered about her at the party, he said, in a way that made me think he couldn't remember, "She looked like a beatnik chick." Eventually she left alone. Her apartment was just a short walk down Avenue A.

"Then I woke up in the middle of the night thinking about him, and I wondered if maybe he would still be there, so I got up and went back to the party to look for him." He *was* there, and it was apparent to him that she had come back for him.

"Nice to see you again, my dear. May I walk you back to your abode?" he might have said in that formal old school way he talked when he was trying to make an impression. They sat outside on her fire escape and he talked about what mattered most, about his recent adventures in Mexico.

"Let me tell you about the magic mushrooms I did with the Indians, and how I found God." This was what she wanted: someone who thought deeply about the world, someone who didn't care what other people thought, someone who would accept her and her nonconformist ways.

WHAT CRAZY MEANT

1963

"What was it like to be so young and partnered with a schizophrenic?" I asked my mother, years later, sitting at her kitchen table in Albany where she lived alone. Thick dust coated the floor, cat hair from her ex-roommate drifted out of the closet, and I casually rewashed the glasses before we drank from them.

"With Frank, I went to gallery openings and dance recitals and we listened to a lot of jazz. We didn't talk much, but we were part of a community of artists, and I finally felt like I belonged to a group who were questioning and challenging everything like I was."

"What made you decide to have a baby with him, even though you knew he was mentally ill?" I asked and watched the hurt look register on her face, a remnant of the way she always felt judged by me.

"It's not like we planned to have a baby. It just happened. That's how we did things in those days. I was madly in love with him; I wasn't thinking about his mental illness or planning for the future. We were beatnik artists, living one day at a time. To plan for the future was something our parents did!" It was the first time she spoke passionately about my father. It made me wish I could have seen them together, when they were young, when she loved him.

"In those first years, we broke up a number of times, but his family encouraged the relationship. Really, Florrie kept us together." My father's mom, Florrie, was always scheming about how to take care of my father, and she saw in my mother a capable ally. It was Grandma who applied for social security disability benefits for Dad when it became apparent that he couldn't hold a job. When my mother quit her job as a social welfare worker, Florrie encouraged her to get unemployment insurance so they could support themselves.

In fact, my father, well-schooled in working the system, once suggested to my mother, "Judy, if you were to put your foot under a truck, we could manage *two* disability checks."

"You put your foot under a truck!" she said, not prone to sacrificing for anything she didn't believe in.

Having grown up feeling like a misfit, my mother loved her new outlaws, a family that believed rules were for people who couldn't think for themselves. At long last, she was part of a clan that embraced her irreverence. This was the family she should have been born into, and she will tell you that she loved being part of the Williams clan at least as much as she loved my father.

With two sources of income, they moved in together to an apartment on 11th and Avenue B on the Lower East Side and lived the Bohemian lifestyle they loved. At first, she didn't tell her family about moving in with her unemployed saxophone and piano player boyfriend. Once she did, they worried about her affair. The idea that he lived with her rather than married her made them ask, "Are you having an affair with a married man?"

In one of many letters to her mother, she complained, "Why do I always have to make you miserable? I'm really sorry it has to be so, but I guess that's the inevitable result of me being me. Maybe I shouldn't have told you, but I don't want to hide things from you, especially when I'm not ashamed. Frank loves me. I know he does. I know all about him and I know he's not married! You probably wouldn't like him, but then again you probably wouldn't like me if

I weren't related to you."

Their apartment was strewn with my father's sheet music and paintings. My mother assumed the role of partner supporting the artist—that generation's reinterpretation of marriage. Living an unfettered life with an artist, a handsome, creative musician, made her happy for the first time. She was in love, maybe more with the lifestyle than with the man.

Everything seemed perfect until one morning Frank woke up and demanded breakfast, something he never ate.

"Judy, it's time you make me spinach and steak, a breakfast befitting a king!" he said. She started to cook for him, but the conceit in his manner was so out of character it unnerved her. Still, eager to please, she did as he asked. When his breakfast was ready, he came to the table and ate as if he were playing a role. He cut into the steak and put bites into his mouth with a flourish. He chewed his food with royal pageantry, as if someone were watching.

"My dear, you know I served in the Army briefly after college and was discharged because I feigned homosexuality," he said, sizing up her reaction. He had, in fact, fostered a flamboyant gay persona to get out of service, one he would roll out for many years to come at parties and family gatherings. Miming with limp hands and a sideways thrust of his hips, his stereotypical rendition of a *Nancy*. He also lost his mind in boot camp.

"Evidently, my dear, they're onto me. Go get your red nail polish to paint my nails so we can fool the bastards!" he demanded. She sat nervously painting his thick fingernails with bright red polish.

They set off down the street. She followed behind him as he sashayed down the sidewalk with his painted nails held limply in front of him, a caricature of gayness, meant to broadcast his proclivity to the spies he imagined were watching.

"They're following us, just as I knew they would. See that guy behind us who keeps ducking into doorways? Let's go to Larry's on Second Avenue where all the Nancys hang out."

She looked behind her and found no one suspicious. She had never seen him like this before, and it made her question her own judgment. Maybe there was someone? He was so sure of himself. Maybe it was she who couldn't see the truth? They sat at the bar with Frank barely talking, his attention on the drink in front of him, as if it held the answer to his predicament. She felt annoyed and confused by how he picked up his drink with his pinkie extended. She was anxious to be his accomplice, but to pretend that his world was real felt like another kind of pretense, another falsehood, like the way her parents pretended and lied for the sake of appearances. She continued sitting at the bar watching him impersonate someone he wasn't, for people that weren't even there.

WHAT WE FELT LIKE

1964

Within days of his breakdown, Frank disappeared. He went to see his mother and then took her Oldsmobile to Vermont to see an old professor he felt called to visit. On the drive north, paranoia took over, and he became convinced that cars in his rearview mirror were mobsters following him. Increasingly afraid for his life, he concocted a plan to save himself. When he got to the town, he pulled in front of a firehouse, obstructing the way of the fire engines, hoping they would arrest him to protect him from the mob.

"Sir, we're going to have to ask you to move the vehicle."

Dad sat waiting in his car, knowing they would call the police. "What is this idiocy? The mob is following me. Surely, you can protect the Messiah from persecution? They will kill me, you know. I'm not moving." Unable to convince him to move his car, the police were called. The car was towed and, after a short stop at the police station, my father was taken to the nearby psychiatric hospital. I can't help but think about how, if his skin were a different color, he could have been considered a threat, even shot and killed.

In the meantime, my mother didn't have any idea where he was. She hadn't heard from anyone—not from him or the family. No word from Florrie that Frank had stolen her car, taken to the road, and been hospitalized. Days became weeks. She sat alone in their empty apartment, convinced the friends they had were

Frank's friends, not hers, so she didn't call on them.

While Frank was missing, a man my mother knew from college showed up for a visit. Ted was planning a European voyage on a cargo ship, and it departed from New York City. She had been attracted to him in college, but they had only been friends. Ted was an art major and had a motorcycle that he once took her for a ride on. This visit, they ended up more than friends. They had a brief, passionate affair, which left both of them imagining a future together. She went with him to the loading dock and they made promises to reunite when he got back. She stood waving him off as the boat left the port feeling in love in a way she didn't feel with Frank or ever before.

A few weeks later, Frank returned from the hospital.

"Judy, I'm back!" he said excited by the sight of her. "I'm a recovered man! It was because of you I survived hell," he said, sitting at the table, shaking his head at the floor. "They treat you like an animal in those places, but I'm out and I have my mind back, baby."

She looked at his pale face and the puffiness under his eyes. He seemed inert and passive compared to Ted's rugged strength and appetite for adventure. Still, she was compelled by how important Frank made her feel. He needed her. She felt guilty. She didn't tell him about the affair. When Ted returned, she would tell *him* she was back with Frank.

But Frank's illness became a third party in their relationship. "Have you taken your medication?" she asked relentlessly. "Where have you been?" she wanted to know each time he came home. She was jealous of the ways his insanity took him away from her. Ironically, later that winter it was Frank who left my mother for another woman.

He announced, "I'm going to move in with Gypsy and that

magical child of hers to help her with the rent." My mother stood crying on the stoop of their apartment building. Fannie, or Gypsy as everyone called her because of the way she could read the future, needed help. He explained her husband had left her alone with two kids. Although Gypsy was compelling, it was her open lifestyle, her young daughter Faye, and another baby on the way that elicited paternal feelings in my father. Faye, a precocious curly blonde four-year-old who danced around the apartment naked, had captivated my father. He felt called to minister to their needs.

"You can't just walk out on me!" my mother yelled as a police officer passed them on the street.

He asked, "Are you okay, ma'am?"

"Fine. Leave us alone," she said, not wanting help from the *pigs*. Ill-equipped to meet her emotional demands, the officer had nothing to say. Did Frank know about the affair with Ted? she wondered. Was this why he was leaving? Or was it her dissatisfaction that had driven them apart? I can picture my father looking off into the distance as if my mother's hurt and anger hovered on the horizon.

* * *

Weeks later, he returned. "Things didn't work out." Gypsy's husband had come back. My mother took him back. Even she didn't understand why. Shortly after Frank returned, Gypsy's husband showed up at their apartment banging on the door, yelling about taking his wife to court for custody of the two children.

"I read all about you in my wife's diary," he said through the closed door. "All about you and your perverted ideas. You will be testifying in court, you sick bastard!"

"What was that about, Frank?" my mother demanded to know.

Dad explained that Gypsy didn't hide sex from the child. She and her husband, and later, she and Frank, had sex openly. If she wanted to, the little girl watched them. She was a very sexual child.

"I put a pencil in the girl's vagina," Frank confided. "That's what this is all about," he complained, as if all the commotion was unwarranted. "She liked it; she was always touching herself down there. Gypsy got uptight about her enchanting daughter. How was I to know she would write about it?"

"He did what?" I said, stopping my mother's story short. "Are you serious? What did you do?"

"You have to understand, Tash. We were reading Summerhill's approach to childrearing; their ideas were about being open with children about sex. We thought that was right!"

The Summerhill School, founded in England in the 1930s, was founded on principles of freedom and self-expression. Students and teachers alike made decisions about rules and governance and even which teachers to hire. It was based on the philosophy that children learn best with freedom from coercion. Many schools based on Neill's Summerhill model were opened in America in the 1960s. Among other areas where children were given license, sexuality was seen as a natural expression that should be allowed. Some graduates reported that mock weddings among older students were common and they were allowed to sleep together on campus. Also, relations between teachers and students were common. I myself went to a "free" school as a child. We weren't having sex or marrying each other in the Staten Island storefront version of Summerhill, but we were a feral bunch who stole and ate whole boxes of Oreos meant for snack and told teachers when we wished we could fire them. I resented the lack of structure and decision-making on the adults' part.

"My bedside table was piled high with Jack Kerouac and Alan Ginsberg. It was a cultural revolution. We were breaking free of the limiting ideas about marriage and sex. We believed babies want pleasure as adults do," she said, always defending her choices on principle and leaving me unprotected in the balance. She stood by my father at the time, and in the end, nothing came of Gypsy's husband's accusations. It was the mother, Gypsy, who would have to defend herself if they went to court, not my father. It wasn't the first time I had heard something about my father having touched someone else's child, but I had ignored it. My body was shaking with recognition. My childhood had been defined by adults who were questioning sexual and social mores but in this story my father's behavior was perverted and unrecognizable. As a teen, I felt my father's gaze as objectifying and I resented and fought for boundaries, but as a child, I never recall feeling unsafe in my father's care.

"Did this make you worry about having a child with him?" I asked, even though it was my father we were talking about, even though I wouldn't exist if she hadn't.

"We just did what we felt like doing back then."

HOSPITALIZED AT BIRTH

1965

I was conceived despite my mother's ambivalence and my father's transgressions. My father was thrilled to have sired his first child. "Being a mother will be the best thing that's ever happened to you, baby," he exclaimed because having children was all important to him. But my mother didn't feel ready, she tells me. It wasn't only that she had doubts about her relationship with Frank; being a mother wasn't something she wanted at the time.

From the beginning, she struggled to get her parents to accept the terms of her relationship with Frank, and she definitely didn't want them to know about the pregnancy. In correspondence with my grandmother, my mother implored her parents not to judge her and Frank for living together without being married. She explained that they loved each other but would stay together only for as long as it felt right. "It's what all our friends are doing. I don't expect you to understand with your weird moral hang-ups," she wrote. Living with a man without being married was bad enough; she just couldn't bring herself to tell them she was having a baby. When her parents were allowed to visit for the first time, she was five months pregnant, but her belly barely showed and she wore a dress that hid any hint of the pregnancy. In a letter to her mother, dated just months before my birth, there were still no clues that she was having a baby. No mention of the baby kicked this week or that she was making clothes for the baby on the way. Only, "Thank you for cash," and some details about the piano they were going to buy for Frank. She kept the pregnancy a secret until the very end.

My father, on the other hand, was overjoyed. "Having this baby will change everything," he announced to friends and family. But then, one morning near the end of her pregnancy, Judy woke up to find him pacing the floor. He was more agitated than she had ever seen him, moving from room to room, peeking out of the windows,

"You see that cat, in the plaid jacket, standing on the corner looking up at our apartment? He's been watching us for hours. Don't tell me you haven't seen him! Did they fucking talk to you?" He glared at her. "They know about the drugs, don't they Judy?" he said about the pot they had stashed in the apartment ceiling eave. Then, he marched out the door of the apartment yelling, "I'm going to find a safe place. See if you can keep your fucking mouth shut for a while!"

It was so sudden. She sat in the mayhem of their home desperate and alone. What had happened? What did she do? Did that really just happen? She couldn't call her family, who still didn't know she was having a baby. As far as his mother went, she wasn't sure what Florrie would say or do. She spent the night alone with the sounds of neighborhood cats screaming and car alarms seeping into her fitful sleep.

The next day heavy with nine months of child and groceries to make Frank a meal when he came to his senses, she trudged to the four-story walk-up. The door was wide open. Their railroad flat had been ransacked. Food was strewn across the floor, and the kitchen drawers were dumped upside down. She put the bags down and found Frank in their bedroom rummaging through the closet. Clothing lay in piles on the floor and he ranted as she stood watching.

"I know they bugged the place. How did they get in? I bet you thought I wouldn't know." He raged at her.

Then, he walked over and grabbed her, and pushed her into the wall. Looking at her with cold contempt, his usually bright eyes dark with suspicion, he did something she never could have imagined. Something so contrary to the man she knew that she didn't believe it was happening till the pain of the first punch in her belly registered between her legs. Then he punched her again!

"Get out!" he yelled. "You can't be trusted."

"*What?*" I say incredulously when my mother tells me this. "He punched you in the stomach?" In the course of my lifetime, I had been the object of my father's mistrust, but I've never seen him become violent. Only once early in preadolescence did he even reprimand me. I had run upstairs in a rage and locked myself in the bathroom. When he came knocking on the door to check on me, I sprayed him in the face with shaving cream.

"Oh, Tasha," he said softly, disappointment in his voice, looking down at the shaving cream on his shirt collar. He stepped into the bathroom, sat on the toilet seat, and pulled me across his lap. Then, he gave me one swat on my behind as if following an instruction book he barely understood for disciplining one's child. I have never seen him raise a hand or threaten anyone, not when he was robbed, not when he was restrained by health care workers, and not when the hookers he brought home stole from him. He could be mean and cutting when he was manic, but never physical. Could he really have attacked my pregnant mother and the baby in her belly—the baby he lobbied for and considered precious? Had he hit her hard enough to make it hard to straighten up and breathe, like a punch in the stomach in a street fight, or was it a slow-motion punch as my spanking had been?

"I can hardly believe he would do that," I tell her.

"Well, it's true!" she said, bristling at the suggestion that she wasn't telling the whole story. My allegiance to my father always left her feeling outside our love. "Frank once threatened to throw Florrie down the stairs. He had been threatening enough that she had to commit him to the psychiatric hospital against his will many times over," she reminded me, but I had never witnessed that side of him. Plus, he idolized motherhood; pregnant women were Madonna-like. And his siring of children was his greatest accomplishment, sanctified by God even.

I've asked my aunts and uncles, and they agree they have never seen him be physically aggressive. Why would a pregnant partner elicit violence from a man who was otherwise kind and gentle? In a review of partner violence among pregnant women found in the DMIHER school of epidemiology and public health studies show mixed outcomes—about a third of women in one study experience a protective effect from partner violence during pregnancy, while fifteen percent found abuse started or worsened during pregnancy as in any relationship pregnancy can exacerbate the tension and stress. I have since then heard from Barbara's family of times, particularly when Barbara was pregnant, when she was afraid of him. One time, he threw her down the stairs and left her with a black eye. I remember hearing about or seeing a picture of her face after. I believe their stories. I know my father was more complicated than my nostalgic remembrance of him and, still, it's hard to imagine his violence.

My father's simmering rage was well-hidden, but I have wondered if it was pent-up anger toward his own mother.

Years later, when I asked him what his relationship with Florrie was like, he complained, and said remorsefully, "We were close, maybe too close. She talked to Dad like he was an idiot, which cost me my relationship with my father." He and his mother were intimate in a way that excluded everyone else. His enmeshment with his mother had driven a wedge between not only him and his father but also the other siblings. Did this incestuous bond taint his relationship with women? I wonder, not for the first time, about my father's shadowy side. The way he used prostitutes and how when he was ill, he treated me less like a daughter and more like a woman. When he believed he had been betrayed by the mother of his unborn child, was it so primal that it took him over like a demonic possession that unleashed his fury? I think I understand something of the violence of betrayal that haunted my father, how infuriating the specter of his schizophrenia was in the face of the responsibilities of being a father.

* * *

After my father's attack, my mother called his sister Irene desperate for a place to stay. She spent the night on her couch and remembers being hungry and the refrigerator being empty and Irene not being there that first night. She chewed the gum she had in her purse and lay awake all night. Panicked at the prospect of having a child alone, she finally wrote her parents. Penned with black ink on what must have been my aunt's letterhead with a golden Madonna seal on the top corner, she wrote:

> "Prepare yourself—you're not going to be pleased with what I have to tell you. In fact, you're probably going to be terribly upset. So, sit down and get ready. And remember I'm not enjoying this either—*I'm in my ninth month of pregnancy* and Frank is sick again."

She told them about how she walked fifty blocks from the Village to New York Hospital on the Upper East Side and spoke with a doctor about the possibility of giving up her child for adoption. Maybe she shouldn't keep this baby? Maybe she should leave Frank to be with Ted? In the end she tells them, "If I've not already made this clear, I will be keeping the baby regardless of what happens with Frank and there will be a matter of finances... It seems to me that if anyone besides myself is to support me, it would be you... therefore, it's up to you to decide if you think you should or can help..." She finished the letter saying, "I hope you won't come to New York. I really don't want to see you at this time, but since Irene has a phone, you might like to call me as soon as you've gotten used to the reality I've told you about."

Meanwhile, Frank committed himself to the hospital, which Judy took as a sign that he wanted to get better. Florrie, who had been in favor of the pregnancy all along, hoping the baby would help my father settle down, let Judy know she could stay with them. Florrie always held out hope for his recovery if only the circumstances were right. Not knowing what else to do, my mother moved into the family home on Long Island while Frank underwent treatment at the hospital.

Pilgrim State Psychiatric Hospital, in Nassau County, Long Island, was the largest of its kind in the country. Considered a state unto itself, the facility included a hospital, a mortuary, and its own cemetery. Between 1946 and 1959, fifteen hundred lobotomies were performed on the most violent cases of schizophrenia and psychosis. I wonder now how much my grandparents knew of what went on there? Were they ever afraid of what might happen to him when he was locked up for months at a time? Did they worry that the arrogance that accompanied his mania might get him in trouble? I know my grandmother, who advocated for him all her life, would never have agreed to a lobotomy—to cut out part of her brilliant son's mind would have been unthinkable—but did doctors always consult with the family? For instance, were they consulted when he had shock therapy?

My father endured over thirty-five courses of electroconvulsive therapy, treatments that stole the memories of his adventures in Mexico and even college days, shock treatments that were done without anesthesia. I have to guard myself from the picture that forms in my mind of my twenty-six-year-old father, strapped down, conscious, a depressor against his tongue, with electrodes pumping current through his already addled mind.

* * *

It turned out that both of my parents were hospitalized at the time of my birth, February 20, 1965. Shortly before my due date, my mother visited Dad in the hospital. He flew around the waiting room in his hospital gown, arms outstretched like an airplane, and taunted her, "You want crazy? I'll give you crazy."

Days later, she went into labor. Florrie and John dropped her off at New York Hospital on East 79th Street to deliver the baby alone. In delivery she contracted a bad staph infection. So, for the first ten days of my life, nurses cared for me. Many years later, my mother suggested this was the reason we didn't have a closer relationship. "The nurses loved you. They kept telling me what a happy baby you were and what a good eater you were. But by the time I was well enough to have you back, you wouldn't nurse. I blame that time apart for why we didn't bond," she said, as if we didn't have the next eighteen years of my childhood to make up for those ten days.

As soon as my mother was well enough, my aunt visited the hospital to share some encouraging news about Frank. "Judy, the doctors have never seen anything like it, but when he got the news that Natasha had been born, Frank suddenly came to his senses. He didn't think he was God anymore, and wanted to come home! He won't be released right away, but he's better, Judy."

My mother returned to the family home with Florrie and John and waited for my father's release. She and I stayed in my father's childhood bedroom, with my grandparents and my father's younger brother John Paul, who was eleven years old at the time, fifteen years younger than his oldest brother. My young uncle loved having a baby to play with. In the months we lived there, he spent hours entertaining, feeding, and holding his baby niece. Years later, he tells me, "I fell madly in love with you when you were a baby. I would put my face in front of you and say '*milk*' as if I was the Cookie Monster and you would laugh. Then, I would up the ante with the word '*cream*,' and you somehow understood that this was even funnier and you had the most infectious laugh." This was the secret my young uncle had figured out—the most reliable love in this family came with a good sense of humor.

A SAINT DIES

My grandfather's cancer caught everyone by surprise. The chronic back pain that bent him over the kitchen table after working his second job catering turned out to be pancreatic and bone cancer. Within weeks of his diagnosis, he was in the hospital dying. The rest of the kids were unaware of Grandpa's condition until the final hour, in part, because my grandmother had trouble facing it. Just weeks before, she had written to her daughter, "He's got a cold and won't stop complaining." My aunts and uncles were still on their way from the Netherlands and Upstate New York, but my father had a sixth sense about visiting him just hours before he died.

"We're going to visit Grandpa," Dad announced when he picked me up for the weekend. It was a drive he knew well, but he was agitated the whole trip and then went looking for the liquor store.

"Where in God's name is it? Don't they know I have the power to heal the man? If I can only toast his life in the name of Christ!" he ranted while we drove, looking furtively on either side of the road. Finally, he pulled to the curb.

"Wait here," said the energized version of my father. I sat patiently, the way children do when they know to keep quiet. His frustration reactive like thorium or one of those unstable, as yet unnamed, elements. He returned with a bottle wrapped in a paper bag. The breeze from the open windows was warm and the fresh air was welcome. Dad pointed to the blue words and read, "Mercy

Hospital! Baby, it's a sign. We may be in time!"

At the hospital reception desk in a waiting room that smelled like medicine and burnt coffee, Dad marched to the nurses' desk and demanded,

"Where is my father, John Joseph Williams? This is his son."

"I'm sorry, sir. What is your name and what unit is he on?"

"Are you stupid, woman? You're the one holding him!" Dad yelled, frustrated that she didn't know *whom* she was addressing.

Once she figured out who Grandpa was and where his room was, she told us, "You can't bring the little girl upstairs."

"Nonsense, this is my daughter."

"I'm sorry, sir. Children aren't allowed because of germs."

"I'm six and I'm not sick," I said.

"No one under the age of twelve is allowed in hospital rooms. She has to stay in the waiting room. Here, she can use these crayons to make a picture," the nurse said, handing my father the crayons and paper. In those days, children weren't required to be supervised at all times! My father looked impatiently around the waiting room for a place for me to sit.

"You wait here till I come back to get you," he said so the nurse wouldn't hear, which I took to mean we would sneak me in. Normally, I might have fought the nurse for the right to see Grandpa, but I wasn't that close with him. He wasn't at home much, and when he was, he had this weird habit of calling me Tush instead of Tash, which made me sound like someone's rear end. Plus, my father was being unnaturally decisive, and I didn't want him to decide anything bad about me in his state.

As my father marched to the elevator, I looked at the lady sitting next to me to see if she could help if I needed something. With a few broken crayons and a torn off coloring book sheet that I folded to the blank side, I started to make a card for Grandpa.

A house with a little stick girl holding her bigger stick dad's hand. Mostly, I watched for the nurse to leave. I knew Dad would come get me when he could. When I went to the bathroom with the idea of finding Dad, the nurse watched me.

I was asleep on the arm of the chair when I woke to my father's voice as he walked from the elevator with two guards at his elbows.

"This is nonsense! Don't you know who I am?" he challenged, assailing them with his supremacy. "You'll regret the day you stayed my hand, for these hands do the work of God," he said, looking haughtily into the eyes of nearby visitors.

"We're going home," he said, taking my hand and heading to the door. We passed the blue Mercy Hospital sign on our way out. We pulled up to Grandma and Grandpa's dark house; my aunt and uncles were at the hospital by now with Grandma.

When they got home later that night, we learned that Grandpa had died. My father's eyes were calculating and fierce as if he was offended by the news.

"They don't know what they've done! If that idiotic nurse hadn't intervened, I could have made him immortal!" he ranted, slamming his way out the door. I lay awake upstairs and could overhear John Paul telling my aunt who had just arrived how things had gone at the hospital while I sat in the waiting room.

"Frankie marched into Dad's room with a bottle in hand. 'I come bearing libations! A toast to a saint,' he announced. He pulled Dad's shrunken body into a seated position, brandishing the champagne, popped the cork and chugged directly out of the bottle as Dad's body slid back onto his pillow. Mom had to call for help," JP said. "The guards came and took him out while Frankie yelled at them, 'You're interfering with my valediction! Take your hands off me!' I hope he doesn't come back," my uncle said bitterly. I lay in bed awake, trying to stay up until Dad returned.

In the morning, he was still gone and it was decided I should go back to my mother's. My Uncle JP drove me back to Staten Island in his sporty Fiat he named Spider; we sped over the Verrazano Bridge taking tight turns and running yellow lights and I didn't want the drive to end.

***

My Aunt Irene tells me that after Grandpa's death, my father was as crazy as she's ever seen him. He didn't sleep; he marched around the house changing the channels on the television and radio and ranted at them, "Why aren't they saying anything about it? This whole thing is a cover-up by the CIA. Don't you think it's strange there's nothing about a fucking saint dying in our midst?"

The family held a three-day wake at Harnett Funeral Home, my grandfather's body laid out in the open coffin for viewing. My Aunt Irene remembers the first night of the wake. "We four siblings stood side by side looking at our father. Frank stood in the middle and we three were weeping, but he stood there like a telephone pole with arms around us. Later, I learned that the frozen affect he displayed was one of the symptoms of his psychosis, but at the time it seemed heartless," Irene confided. Frank left the wake early with his good friend Don Newlove. Don had shared an apartment with Dad in his college years and stayed in touch with him from his days in the East Village. The rest of the family returned from Harnett's to the pair of them sitting and talking, and Newlove was drunk. "Despite Newlove being a recovering alcoholic, Frank had given Newlove a big glass of scotch, but he himself was drinking water and encouraging his friend to drink. Newlove was saying, 'When my father died, I pissed on his grave,' which amused Frankie to no end. It was something we couldn't bear to face; we just walked in and passed by them as quickly as possible. Frankie seemed actually evil that night, and I had never thought of him like that before or since," she said, weeping.

My father refused to go to the burial. He holed up in the house with the TV blasting, listening for the messages only he could hear. When they returned from the services, he assailed them with questions: "So, how was the funeral? Lots of flowers? Lots of fucking priests? Good send-off for the old man?"

"You're a monster, a fucking monster! Get out of this house! Leave us alone!" my aunt shouted, punching at him as he held her out of reach, protecting her from hurting him as much as he was defending himself. She ran upstairs, threw her things back in a suitcase, clomped down the stairs, and said, "You coming?" to her younger brother in the living room. He jumped off the couch, and together they headed out the front door to his car and drove away, leaving their mother and youngest brother to deal with my father's psychosis.

For another sleepless night, my father continued to listen for messages on the blaring television. Grandma lay in her room with the door closed, trying to block out the noise, and JP tried to sleep upstairs. When Grandma came into the kitchen for coffee in the morning, Frankie was preparing his breakfast in the black cast-iron frying pan and announced he was making "a trinity of eggs befitting the Messiah." That afternoon, Grandma had a meeting with the insurance man about Grandpa's life insurance policy, and my father kept turning up the volume of the TV louder and louder.

"Frank, for God's sake, turn that down! We can't hear ourselves think over here," Grandma yelled.

"For God's sake, did you say?" my father fired back at her. "Is that what you think you're doing? Is it for God's sake? Did you get the old man's money yet?" He walked over to them and loomed over Grandma and an alarmed insurance agent. "I, for one, will have nothing to do with the money changers and their blood money. Get out of my father's house."

I can picture my grandmother's face. The way she guarded her feelings by refusing extended eye contact. "I'm very sorry; my son's not well," she would have explained, a refrain she was all too familiar with by now. The agent rushed out, and Frank returned to the blaring TV for the next message. When my exhausted grandmother finally fell asleep in a chair, my father took her keys and drove off in her car without leaving a word for anyone about where he was going, his whereabouts unknown for weeks.

* * *

Not knowing what to say or do, my mother left me alone. "I just don't understand what you need," she complained when I didn't go to her, as if I could help her understand attachment and loyalty between a child and parent when she didn't feel it herself.

She tells me now, "I knew you were in pain, but I didn't know what to say."

Neither did I.

MRS. POWELL'S

It was an elegant white gambrel colonial with two pillars framing the front door, which Grandma had coveted from the yard next door all her married life. When the next-door neighbor, Mrs. Powell, died that same year, Grandma used Grandpa's life insurance money to purchase the house.

Having a separate home of her own was a necessity, but that house felt like a masquerade, like we were tearing a page out of someone else's American dream. Much of the fancy furniture had been left in the sale—the elegant red velvet settee we never sat on and blue glass coffee table that reflected the afternoon light, where we never put our coffee cups. It felt like living in the master's house. Even though the pots and pans, hand-me-down china, and Grandma's clothing went into the cabinets and drawers, it never stopped feeling like Mrs. Powell's house.

My unemployed father lived alone in the family house next door and slept well into the afternoon. On weekends when I returned from playing with other kids or visiting Grandma, I would find him alone playing piano in the musty cellar, in a room converted to a bedroom for him as a teenager. The black and white linoleum floor was peeling up and dim light filtered in from a small window through a dirty makeshift curtain that hinted at the adolescent privacy my father wanted all those years ago, but now couldn't escape.

He sat at the upright piano with his back to the door. His

hands gently thrummed improvised tunes on its broken ivory keys. A cigarette burned between his lips and sent smoke winding into his eyes. "Come sit next to me, baby." His eyes gleamed. "Listen to what this song has to say." His simple rendering of Coltrane's "My Favorite Things" spoke volumes to me about the way his life was measured by the loss of the things we prize; steady friends, family, and work were all beyond his reach. Through the music, he could convey a yearning he usually kept to himself. I sat next to him soaking up the isolated world of his quiet coping and felt the sadness like an enduring guest.

Grandma also got up in the early afternoon for her late shift as an administrative secretary at the hospital. It was better not to go in until she could breathe smoke again, until she had finished leaning on the edge of the kitchen sink, "hacking up a lung," and had had her first cigarette and a cup of coffee. She was ready for an audience once she was at the kitchen table in her house dress, her chest hollow on one side from the mastectomy she'd had years before. We sat for the hour when Dad came to for her counsel, for what he called "sessions." They smoked and talked, and I would get a slice of Entenmann's coffee cake and the favor of being in the room while the adults made sense of their lives. Dad's coffee was always so full he had to lean down for the first slurp. Grandma sat quietly, her gaze steadfast on her son, sucking on and exhaling smoke like a dragon.

"I can't seem to get anywhere with this illness," Dad said, after sitting in silence for a time. "I've been working on a painting of the sun as pure idea... I want to show how the mind gets so bogged down in the reality of everyday life and fights for spiritual release in the energy of the sun," he confided, self-aware in a way that she found heart-wrenching, listening and quietly exhaling like a balloon deflating slowly and then dragging on her cigarette again. She understood her son was grappling with things she couldn't see or understand, and she was steadfast to his cause.

"I wish I could adapt the attitude of his contemporaries, who say he brought about his own troubles," she wrote to my mother's mother, Annabelle. "But I know better. I've watched and shared his torment for too many years and have been on the seesaw of hope and despair with him."

She would sit with him until it was time to get ready for work. She pushed open the swinging door that separated the kitchen from the living room and her bedroom in the back. Sometimes, I helped her clasp the bra with the false boob tucked in one side, but usually she did it alone, returning dressed and ready for her shift. "Where are my eyes?" she said, coming back in the kitchen looking for her glasses. Eager to help, always looking for a way to share her burden and earn her love, I found them and eagerly draped the glasses chain over her head, coronation-like.

Except for the great books club she started and the theology group she led, my grandmother was a frustrated intellectual. She lived in a world where being a smart woman didn't pay the bills or lead to advancement. She worked long hours for a working wage and no more. Instead, she channeled her entrepreneurial spirit into a variety of schemes aimed at raising the family's prospects. The one that came closest to succeeding was her design and business plan for confirmation tunics. In her mind, the robes would become as essential to confirmation in the Catholic Church as graduation gowns were to commencement. She designed white robes made with a red flame on the breast, symbolic of the enlightenment promised of the sacrament. Betting on this idea to make them rich, she pre-ordered the gowns through Walsh Conley, the local distributor of religious goods, then called and pitched the idea to the bishops and priests she had befriended over the years.

Her plan was that Frank and my mother would head up the first franchise and deliver the rentals. I found a home video of young girls and boys marching double file toward the church in Grandma's confirmation tunics, with the emblem of a red flame on the lapel. My uncle confirmed they were rented out at least once, but the balance of those boxes of confirmation tunics sat piled in a corner of the house for years. It was an idea that never got any traction. I wondered if it had to do with the fact that she was a woman with a big idea, "too big for her britches." The tunics were a talisman for the way she continued to hang her hopes for advancement of her first-born son despite the odds. "Always betting on the losing horse," is what my uncle said.

With Grandma at work, I would be alone with Dad except for the comings and goings of the tenants Grandma found for Dad's house. In the early days, there was a host of characters, dealers and prostitutes my father attracted plus one or two people Grandma found to rent a room. I slept in Dad's room and avoided most of the tenants. Christopher K., an art student in the neighborhood who Grandma encouraged to be a friend to my father, was an exception. The third of eight children, he was only too happy to get out of his childhood home, and he felt valued for his artistic aspirations in our family. When Christopher brought his serious girlfriend Collette around, beautiful Collette who loved me, I became attached. Christopher tells me years later that I pulled them aside and told them, "If something happens, I want you two to adopt me."

At eleven p.m. I would head over to Grandma's. Like my father, I sat with Grandma for her attention. I watched her at the kitchen table as she sucked the smoke deeply into her lungs then flicked the ash off her cigarette with long elegant painted nails, her one vanity. She had an air of royalty, like a woman who was above her circumstances. As a child, I found her steadfast stoicism reassuring.

Through her, I understood the ways illness prevented Dad from having a job or being like other fathers, but also, she listened to his ideas and always believed in him. In this way, she was a model mother.

"You of all people know how much he endures, Tash," she schooled me, and in this empathy for my father, my grandmother and I were united.

"How was your father today?" or "How are you liking the Free School these days?" she asked as I grew into my job as my father's keeper.

When it came to myself, I was less patient. "I don't learn anything," I complained. "They worry about my spelling. Even though they know what I mean!"

"You don't think spelling is important?" she asked, because discussing ideas was how she cared for people.

"They want to test me for dyslexia, but I told them there was no point."

"What did Judy say?"

"She left it up to me to decide."

"Maybe you should consider it?" Grandma had dropped out of college to support her family at a young age and knew firsthand the cost of not having an education.

"There's nothing they can do. Plus, they should look at my ideas, not spelling!" I said, shutting down the question of my deficiencies.

At eleven-thirty we went into the living room to watch *Johnny Carson*. It was the only time we went in the living room, except when my father was raging in the kitchen. Then, my grandmother hid behind the swinging door, at the square side table in the corner of the formal living room, to commit my father, her long nails clipping the dial of the rotary phone, which would not be rushed.

"A danger to himself," she recited more times than any of us could count.

But often it was just Grandma and me. "Do you have any lotion?" I asked, ready to take care of the woman who took care of us. I rubbed expired Vaseline intensive lotion on her rock tight shoulders and massaged out the blackheads, which collected in the pores of her neck from the metal chain that held the eyeglasses she took on and off all night to type and greet patients. Sometimes, she let me brush her brittle gold-colored hair that smelled of hairspray while we watched TV. In these small ways, she would allow me to take care of her, but she never asked. We sat in the living room, thin slices of Pepperidge Farm coconut layer cake on the folding TV trays in front of us while we watched the Carson monologue. Grandma smiled but never laughed at the jokes, which I only partly understood. But I watched her smirk at Johnny's sarcasm; I took note of the ways being a wise-ass could earn her esteem.

She went to bed when *Carson* was over, but didn't tell me to go to bed. She didn't worry about bedtimes, or mealtimes. She had bigger fish to fry. She and my mother were in agreement that people were their own best judge. But Grandma was the opposite from my mother in the way I felt seen and important to her.

I stayed up late into the night and watched *Perry Mason* and *Kojak*. Kojak and his lollipop-sucking tough remarks matched the approach of my family. I watched TV until I got tired and took myself to bed, either in the laundry room, where a single bed was curtained off in one corner of the room, or next door at Dad's house. Grandma's bedroom was the sun porch adjoining the living room, a glassed-in room, exactly where I would have slept if it had been my house. I once had a dream she was throwing stones at neighborhood kids from this exposed room where she was vulnerable to attack. My grandmother would be the first to throw stones to defend against intrusion. I had to stop her, to divert her great boulders, before the kids aimed larger boulders back at her. I had to keep the glass enclosure intact.

While our family struggled under the pressures of my father's mental illness, Hempstead, Long Island was straining against racial integration. Neighborhood demographics were shifting from white to brown. The new corner house on Baldwin Avenue was visibly from the old guard. It had a magnificent flowering cherry tree in the side yard by the driveway. Every spring it bloomed soft pink billowy flowers that reminded me of a southern plantation. If I had to place us in the shifting racial demographics, we were like tenant farmers. We gained enough advantage in our whiteness to aspire to rise to the educated class, but we still resided in the master's house. My aunt and uncles succeeded at being the second, third, and fourth in the family to get a college education, but my father's life was always marked by the ways his illness kept him and my grandmother from ever getting ahead.

AFRICAN PRINCESS

Sometimes Dad brought home his "ladies in waiting," as he called them. Grandma preferred not to know who came and went. When I arrived for the weekend, the woman I remember best had made herself at home. She stuck her hand out to me to kiss, saying, "You can call me African Princess," and I was fascinated. She was a petite, slender woman with a short, cropped Afro and large dangling earrings that framed her fierce eyes.

Dad picked up African Princess standing on a street corner in Ocean Beach in the middle of the winter, hungry and cold enough that she got into his car with the promise of coming home with him and getting warm. They made some kind of arrangement, Dad looking for company and African Princess happy to stay. "I take care of my ladies," he said high-handedly, as if he was keeping her out of harm's way by being the good John. She sauntered into the room, as if she owned the joint. She had a kick-ass regalness, which no one dared challenge. She sashayed from the back bedroom, her hips swinging from side to side, a bathrobe loosely wrapped around her slender body and slippers that brushed the floor, like a snare drum.

"Hey, baby, we's outta' cigarettes. Whatchu gonna do 'bout that?"

"I'll go to the store soon, baby," Dad offered.

African Princess commanded everyone like the *Cleopatra* my father imagined her to be. And in a don't-mess-with-me kind of way, she gave Dad a purpose for a period of time. "Someone need to clean up around here!" she complained and my father laughed, savoring her like a rich bitter drink that added flavor to his life. Still a good-looking man, you could tell by the look of admiration in his eyes that he relished her verve, maybe because to be tough in our family was heroic or maybe because it reminded him of the audacity his medication all but stifled.

She leaned into the corner of her seat, elbows on the table, with her skinny legs wound around each other, waiting for my father to wait on her. "You got rum and coke?" she said, an unlit cigarette in her mouth, waiting for a light. Her barely hidden disdain for others burned in her hot obsidian eyes. Freddie, Dad's pot dealer, was often hanging around. He scrambled to flick his Bic for the *princess*. He turned into a big suck-up around her; we all did. He generally showed up when other people were around. He was a young man, well built, with a medium short Afro and a thick seventies mustache. He wore a bright red leather jacket, and I loved the way he dressed like he had somewhere to be and the way he flirted with me, a nine-year-old girl pretending to be a young woman.

I sat at the table like I belonged. When a joint was passed in my direction, I smoked, inhaling cautiously. They teased me about getting high for the first time and I said, "Yeah, right." It was the first time, but they didn't need to know that. The Commodores' "Just to Be Close to You" played in the background, and I believed Freddie came to see me.

"Yo, man. I got these new wheels, just waiting to get the dough to get the insurance going, and then I'll be riding in style," Freddie bragged.

"Shut up, you fool," African Princess spat at him with a severity that made my father drag harder on his cigarette and focus on aiming sugar into his overfull coffee cup. Dad and I, happy to have some company, hoped he wouldn't go far. Freddie was a fixture in the neighborhood, and African Princess wasn't gonna last. She had no patience for stories. She expected goods and payments. She aspired to bigger stakes, which appealed to my dad's sense of adventure, but his plans were usually short-lived.

"I've got a beautiful idea. When I get my check, we'll score and turn a profit, baby," Dad said, promising her a better life. She sat at the table, her long fingers elegantly smoking my father's cigarettes.

"You all talk, where it at?" she challenged, her head lifted to exhale over him as if to make him invisible. I was fascinated by her ruthlessness. I wanted to be as tough and in control as she was; ruthless looked good on her.

She ate his food, smoked his cigarettes, drank his liquor in celebration of cashing his social security check. In the morning, she left with all the money in Dad's wallet while he was asleep. Pain and disappointment creased his face, standing at his dresser in his Haines briefs, to find his empty wallet. "Why? For God's sake! I was going to spend it all on that whore anyway," he said, shaking his head as if this were the last thing he anticipated. Even I knew to expect this; people were always taking advantage of my father. But part of his charm was how he was eternally hopeful that people would be better than they were.

"Come here, my princess," he said, patting the bed next to him. "At least you're not leaving me."

O CANADA

Dad's mom and I were bound by our mutual love for my father, but summers in Canada with my mother's parents offered refuge from the complications of my parents' lives. Every summer from age five until I was fifteen, I spent the summer with Annabelle and Mell at their lake cottage near Bracebridge, Ontario, five hours north of Buffalo, New York. Terrified of flying herself, my mother would take me to the gate for the flight from Newark to Buffalo and pick me up again in late August. The stewardess gave me junior pilot wings for flying alone and a tour of the pilot's cockpit, full of switches and gauges and friendly co-pilots before taking me to my front row seat.

My grandparents and I drove to the cottage on Skeleton Lake—five hours from Buffalo to Bracebridge—and stayed until August. I slept splayed out on the backseat of Grandpa's Lincoln Continental without a seat belt, until we arrived at our roadside picnic area where Grandma pulled out butter and salami sandwiches wrapped in wax paper, hard-boiled eggs, and cookies which I ate with a hunger I staved off all year.

A five-hour drive meant we left early in the morning and arrived midday. Grandpa coasted into his usual spot on the grassy field where we parked and would set up croquet for summer games with Grandma. We gathered our gear and groceries into a wheelbarrow and carried our bags along the pine-cushioned path to the cottage. It was a quarter of a mile to the tip of what we called

Peconic Point. The muffled quiet and smell of the pine and lake air cushioned us from the outside world.

Their cottage was a simple one-story rectangle with red asbestos shingles that sat on the top of a rock that sloped into Skeleton Lake. The inside had an open layout: one big room for living and three bedrooms along the back wall. It had tongue-and-groove pine walls and linoleum tile floors. Three large picture windows overlooked the lake in the living room and two wicker chairs sat facing the windows where Grandma and I sat to watch the sunset on the lake. Behind the maroon cotton couch was the kitchen area. A large square oak table with a yellow vinyl tablecloth sat in the center, and there was a counter and sink on the outer wall facing the lake, where we peeled potatoes and washed and dried dishes. An armchair next to the door at the entrance to the living room area was where Grandpa sat, facing the kitchen with his feet propped on the ottoman. On the table next to him was his transistor radio broadcasting the ballgame or news and occasionally the big band music that he loved.

The three bedrooms at the back end had doors and walls that stopped short of the ceiling. Grandpa and Grandma had separate rooms, like they did at home. I slept in a cot in my grandmother's room. I loved being with her. I didn't mind the lack of privacy. The third bedroom was a guest room where Uncle Joe, my grandmother's brother, stayed when he came to visit for several weeks at a time. At the far end of the kitchen was a room with a toilet and a basin for a sink. Bathing happened in the lake.

Grandma was four foot eleven inches—the same height my father's mother was and the same height at which I will stop growing. She was a spunky, petite woman who wore primary colors— red plaid pants together with striped shirts and beads that hung bosom-level. For outings to the store, her heart-shaped lips were always painted red, and she powdered her pert nose to remove the shine. She had an ample bosom for her size. As a child, I was underdeveloped, but as an adult I will have Grandma's breasts. Because she was deaf and hearing aids were clunky, her wide brassieres came in handy. Her hearing aid clipped to the center, her chest whistled under her shirt when the volume was too high. I leaned into her powdery smell and gentle breathing when we sat on the couch together. She was mine and I was hers.

My mom, Judith, as she had me call her as a child, never joined us at the cottage. I didn't miss her, but sometimes I felt her absence at Grandma and Grandpa's, as if their love reminded me of what I wasn't getting. The year before my half sister was born, when I was eight and vying for my mother's attention in demanding ways, my mother told me, "I love you but I really don't like you." She was relentlessly honest that way. I also didn't like her, and sometimes I wondered who didn't love the other first?

Over time I came to understand she didn't like her parents either. She rarely visited because she had decided long ago that they didn't like her: a cycle of not loving or feeling loved. Grandma and I both lost my mother in the course of our lifetimes. Perhaps it's fairer to say we both rejected the detachment and autonomy my mother demanded. So, we made the most of our once removed alliance. I was hungry for care and home-cooked meals, and my grandmother lavished on me all the love my mother had rejected and all the meat and potatoes I could eat.

"Why do grandmothers love their grandchildren more than mothers do?" I asked once.

"It's not that your mother doesn't love you, Tash. It's just who she is."

* * *

Uncle Joe came to visit for weeks at a time. After serving in the First World War, he earned the title of mechanical engineer as a tradesman, though I have no idea what he engineered. He always wore a button-down shirt with a pen in the pocket and his hair slicked back. He was the kind of uncle who sent my letters back red-lined with grammatical corrections, and he played cards as if the author of Hoyle's rulebook were watching. When Joe was up, we played slow games of gin rummy, where Uncle Joe tediously engineered all the possibilities in hand. We all grew weary of his taking the game too seriously, but only Grandpa, who wasn't a fan of having his brother-in-law around all the time and whose arthritis made his hands ache, would throw his cards on the table. "For God's sake. I'm out!"

* * *

Nearly every morning after breakfast I walked the mile down the gravel road to my summer friends. The Bournes had two daughters, Donna and Leslie, who were my age, and we spent each sunny day in the lake. Grandma often joined me for the walk to their house because we liked being together. I felt bad leaving her all day but she let me know it was important to her that I had fun. She would return to the cottage and the wildflower bouquet we picked on the way would be waiting for me in a vase on the table. I always came back before suppertime.

Donna, Leslie, and their parents, Eva and Jack—or Dear, as the family affectionately called him—were my Canadian family. I liked to think I livened up their Canadian restraint with my Yankee confidence, but deep down I yearned to be part of their nuclear family. "Will you pass me a fork, Dear," I asked, claiming an intimacy I felt eating lunch together every day at the dock. I soaked up the lightheartedness of Jack and Eva as they joked around and pushed each other into the lake. I felt guilty eating and drinking their pop every day, so I earned my keep by trying to be funny, "It's soda where I come from, ay," and they laughed.

Leslie, Donna, and I played mermaids on the floating dock. We clumped algae on our heads and bobbed in the shallows of the lake. I was included in their lives and never talked about the details of my own. I wouldn't find out for many years to come that Leslie, their youngest daughter, suffered a lifelong battle with anorexia, or that Eva felt stifled in her role as full-time mom. To me, the way Eva cared for her kids and loved Jack, and the way they took me in, made them the perfect family. I didn't consciously hide my life from them, but as far as they were concerned, my grandparents were my only worry. "I should get home," I said, when the sun got low in the sky.

An avid reader, Grandma would be sitting on the coach with a *Reader's Digest* condensed book on her lap when I returned. We prepared dinner together. Always, there were potatoes and a vegetable to go with whatever meat was the center of the meal. Kielbasa, pork chops, and chipped beef were staples. Instead of helping, Grandpa yelled at us when the pots and pans rattled too loudly.

"Damn it, Annie, what's all that racket!" he complained, as if her hearing aid wasn't whistling its own objections in her ear. She would look at me knowingly, and I would pat her downy, salt and pepper hair to show her I loved her and that Grandpa was being a jerk. If we had something to talk about out of Grandpa's earshot, we would hike up the rocks behind the cottage.

"Why do you stay with him?" I asked her once.

"You wouldn't understand this yet, but we take the good with the bad," she said. In my world, the adults came and went according to how they felt at the moment.

On rainy days, I stayed with them at the cottage and loved to eavesdrop from the cot in the bedroom while my grandparents complained about the life my mother had so conspicuously built apart from them.

"Is Judy still with that man?" Grandpa would wonder aloud about my mother's latest boyfriend to answer the phone. "Too bad she never comes to visit," he would say, nostalgic for the connection that was hard to have with him. I could picture my grandmother's brow furrowed in shared disappointment.

"At least we have Tash!"

We had each other. I futzed around the cottage with Grandpa while he cursed at things that went wrong. Other times we went out, just he and I, in the rowboat with its small above-board motor. Grandma hated the water, maybe because her ears needed to stay dry. Grandpa's favorite thing to do was to slowly tour around the perimeter of the lake, gently whistling through his teeth as he noticed the changes in the shoreline. I loved my grandfather, but you had to take him on his terms. He was a lot like my mother that way. His pat on your hand, when sitting next to him or wordlessly stacking wood with him, was as much as you could expect. So, when he said, "Look how strong she is, Annie," when I carried an armful of wood to the wood stove, I felt especially worthy.

At dinner I ate seconds and sometimes third helpings and filled in my thin frame— always returning to my mother tan and grown. We sat at dinner; the sounds of our eating punctuated by my reports of the day. How far I swam, what we found on the shoreline. After Grandma and I did the dishes, we drank ginger ale floats with vanilla ice cream or each had two pieces of candy from the box. Our neighbors would comment when I got home, "You put some meat on those bones this summer!"

The summer stretched out in a way it doesn't anymore. Eventually, we would load the wheelbarrow full of our luggage and supplies for the trip back to Buffalo. Unlike leaving my father, I wasn't sad to leave the cottage. My grandparents would be just the same when I saw them next. They would survive the time apart while I ventured back to school, and to the chaos of my parents' lives. I could depend on the constancy of our summers and their love for me.

TED

The summer of 1973, when I was eight years old, my grandparents made the long drive from Canada to Staten Island to bring me home. In part, I think, they wanted an excuse to see my mother, who never came to the cottage and only sometimes visited for Christmas. We arrived at an unlocked apartment and found my mother had a new lover. They had cut an opening between the two apartments.

They stood together, arms over each other's shoulders, dressed in similar tank tops. The sun highlighted their long armpit hair in the opening between the apartments, its ragged thresholds connecting the sloping floors of the two apartments. I hated their unruly hair and their same clothes. "We're living together!" she announced. "Come see your new room," she said, smiling like I should appreciate all the change and Ted's new unannounced position in our lives. My old bedroom was now their room. I would be moving into Ted's old room, his creepy old room off the kitchen, that felt like he had left something of himself there.

My grandparents had a telephone party line at the cottage, two short rings and one long. Over the summer I sometimes hoped it would be my mother calling. It never was. We never talked when I was away for the summer, but this new living arrangement seemed phone-call worthy. She could have told me that he was moving in. I also didn't know she knew Ted from college or that he had been her lover briefly when my father was in the hospital.

The new double-size apartment entrance was through Ted's apartment door, which opened to his living room and kitchen. The wall between the two rooms had been opened to studs with horizontal shelves that held coleus and spider plants and his prized pottery. The kitchen had a bathtub with a piece of plywood on top to serve as a kitchen counter. Dirty dishes collected until someone washed them, either because there was no more space to pile them up, or because it was time for a bath. When did they take baths, I wonder now? When we lived alone, I took a bath every few weeks out in the open of the kitchen. Janis Joplin shouted out "Me and Bobbie McGee" while my mother did laundry in an old school washer with a rolling wringer to squeeze the clothes dry. Then she hung them out to dry on the line off the fire escape. The apartment smelled like clay and cat litter for Ted's cat, Critter. Critter was an old gray tom cat with an oozing wound on his tail, as if someone had shut his tail in the door and it had never healed.

The apartment was bigger but there was less room for me.

Just off the kitchen, my new small bedroom had a window, sealed shut to keep winter breezes out, which looked out onto the New York Bay. Over time they would build me a loft bed to make room for a dresser and table under it. A set of shelves made with wood from the piers was in the corner where I would spend hours playing Barbie. I pretended Barbie, with her hourglass figure, and Ken, in his camouflage outfits, were on far away African adventures in Barbie's pink jeep. I made Ken dependable and Barbie bossy in high heels. I listened to the Beatles "Hey Jude" cranked loud. I kept my bedroom door shut because instinctively I knew it was better not to let my mother or Ted know what I cared about. It was in the privacy of my room with the record player blaring that I imagined being powerful enough to change my world. Singing "Revolution" as loud as I could.

Ted was a Renaissance man, a potter, painter, and musician. His dirty blond hair reached down his back in a ponytail. When our new blended family took walks along the New York harbor, his meandering stride was deceptive; no one would know this tall, handsome Scandinavian man with angular strong features was a man you should think twice about messing with. The elegance of his pottery and steady strokes of his bay landscapes didn't show the way he was just waiting for a fight. I liked his paintings and pottery. I would go downstairs to watch him turn or glaze a pot in his ground floor studio where he sold his wares. I wanted one bowl enough to do a hundred chores to earn it—a cereal-size bowl with egg-white crackle glaze.

But it didn't take long to understand he was a man who took positions and expected to have his way. At the arts league he belonged to, he fought over where paintings were hung and paying his dues. He would argue with the woman in charge, "So you think it's right that I pay the same as you and my paintings are in the back room?" cornering her with his finger in her face. "You need to play fair," he threatened until her husband stepped in and he backed down. My mother and Ted were well suited on that front; they both demanded that other people see their points of view but also didn't care what people thought.

My biggest objection to our new sleeping arrangements was the cockroaches that ruled our house at night. With my new room off the kitchen, I had to scamper across the kitchen floor to pee—past the dirty dishes where the dreaded roaches swarmed every night. I sat on the toilet in the small tiled lavatory next to the kitchen with my feet held off the ground and then scurried back on my toes to the safety of my bed. I detested the roaches and their audacious trespassing when the lights were off. But there was something fascinating about their sleek, ruthless bodies built for survival: how their tiny oval eggs lay in the dark cracks, and the baby roaches that hatched and multiplied where we couldn't see. There was something revolting and captivating about their numbers and how they could squeeze into spaces and thrive in the dark.

LANGUAGE OF SURVIVAL

When God spoke to my father and he took off, roaming the streets in unfamiliar cities or detained at the Canadian border for declaring himself the Messiah, I felt his absence, like a death, like I ceased to belong to anyone. I had this suffocating sense of mortality that closed in on me at night like a heavy blanket. I would pray to God for understanding. "Why is this his life? Why are all the adults falling so short? What is wrong with me?" I cried quietly in bed.

Our neighborhood in Stapleton, Staten Island was made up of poor black families who lived in the projects and white working-class Irish cops and Italian mafiosi who lived in the single-family homes. *Black is beautiful* graffiti on our apartment building door spoke volumes about the naive hope of integration in the sixties and seventies. Motown wafted out the windows, and bold-colored laundry flapped in the breeze on the clothesline. My mother and her friends imagined themselves part of a cultural revolution for all, but they were poor artists by choice, while most of our black and brown neighbors were locked into generational poverty. Despite all the peace and love talk, we continued to fail to deliver on the pact of reconstruction.

I watched from the sidelines as girls from the next building played Double Dutch, girls with plastic clip barrettes at the end of twisted cornrows, their skin shiny and brown. "Cousins" and "sisters" joined in syncopated motion, teetered back and forth, like a rocking horse, to enter the beating ropes chanting, *"Miss Mary*

Mack Mack Mack. All dressed in black, black, black..."—songs they just knew. *"Hambone, Hambone have you heard? Papa's gonna buy me a mockingbird"*—rhymes and rhythms known and absorbed like white privilege was ours to have.

* * *

Next door was an extended African American family we came to know and love. Gwen and Gary, and his parents, siblings, and cousins all lived in two apartments. Gwen was pregnant with their first baby. Gary often sat outside the building, a pick stuck in the perfect roundness of his Afro and a conga drum between his legs. "Where you been, Aunt Tasha?" he sang out to me on the block. I loved his sweet falsetto harmonies as he sang— "Papa was a Rolling Stone"... the conga drum he played syncopating each beat. The sound of making do echoed on our street like a broken promise. The adults laughed and smoked reefer together and had the occasional backyard BBQ, but we never went to each other's homes. We lived next to each other in different worlds. I was aware, even as a young child, that our communities were separate but not equal.

But they had something we didn't. I remember one time they invited me to come up for lunch, maybe because I was so undersized or maybe because I asked what they were having. We sat around a small table, and Gwen, the grandparents, and kids ate spaghetti with butter. One of the baby cousins sucked on a lollipop. Gary had a dentist appointment for a bad tooth, and there were work schedules and childcare to figure out. I was too young to watch their baby but old enough to notice the way they took care of each other. I envied how they allowed candy for lunch and how they helped each other figure things out. I wanted to belong to the community that spoke the language of survival: "Who you looking at?" and "Don't be talking about my mother," were a promise to stand by each other. As a little white child with a hippie mother who didn't stick it out with anyone, I had no claim to that surety.

* * *

Instead of going to the district public school, I went to a private-run Free School from first through third grade. It wasn't free, but parents were instructors alongside one head teacher, which made it more affordable. Students were "free" to decide what and how they wanted to learn. We even had a say on hiring and firing. I resented the lack of structure and wanted to go to a "real school," but my mother believed in the model of education where kids knew best, and public school wasn't that.

Our school met in the basement of St. Paul's Episcopal Church. We were children whose parents wanted progressive education or wanted out of the "rough" public school. We roamed the woods behind the church and claimed encampments in the bushes. I spent the better part of a year drawing the church and researching its history for a local historical society; figuring out how many stones were in the walls of the church was my math work that year.

Of all the parents who taught at the school, it was Mr. Brown, an organic chemist, I liked most. We sat in our basement classroom with plastic models, elements that we combined to make organic molecules that made up the world around us. The idea that atoms and compounds could be linked together appealed to my interest in God's plan, which like my father, I yearned to understand. One day we visited his laboratory workplace where we gained entry with his plastic ID. We stood watching the machines that manipulated molecules to make plastics. At the age of eight, I could imagine myself at a job with this kind of purpose and influence: mimicking nature, manipulating the very biomolecules we were made of.

But I happened to hate his son, Cory, because his pageboy

haircut was perfectly round and impossible to mess up. Also, because he had the family I wanted: a gainfully employed father and a mother who wore aprons, cooked meals, and took care of her children. With the freedom to challenge authority and a pent-up fury at my mother's indifference, I told my teachers to "sit down and wait for kids to ask for help." I brawled with classmates for a turn with the jump rope or my favorite game, kids who were free to do as they pleased but who didn't understand you weren't supposed to put your needs ahead of another's. When Cory wanted a turn with the toy in my hand, I grabbed him by the hair and bit his arm. When the teacher broke up our fight, I was grateful and furious; she had no idea what I was fighting for but neither did I! I was always testing what the adults were made of, if they could handle me, if they would stick around.

* * *

The Solomon-Oleyetos across the hall from our apartment were my stand-in family. Ofelia was a tall, beautifully pear-shaped, knock-kneed Cuban immigrant, an intellectual whose dissertation was built on index cards found on every surface of their home. She studied the life of a Spanish writer and critic of fascism in Spain, Sofia Casanova. Ofelia had lived under another dictator in Cuba and fled when Castro's regime took everything the family owned. As a child, I only knew she cooked delicious food and disappeared for hours at a time to write her book.

In third grade, I started babysitting her toddler boys after school for a dollar an hour while she wrote. I warmed Progresso minestrone soup for us to eat, and on occasion, mistakenly zipped their little penises into their pants, to screams of pain and promises of candy if they just wouldn't interrupt their mother's work.

Alan, her partner, was a short, rotund man with a large, hard belly and short legs. He was a pacifist who went to prison instead of fighting in Vietnam and was the first ideologue I knew. He did things like chew his food a hundred times before swallowing it. But his proclivities—the *Playboy* magazines under his bed and the way he tickled his children and me on the floor of their living room until we begged for mercy—seemed inconsistent with his peacenik principles and I was a child bruising for a fight. I resented his control and didn't trust him, but he adored Ofelia and so did I. Her self-assured, Latin-infused confidence was like an expensive perfume I secretly felt I didn't deserve. She was the first of a series of mothers I kept close.

When I arrived at their apartment door, which was most days, she would laugh melodically with her Cuban accent. "Oh Natasha, my dear, what *are* you doing wrapped in that scarf?" One part skeptical of the freedom my mother gave me to dress in whatever I wanted and one part enamored with my independence. I sat in a corner of their living room cutting out pictures from magazines of the brides I aspired to be, imagining myself in a beautiful gown ready to start a normal family. Compared with the empty quiet of our apartment across the hall, Ofelia's house was alive with the Cuban-flavored Spanish that syncopated conversations with her sister Nellie and the Puccini and Verdi arias that played endlessly on their reel-to-reel player. I stayed as long as I could hoping for an invitation to eat the matzo ball soup and *arroz con pollo* that simmered on the stove. I went home as little as possible.

My closest friend, Jenny, lived between school and our apartment, beyond the projects at the top of the hill. Jenny went to the Free School because her mother felt the public school was too dangerous. Her mother, Binnie, was agoraphobic and never left their apartment. Jenny and I shared a bond over family members who needed us to be there, and I was always welcome at their house because Binnie wanted Jenny home. We jumped on the pull-out coach where Binnie slept in the living room of their basement apartment, singing at the top of our lungs, *"Binnie, Binnie, Binnie and the Je-e-e-e-t-s."* We yelled over the relentless squawking of Peter and Henrietta in their hanging cage: "Pretty bird, pretty bird," they screeched. Binnie smiled, exhaling smoke from her toothless grin, grateful for the four walls, the love, and her namesake song.

In the blue of her mother's chain-smoking, Jenny and I played Barbies for hours. She understood the importance of fairness. Each of us took turns picking the doll, the clothes, and the furniture to furnish the apartment building we built out of her bureau drawers. "I want the sequence dress."

"I'll take Ken."

"The sofa's mine." We bargained, until we had created the best possible set-up. Then it was time to clean up and go home before the streetlights and dinner time.

When I couldn't face going home or "ran away," I hid out on the back stairs to Jenny's basement apartment. Jenny brought me a peanut butter and jelly sandwich while I waited for my mother to notice I was gone. When it started to get dark, Binnie told me I better get home.

One evening walking through the park between Jenny's and our apartment, Darlene, one of Gary's cousins, ran up and pushed me up against the wrought iron railing, demanding, "How much money you got?" I pulled out the dollar in my pocket and she snatched it, pushed me, and ran off as if we were strangers. Hot tears streamed down my face. As much as I felt a kinship with kids who like me had to be vigilant, who knew how to keep their needs below the radar, in that moment I was just a white girl who had a dollar Darlene needed more than me. My own survival would require I get tougher and learn how to survive outside the pack.

DEMON CHILD

When Dad picked me up for the weekend that spring night, he announced, "It's time I took you to see this important film, my dear." We were going straight to the theater to see *The Exorcist*. I was eight years old and didn't know anything about the film, but I was excited to be going out with Dad.

The only other movies I remember seeing with Dad were *Song of the South* and *Bambi*. Even though I didn't like cartoons, didn't believe in characters that could fall off cliffs and stand up again, he took me to Disney films. Maybe he had an idea that parents should go to movies with their kids, like he tried to be a good brother by showing his younger siblings how to play ball and work a paper route. The day we went to see *Bambi*, the theater was full of families in the seats around us who talked over each other, kids demanding attention from parents and fighting over who held the popcorn. I listened and watched through our ambient quiet while Dad and I sat, candy in hand, wordlessly waiting for the lights to dim.

"Did you go to the movies when you were a kid?" I asked.

"Well, Tasha..." he started like he had a marvelous tale to weave but never finished; I was left to imagine the tangle of thoughts he couldn't unravel or felt he had to protect me from.

The movie finally started with a picture-perfect woodland scene. The fawn and its mother pranced and grazed on the brush until menacing music warned of danger. "Run, Bambi, run!"

the mother cautioned, and then a gunshot exploded and Bambi rushed into the thicket. After the fawn came out alone calling and calling for his missing mother, a lone stag appeared majestically on the hilltop, and it was apparent by the tilt of his head, that this was the father, heroic and steady, who would guide him through a motherless world. Sitting in the darkened theater, I heard my father sniffing rhythmically to keep his nose from running, his face wet with tears.

I had never seen my father cry. "Are you crying?" I asked. It didn't seem possible that this animated world would make him sad. Plus, I knew one could survive without a mother.

"It's a sad movie," he said, wiping his nose with the back of his hand. Usually, he managed his grief privately. I never knew what he was feeling; instead, I imagined his pain like it was my own. But here in the dark theater with his young daughter next to him, his tears flowed like a diverted torrent. Some brain studies show schizophrenics experience emotions at least as intensely as the rest of us. But the part of the brain that anticipates, makes sense of, or responds to experiences lights up in the brain differently, like it is caught unaware every time and doesn't know how to respond. One study shows how, compared with the normal brains that react to relational images like puppies, schizophrenic brains light up more to symbolic, neutral images, like a chair. I think about how my father was always searching for meaning in symbols. Maybe cartoons were like chairs or caricatures of people that made it easier for my father to feel something? I would never see him cry again, but it made me want to take care of him. He needed me. I took his hand as we left the theater, proud of his big heart.

* * *

Tonight, he was determined for me to see *The Exorcist*. He

marched me up to the ticket window, his thick hand holding mine. "How old is the girl? You do know this is an R-rated film? Are you her parent or guardian?" the salesgirl asked.

"Of course, she's my child," he said, offended at the insinuation that the Messiah didn't know his own seed. "She's twelve, just small for her age," he lied, and I worried she wouldn't let us in. He pushed his cash under the glass to end the interrogation and she handed us our tickets. We ignored her concerned look as we marched to the concession. "We'll have an extra-large popcorn and Good & Plenty," he ordered, always the biggest and most with him. I followed his march into the dark theater to a seat near the aisle.

The movie started with a beautiful call to prayer. Men swung picks at a dig. The sun rose God-like in the sky to meet the prayer. Something important was dug up.

I sat in the dark, beside my father—the bucket of warm popcorn on my skinny knees as the scene changed to a prepubescent girl being raised by her mother in what seemed to be a normal life on an ordinary fall day. But the film quickly turned dark and scary. Something takes hold of the girl. She has scratches on her pale, puffy face. Her body's slammed into the bed by a demon inside her. I sat horror-struck as I watched the girl transform into a beast, her face blotchy and purple, her skin bulging and erupting from the violence of her possession. As if being molested by the demon from the inside out, she yelled, deep-throated, at her mother and the priests, "Fuck me, fuck me!" and thrust her pelvis at the priests standing at her bedroom door. Her transformation from girl to beast was so sexual it was mortifying. My body was shaking. Even the priests seemed to be hurting the girl in their effort to exorcise the demon. They raised crosses and intoned their *Our Father's* like weapons against the possessed child. It was the failure of the priests, their powerlessness in the face of the demon-girl that I found most disturbing.

The scene where she drives a crucifix into her crotch and pulls her mother's head violently between her bloody legs, demanding "Lick me, lick me!" was when people began walking out. I sat shaking, breathing shallow and holding myself still in order not to be seen. My father leaned over to see my reaction. He didn't say anything, just looked at me. I couldn't move. When the film ended and we got outdoors, I stormed ahead of him.

"What the hell is wrong with you?" I shouted, while people pretended not to look at the eight-year-old girl screaming at her father. I stormed ahead of him to the car, my stomach in knots. I sat in the back seat, as images replayed in my mind of the child's swollen head spinning around her neck, green vomit spewing into the face of the priest. "I hate you," I erupted. "Why the hell would you take me to that movie?"

"Well, Tasha, I had my reasons. I have a special message to impart you know," he said thick with connotation. "As my daughter, you're at risk."

"Fuck you. You don't know what you're talking about. You're an idiot," I raged at him and felt bad but wouldn't take it back. We didn't speak in the car. When we got home, I went to my bedroom and slammed the door. I threw myself on the bed and cried. My father was trying to show me something. But that knowledge, that power made me feel dangerous, as if I might squeeze the life out of anything precious or fragile with my premature self-rule. Like in a recurring dream I have of a family of baby mice in my bed, so delicate and soft that I imagine crushing them.

WE BEAT THE DEVIL

The next day Dad announced, "We're going to church, Tasha. Get dressed." We were headed to the local Catholic parish in Hempstead, where we had been before when God called Dad to worship. He wasn't a regular churchgoer; mostly we went around Easter time, when he identified most with the rituals of the resurrection of Christ. Usually we got there late, just in time to line up for the priest to press paper-thin wafers to my unbaptized tongue, which was strictly prohibited. "Go on up and take the sacrament," Dad encouraged, since in our family rules were considered suggestions for people who couldn't make up their own minds.

On this day, we arrived in Grandma's maroon 1948 Oldsmobile to an empty church parking lot. I was dressed in my eight-year-old best, a lightweight, sleeveless, peach-flowered dress, that wasn't warm enough for the day.

The church was dark and quiet as a crypt. It smelled of wax from the rows of prayer candles in the votive stands. I remember a silver chalice with embedded gems that sat on the altar, spotlighted with gentle lights. I was drawn to the beauty of the church, everything so reassuringly in place. I preferred being there without the judgment of the priests and the paces of the mass—the standings, kneelings, and sittings-down of the ritual. I walked up to the bloody figure of Christ with a crown of thorns lit up behind the lectern. I wondered how he bore the nails through his hands with such understanding in his face. There was something familiar about the betrayal and the faith in his face. My father watched as I stood looking at the larger-than-life crucifix, until, as if he had made a decision, he announced, "Stay here, I have to find the priest," leaving me in the chapel alone.

There were shafts of blood red and dark blue light streaming through the stained-glass windows on the cold wooden pews. I stood alone and wondered what to do, not understanding why we were there, not feeling anything that I can remember but recalling the scene in muted tones as if filtered through gauze. There are four kinds of memory—semantic, episodic, procedural, and emotional—all processed in different parts of the brain. They say memories stick when there's an emotional charge. Sometimes events will be scrambled or less organized, sometimes you won't remember what happened, other times you may just not remember how you felt. It will be forty years before I know why this memory stuck.

I can imagine I heard my father's agitated voice as he spoke with the priest in the other room. "Damn it, man… can't you help us?" Or was it as quiet and empty as I remember? On my toes to reach, I dipped my fingers in the basin of holy water at the entrance and made an unspoken prayer to whoever was in charge, touching my forehead and then either side of my chest to make the sign of the cross, hoping not to offend any higher power by not knowing which side came first. I was reaching back into the basin just as my father walked back in the room, with the priest trailing behind him, yelling, "You're an ignorant sheep," and the basin of holy water tipped and spilled all over the front of my dress. The priest looked at me disapprovingly, as if our visit was a problem for him and now I had made it worse by spilling the holy water.

"I'm sorry," I said.

"My dear girl, you've been anointed!" Dad said, elated, as if my wet dress was just what he wanted.

The priest was unimpressed. "It's time for you to take the girl and go."

"Don't worry, my child, it's a sign from God." Dad put a hand on my shoulder and guided me toward the door. I felt responsible about the empty stoup of holy water but was relieved to be leaving. My dress stuck to me in wet flimsy layers and was chilly on my body as I followed behind my father's brisk steps.

"What was wrong with that priest?" I asked, trying to keep up. "It's not like we committed a crime."

"He's a fucking idiot! Pretends to be a man of the cloth but he's just a moneychanger, a dealer in salvation," he answered, aggravated and energized.

Relieved to be back in the warm car with its familiar smell of cigarettes and Grandma's hairspray, we drove away. Our tires screeched as we turned into the anonymity of Hempstead Turnpike like we were getting away with something, which it felt like we had.

I tried to be funny as we drove past the strip malls.

"Why is it that every diner is Greek?" I quipped, but my father barely looked at me. Usually, he laughed when I made a joke. But he was distracted by something more than the priest. "What was a sign from God?" I asked, impatient to understand what had happened. After a long silence, I prodded, "Dad?" Still no answer. Then finally,

"You have been purified by the holy spirit, my child. We've beaten the devil at his game!"

TO MEET THE HORIZON

"We're going to visit Aunt Rosalyn for an adventure," Dad announced when we got home. We climbed back into Grandma's Oldsmobile, stopped at the store for cigarettes and a gallon of Gallo wine, and headed out to the Hamptons. I was always happy for a trip to the beach.

Aunt Rosalyn, as we referred to her, was a heavyset Long Island woman whom my grandmother counted as a close friend. She loved how rich and unapologetic Rosalyn could afford to be. In turn, Rosalyn looked to my grandmother for advice. Grandma had a surety about her, a hard-won perspective that she doled out like a mafia don at the kitchen table. Rosalyn, with her white convertible Cadillac, high heels, fancy handbags, and privileged life, was a regular among my grandmother's devotees, who shared her secrets over coffee and cigarettes. In turn, our family was welcome to visit Aunt Rosalyn's second home at the beach in Southampton, Long Island. I don't know if anyone had ever taken Rosalyn up on the offer before and we would never visit again.

The house was offset from the ocean with a manicured garden of beach grass and begonias. The pebble driveway crunched under our feet as Dad and I approached the door, past the four-door garage, where Rosalyn's many cars and her live-in driver, Lenny, were housed. Lenny was a skinny, quiet man. He would run errands, take her places and wait; like the perfect "help," he was attentive but not intrusive. Years later, when I was old enough to consider their arrangement, I wondered if they were lovers. He stuck around despite the fact that Rosalyn never stopped talking, pinched people's cheeks too hard, and didn't listen when you answered her questions.

"How are you, hun?" she asked, grabbing my face between her hands.

"Lenny, get them something to eat! It's so late. You must be hungry and tired. I didn't know you were coming. Did you call?" Rosalyn asked. She acted happy to see us but looked uncomfortable. In a house as well-kept as a museum, the refrigerator was empty, which might have been her weight loss strategy. Lenny went to the store and came back with a block of cheese and box of crackers for us to eat. We ate the makeshift dinner and she showed us to a room with two twin beds. Dad stayed up talking with Rosalyn after I went to bed.

The next thing I remember is my father's hand rocking my shoulder to wake me up.

"Tasha, I have something to show you," he urged, walking toward the door in the predawn light, his hands curiously animated. Getting up early was a departure from our usual morning routine. Happy for the adventure, I climbed out of bed and pulled on my sweater. My skinny arms and legs were cold in the moist morning air.

Rosalyn must have heard us, because she stepped out into the hallway wrapped in a robe and asked, "Where are you going at this hour?"

"To meet the horizon," Dad said. "That's where many great minds have gone for inspiration."

When I relayed this memory to my father years later, he told me that Rosalyn, alarmed at the idea of my manic dad alone with me at the beach, threatened to call the cops if he took me to the ocean at that hour.

"You do what you have to do," my father might have said, undeterred in his mission. I don't recall the police being called.

"Where are we going?" I asked, stepping lightly with bare feet on the pebbled driveway.

"To watch the sunrise, my dear," he said with importance. We got to the sloping dunes and sat on the cool sand overlooking the ocean as the sun, yellow and globe-like, rose into the sky like a mighty presence. "It's time we practice the Our Father," he said. I sat close to him for warmth and listened to his incantation. "Our Father who art in Heaven, hallowed be thy name," he began. Our voices merged, "Thy kingdom come. Thy will be done on earth as it is in Heaven."

MY FATHER'S CONCUBINE

The child psychologist, Don Catalena, sat elegantly, one slender leg crossed over the other while he asked questions. "What is life at home like? What happens when you wet your bed?"

When I first started wetting the bed, I would flip my blanket and sheets down in the morning so they would dry by the next night. I told my grandmother that I was embarrassed and couldn't sleep at friends' houses anymore because I was afraid of an accident. Florrie called my mother and suggested she take me to see someone.

I saw him once or maybe twice, but I remember feeling cared for. He advised my mother to set her alarm in the middle of the night, to wake me up to pee and check if my bed was wet. If I had wet the bed, we took off the sheets and replaced them with dry ones. As if all she needed were instructions on mothering, she woke me, reminded me to pee, and was patient. This kindness on my mother's part, getting up to check on me and the comfort of the line-dried sheets were all I needed to cure my bedwetting. Children wet the bed when parents are in conflict, with a new baby on the way, or from stress. All of which were true. My mother was newly pregnant with my unborn sister, and Ted and my mother were fighting more often than not. Fights that turned to slapping and pushing and screaming. Fights I heard from the backyard where I kept my distance

*　*　*

That winter, my father was corresponding with Sarah H., the adult daughter of the family that lived in the downstairs apartment of our building. Sarah was beautiful with soft, kinky dark blonde hair and lush lips. Sarah's mom was African American and Sarah's father, Dr. H., was white. He was a professor of the literature of Nabokov and Anais Nin. He was infamous among his students for espousing the virtues of one's natural drive toward pleasure, even incest. He posited that it was a natural instinct that many great artists and kings were inclined toward. His daughters were schooled concubine-like to play instruments and read literature and poetry, and rumor had it, their father taught them the fine art of satisfying a man's sexual needs. The oldest daughter, Dulce, was reported to be a high-class call girl. I remember Dulce visiting her parents in stylish pantsuits with bellbottom flare and a felt hat with a peacock feather that rippled in the bay breeze.

The younger daughter, Sarah, had a series of unlikely boyfriends who were neither cultured nor worthy of her talents as a cello player and a woman of literature. I imagine it was a way of getting back at her father.

Big Brown, a homeless brown giant Sarah brought over from Manhattan, lived in the abandoned van in the backyard for a summer. On hot summer days he walked the neighborhood barefoot with his huge distended belly hanging shirtless over a dirty pair of chinos. He was weirdly mild mannered and demanding at the same time. He would knock at our apartment doors around suppertime. "I'm sorry to bother you all, but you have a little something you could spare?" he would ask, his huge bare belly so in need of filling. There was something so dissonant about the man who mumbled apologies for being in the way, but who made his presence so inescapable and was so huge he could lift you in the air with one hand.

We didn't understand why Sarah was attached to this man who was as objectionable as she was refined, but he became a fixture in the neighborhood for a period of time. Sometime later Sarah had a child named Sylvia. The father was an African American boxer who didn't stick around, so she was back in her parents' apartment with Sylvia, who was several years younger than I was.

Sarah and my father began corresponding after my parents split up. They saw each other when Dad came to get me. Then, when Dad went into the hospital, they wrote letters to each other. Just weeks after his release, Sarah moved in with Dad, and they were planning to be married.

My father, dashing and handsome and eager to support her and her daughter, was her ticket out of the family apartment and off of Staten Island. It wasn't the first time my father was drawn to caring for a woman and her young daughter. Although Dad may have been an improvement on Big Brown, her parents didn't approve of the match. It was my grandmother who helped them plan the wedding, a wedding Sarah's parents did not attend. I have a picture of me in the wedding party, but I have no memory of it. In the picture my father is smiling like a Cheshire cat, with Sarah and me looking like we've been pasted into the picture from another less happy moment in time. Sarah's daughter, Sylvia, is conspicuously missing. There's another picture of my father with his tuxedo and bow tie on, a lock of hair falling jauntily forward. He's walking down the pathway next to his parents' old house, the bright white snow contrasting elegantly with his tux. You can see a lilt to his step even in still life; he is a man who has everything he wants in the moment.

I wanted to live with my father, his new wife Sarah, and her young daughter, Sylvia; I wanted to get away from my mother and Ted. When I told my mother, she said, "If you want to live with your father, that's up to you. Call Florence to see what she says." Where my father was concerned, my grandmother made the decisions.

"I want to move in with Dad." I lobbied, "I don't like the Free School. I want to go to a real school, and I hate Ted." I don't know how much Grandma knew about Ted and Mom's relationship. None of us talked about the nights my mother was being slapped back and pushed against the bedroom wall. But on the topic of living with Dad, Grandma generally bet on my father's prospects improving and our new blended family could be just the thing. Everyone agreed. I would finish out the school year in Hempstead and live with Dad, Sarah, and Silvia.

Sarah hung curtains and put vases of dried flowers in the living room. Sylvia, who I had never met, was six when I was nine. She was a shy girl with big hair and light brown skin. We were strangers to each other really; her mother wasn't mine and my father wasn't hers. Like characters in a surreal play in which my dad and Sarah were trying to rewrite their lives, Sylvia and I acted like siblings, and feigned being a family living in my father's childhood house.

* * *

The light switch in the hall was industrial grade and clicked obscenely loudly in the still of our empty home as if to call attention to the space we couldn't fill. Sylvia and I each had our own bedroom, upstairs off a short hall with brown linoleum tile, hospital green walls, with a bare light bulb in the ceiling. My room was sparsely furnished with a twin mattress, a closet, and a small religious icon of Mary and baby Jesus on the wall. I don't remember meals or outings or bedtimes. I have one memory of Sylvia playing dirty doctor with me in my bedroom. The bedroom door closed as genitals were touched and secrets were kept. When I was old enough to have heard the stories of their family, I worried privately that I was joining in the legacy of the family's sexual misconduct. But no one was watching us; there were bigger problems on the horizon. Dad became manic and increasingly paranoid about Sarah's parents being in cahoots with the mob, about some professor he needed to communicate with. Within months our new family was coming apart.

One afternoon Sylvia and I returned from school, and Sarah had their suitcases packed and waiting. "Come, Sylvia," she said softly, as she took the two suitcases and her daughter's lanky hand and walked out. My father was asleep. Grandma had convinced him, if he didn't want to lose his new family, he needed to take his meds again, but Sarah had already decided to leave us.

"Dad, it's time to get up." I rolled his back with a gentle back and forth, to wake him.

"It's time to get up, Dad."

"Scratch my back, baby," he mumbled, over-medicated, his face mashed into the pillow. I sat on his back, the smell of his skin like home, his freckles a tactile reminder of the genes we shared. The freckles on my nose and cheeks were from Dad's people: a muddled mix of Irish Catholic and German Jews, a family that instinctively closed ranks to protect their own. Dad's illness was our liability. Outsiders could come and go but we were united in his care, unlike my hippie mother—a German, Dutch, and English third-generation immigrant who hated her family and was loyal only to Ted.

Grandma let me stay through the weekend but then it was time to go back home to Mom's.

SOMETHING WRONG

When I wouldn't come out for dinner, my mother called through the door, "There's dinner, come out if you're hungry." Maybe she didn't know what was happening? It wasn't as if we spoke openly, even among the family, about my father's breakdowns. It was as if part of our dignity came from not trying to understand what we had no explanation for. As a child, I took my cues from them. I had no words for what I was feeling and took comfort in the company of our quiet. I also knew there was nothing anyone could do, and I knew my mother would only make it worse by demanding to understand how I felt when I didn't know myself. Privately, late at night, hands pressed together in prayer, I turned to God.

"Please help me, make me a better daughter," I pleaded, sure that my own survival instincts were hurting the people I loved and would be made better if only I could get it right. Surely, there was a higher power that could fix what I couldn't.

My solution to the undertow of sadness of my father's life and my mother's indifference was to continue my crusade for normalcy by going to public school for fourth grade. After three years in the parent-run Free School, I wanted "more structure," I told my mother. She agreed to send me to PS 104, a notoriously underfunded and badly-run school that mainly served families from the town projects.

My new homeroom teacher's approach to teaching and learning was a set of mastery-based subject cards. In the morning, I picked a card in the subject of my choosing, read a paragraph or more, answered questions on the reading, and checked my own work with the answer cards. I didn't always make the distinction between what I knew before I saw the answer and after. "I know the right answer now," I rationalized, and happily handed in my self-checked nearly perfect score to our teacher. Now this was *real* school, taught in a big brick building with two metal doors leading out to the sidewalk. Here we got grades and had teachers you knew only by their last name.

One afternoon, walking home from my new school on the other side of the town park, I passed two girls cornering a classmate of mine in a storefront entryway.

"Give us your money or we'll kick your ass!" they demanded as I was walking past. Their victim, Levi, was a tall, dark-haired Irish boy with freckles and a glimmer in his eyes. I liked him and even hung out with him in the schoolyard sometimes.

"Hey, leave him alone!" I shouted, defending him because the girls outnumbered him and because they were wrong. Caught off guard, they ran off.

The next day, walking home from school, a boy I had never seen before challenged me to a fight. "Hey you. You should mind your *bidness*!" he said menacingly, and I knew it was about the girls I had scared off the day before. I started to walk away from him, as kids gathered around us. I decided I wouldn't react unless he hurt me; it wasn't his fight. He kicked me in the back and stomach while I walked toward home, which didn't hurt through my coat, until he aimed higher and kicked me in the head. Even with the fur-lined hood of my faded purple coat, his kick snapped my head back. I spun around and grabbed him by the collar and threw him to the ground with all my might saying something girl-superhero-like, "Now you hurt me, motherfucker!" and he didn't get up to fight back.

I could hear the other kids talking. "Oh shit. She little but she strong." He didn't throw another kick and I walked away with a mixture of hurt that no one stood up for me and pride that I didn't need them to.

Heading down the block toward home, the two girls from the day before yelled from behind me. "Hey, wait up. Where you going? What's your name? You new around here? Wanna hang with us?" they dared.

"I have things to do at home," I lied.

"We'll walk you home," they pressed.

I kept walking with them as I tried to suss out if they were going to try to beat me up when we got away from the school grounds, and if not that, how I could get rid of them before we got to my apartment.

They ended up walking me all the way home despite the silence between us. I took them around to the backyard, not wanting them to know my apartment number, and as luck would have it, my mother was taking the laundry down from the clothesline. I could do this all from the anonymity of the yard, I hoped.

"Mom, do you still need me to help you with the laundry?" I lied. "These girls want me to go with them but I told them you needed my help."

"I don't need your help!" she said, smelling deceit like a hunting dog smells prey. It was so like her to completely miss cues, to not understand the tone of my voice or the unusual nature of my offer, to never know when I needed help.

"Wait here," I hissed. "I'll be back!" I rushed past the girls to set my mother straight.

"Don't you understand anything?" I exploded in our kitchen, as she stepped in from the fire escape with a basket of dry laundry.

"I'm trying to get out of going anywhere with these girls. They had someone beat me up today!" I yelled, giving her an opportunity to stand by me. But she had this thing about honesty.

"You can't lie to them. You have to tell them how you feel," she said, as if being dishonest in this case would bias the outcome of my life irreparably. She collected welfare rather than work. I had seen her steal a can of bug spray when we didn't have the money, and she picked one crazy man after the next, but I was supposed to be honest with the school bullies.

"Why is the truth more important than me?" I cried. "You're a fucking bitch!"

"Don't you talk to me that way!" she said, slapping me across the face. I grabbed her by her shirt and tried to swing her to the ground like I had done to the fifth grader outside school. I pulled with pure rage coursing through my arms, wanting to matter to her, wanting to hurt her. She fought me back, anchored her feet and grabbed at me, and we scratched and slapped each other, both of us heaving hot air at each other's faces with fury. Then there was a banging at the apartment door. The girls had found their way to our apartment.

"Yo, you coming back out?"

"Go away," I screamed through the closed door, choking on my anger, hot tears streaming down my face. "I can't come out right now!"

I had never hit my mother and it marked that imperfect coming-of-age moment that comes when a child realizes the person in charge is no righter and possibly no stronger.

LUCKY

The summer after fourth grade, my mother and her new boyfriend, Ted, got the idea to go on a trip to West Virginia with the plan of finding land to homestead. Ted wanted more space; he wanted less people in his space and living close to the land was calling to him. Appalachia was calling a lonesome cry to his wilder side. Ted spent long hours working on our old Volkswagen Bug to get it ready for the trip, a car we affectionately called Green Vomit because of the uneven green surface of the rusted patches of its body. He whistled through his teeth while he replaced spark plugs and tuned up the engine. A cigarette tucked behind his ear for a break.

* * *

One late spring day before we left, my mother was working in the community garden behind our building. Some families wanted to put a fence around the garden, but Ted was dead set against being fenced in and the backyard was no exception. That afternoon my mother came upstairs and announced that our across-the-hall neighbor Alan was putting up fencing. Ted grabbed the car keys, and ran out. I could hear the throttle of the clutch and the VW engine clicking as he drove around to the backyard. He gunned the engine, drove onto the sidewalk, into the yard aiming the car straight for Alan, who was hammering posts for the fence that Ted didn't want. Alan jumped out of the way and ran upstairs to the safety of their apartment. Ted jumped out of the car, pulled the posts out of the ground, and dumped them on the street. Then he backed onto the road, and parked our VW back out front.

After, Ted sauntered into the house and sat at the kitchen table, across the hall from where Alan was taking shelter in his Quaker informed nonviolent resistance. He leaned back in his chair with his boots on the table in front of him, with a home rolled cigarette in his mouth. Ted laughed quietly, smiling as he blew smoke in the air like he enjoyed the sport of it. "He deserved it, the bastard." Ted made enemies easily. He fought with other tenants of the building and members of the arts collective. He picked fights over wall space and clashed with neighbors over the shared yard and generally was not well liked. I held it against him that he'd taken my father's place, that my mother had swapped my schizophrenic father for a more selfish version of crazy, but I knew enough to stay on his good side.

* * *

When the car was ready and our bags, tents, and supplies were packed for the month-long trip, we headed west. We drove long hours on the highway, my mother making declarations about how this or that town felt more or less like a potential home, and Ted sullenly blew smoke out the window. When we had reception, we listened to top 10 hits that summer, including "50 Ways To Leave Your Lover," which I hoped she was listening to.

I sat in the back seat and read my first book, *Looking for Mr. Goodbar*, the 1970 crime drama about a young teacher who meets her soon-to-be murderer at an afterhours club. I couldn't put it down. Since dyslexia made me a late reader, my mother was pleased—I was finally reading and whatever I wanted to read was fine with her.

On one of our rest-stops we met a family who invited us over for a visit; Ted could be charming when he wanted to be and my mother was happy when they were adventuring together. I remember the warm afternoon in the large, lush expanse of the backyard with our momentary friends. The sun was high in the sky and their two daughters and I traipsed through the grassy acres behind their house hunting four-leaf clovers. After a long time of only finding three-leaf clovers, picked and discarded by our hopeful hands, I got frustrated. I got the idea to combine two clovers, each with a leaf torn off, and announced we would have to make our own luck. We laughed about it with the adults and drank cold lemonade. We returned to our campsite on what was to be the last day of sun for a long time.

* * *

It was a summer of rain. Over the course of a month, it rained more than it didn't. We spent weeks camping and hiking the Appalachian Trail in the rain. Every day we packed up our wet camp and hiked up the wet rooted paths and every night we set up the tent in a downpour.

Somewhere in the heart of Appalachia, in town getting supplies, we met an old man with whom Ted struck up an unlikely rapport. I'll call him Leroy since I've no recollection of his real name. Leroy and Ted got to talking about our camping trip and the rain that wouldn't let up and the man invited us to come stay with him.

The thing about the man I do remember was he had no legs. He wore his pants tied in a knot at his crotch and he got around in some kind of cart. Maybe he wanted a ride from town back to his house? Maybe we followed him home? He lived in a small house and maybe that was why he didn't have a wheelchair because it wouldn't have fit. Maybe he was just too poor for a wheelchair. He pulled himself from one room to the other by leveraging his weight on his arms and hands like a dog with only front legs. He lived in a two-room shack, with a back bedroom and kitchen living area. It had basic furnishings, like a table and chair that he could lift himself onto. He had a nasty dog on a chain that he fed from the porch. Accustomed to free rein at a young age, I roamed his land with its rusted appliances and old car parts scattered on the land, while Ted and the old man drank beer on his stoop, my mother off somewhere reading.

The old man offered Ted and my mother the bedroom to stay in since they were a couple. He insisted that I could sleep on the couch. Which makes me wonder now where he planned to sleep. In fact, I have no memory of the talk about the sleeping arrangements, but my mother told me later this was what the old man wanted and she had a weird feeling about it. Ted sided with the old man trying to convince my mother to sleep with him alone. She refused, and in the end, she decided to leave me in the locked car to sleep. It would have been in character for her to ask me what I wanted to do, so maybe it was my idea, but I remember waking up cold and resenting them for leaving me alone in the car.

This weird man, who I imagined had no friends and many enemies, became perversely important to Ted, as if he saw something of himself in the man. Leroy and Ted acted like long-lost family, the two of them snickering at private jokes and communing like evil stepbrothers. This dirty man who left his garbage out in the open and seemed to trust no one loved Ted. The old man even offered Ted a pair of new khaki pants that were too big for him and fit Ted perfectly. Ted meandered to and from the car and the shack with his new pants on, more at home than I'd ever seen him.

My mother and I were uncommonly united in our aversion to the old man, but the more we lobbied to go, the more attached Ted was to staying. It was as if our discomfort fed his affection. He seemed to want to test the bounds of what we would accept, like our rejection of the man was a rejection of something in Ted that we needed to accept.

My mother finally decided she'd had enough. She packed our bags back into Green Vomit and climbed in ready to leave without him. We locked the doors and put the car in gear to drive away. When Ted saw us in the car and realized that she was serious about leaving, he came running outside, yelling at her to wait and jumped on the roof of the car to try to stop her. But it was too late, she had already made the decision to leave and once she decided something, it was done. She kept her foot on the gas.

In an effort to get my mom to stop the car, he rolled off the roof onto the hood and on the ground in front of the car. My mother says she was sure he lay vertical to the wheels so we would run over him but not on him. But our wheels hit Ted's body, and he screamed. She braked without hitting the clutch and the car stalled. "Oh my God," she yelled.

"You ran me over! You tried to kill me, you bitch!"

"Fuck, are you all right?" she cried from the driver's seat where we stayed in the safety of the car, afraid to get out, afraid of what he might do.

"My pants and hair are stuck under the wheel and I can't get up," he said quietly, sounding dangerously calm. Ted had a long ponytail, and it was trapped under one wheel and his pant leg was under the other wheel. She was afraid to drive forward or backward for fear she'd really hurt him. We got out, and my mother saw only one way out—she had to cut his long hair trapped under the wheel and cut the pants to free his leg. Then he might be able to twist out from under the car. But Ted refused. "You can't cut my new pants," he yelled absurdly. Like Sampson, he would keep his long hair and the pants the old man had given him. It was as if this was exactly what he wanted all along: to be stuck and in danger, because that's where he felt most at home.

"You're out of your mind. I'm cutting these pants!" she said, taking the old man's scissors and cutting angrily at the seam and then cutting his long ponytail to free him. As soon as he rolled out from under the car, my mother scrambled back in the car.

She locked the doors and we started to drive away again. Ted banged on the windows and limped after us, but she drove faster. We lurched down the deeply grooved dirt driveway to make our getaway, Ted, limping after us, waving his hands in the air until we lost sight of him and turned onto the open road.

She cried and drove all day and through the night, while I listened to her cry and slept in the backseat. I felt sorry for her but not sympathetic, not the kind of sorry that made me love her more, but the kind that made me feel bad about myself for not caring. I resented her for choosing another crazy man when she wouldn't stay with my father. I felt alone in the car with my mother, the drama of her life would always overshadow my needs and I would never be wild enough to be interesting to her.

In the early dawn, my mother needed a break, so we pulled over and sat on the sloping shoulder of the thruway as cars rushed past us. I smelled the rotten egg smell that signaled we were in industrial New Jersey and near our Staten Island home. I pulled my legs to my chest, while my mother held her head in her hands, crying. "I'm a terrible person. I could have killed him. I'm sorry, Natasha," she said, as if our safety wasn't the real issue here. "I'm sorry for putting you through this. I just don't know what to do," she said.

What was wrong with her? I thought.

"He deserved it, the bastard," I said instead.

"I think you should go stay with your father for a while," she said, and that was fine with me.

NOT MY FAMILY

With a baby on the way my mother took Ted back. He was there when I returned from Dad's. She tells me she was so horrified to have run him over that she was relieved he came back to her. If he could love her after *that*, she couldn't be all bad.

Ted became increasingly withdrawn and uncommunicative. As the pregnancy progressed, they fought more, and it became more violent. When he wanted to have sex, and when she demanded an explanation for his distance, they fought. They fought in the nude, like white, underweight sumo wrestlers without the loin wrap. He pushed her bare back into the wall as she shoved him away. When I tried to break up the fight, she yelled at me, "Get out of the way," as she reached to pull his hair and he slapped her face. I left the apartment for the quiet of the abandoned VW bus clubhouse in our backyard that big brown had vacated. It was here that I stashed candy bars to eat out of sight. This was also where I ruled the games my friends and I played, with a confidence no one dared to challenge. I was the examiner in dirty doctor, the lead singer in the Andrew Sisters concerts we staged, and taskmaster for the holes we dug to China.

I managed to stay on Ted's good side. I did what some children manage to do when they're in the face of a predator. I paid attention to what he liked and kept the peace. Some nights we played Yatzee, or Ted and I improvised "Heart and Soul" on the piano. He held the tempo with the base while I riffed with the melody. When

I fell asleep on the wicker couch in our kitchen one afternoon, I dreamt that chickens were pecking at me. I woke up to find Ted sitting in a chair facing me while I slept. I imagine it had been him poking me until I woke up, instigator that he was. I instinctively kept my distance, close enough to sense his moods but out of the line of fire.

Ted stopped coming out to visit with friends in the building, preferring to smoke his grass alone, sitting with his work boots up on the table edge blowing smoke in the face of his own isolation. He became paranoid about his pot, which he was sure was being pinched, and money he thought he had, but didn't. "You're a sneaky bitch, aren't you?" he accused my mother half-jokingly, trying to make sense of what he thought was missing.

One morning their fighting got out of hand, their bodies slammed against the walls in the other room. "Help me!" she called out. I ran in to Ted's hands wrapped around her throat. My mother gasped for air, and I pressed myself between their naked bodies to force his hands off her neck.

"Stop it!" I yelled at both of them, pushing them apart, so she could get away. Then I ran out and across the hall to Ofelia to get away from their naked violence. My mother also came running, onto the ivory hall tiles, legs scampering, bush showing, and little breasts dangling in the night air. I hated her tiny breasts with erect nipples that had never fed me and dangled now for all to see. Eight months pregnant, her huge belly was tight with my baby sister on the way; a neighbor handed her a shirt to cover up. I hated her for having a second child when she didn't seem interested in mothering the one she had. I watched mortified by their exposed bodies and public fighting. I stood at Ofelia's side, across the hall, watching as if it wasn't my family.

One of the neighbors had called the landlord who showed up

with a shotgun and banged on our apartment door. Ted opened the door with a belligerent, "What do you want!"

The landlord stood into the doorway with the gun at his side. "I want you out! I won't have this in my building!" he said. I loved the landlord in that moment and the way he made Ted listen. My mother's demand that he listen to her got her a slap in the face, but he wouldn't dare hit a man with a gun in his hand.

My mother doesn't remember the landlord coming but remembers running down to Mr. Lobel down one floor, an older man who lived alone, whose apartment was piled high with *New York Times* newspapers. Mr. Lobel's apartment was where, if you knocked on his door you could get a magic wand he made out of newspaper that extended and retracted with the flick of a wrist. His son went on to write the *Frog and Toad* children's books and I imagine his inventive father was an inspiration. My mother ran to Mr. Lobel's and I went to Ofelia's; it didn't occur to either of us to stay together.

"I don't know why she stays with that man," Ofelia said that night, "especially when your father is such a prince." I agreed. I wanted to stay with Ofelia, to not go back to a mother who wouldn't protect herself, who chose men who could never meet her needs.

My mother stayed with Ted, and, in several weeks, my half sister, Laura, was brought into the world with the help of forceps that left little bruises on her newborn temples.

BARBARA THE MADONNA

In 1975, when I was ten years old, my father met Barbara, the woman he would spend the next fifteen years with. They met in group therapy at Pilgrim State Hospital, both diagnosed with paranoid schizophrenia. He had a Messiah complex and she had a Madonna complex. Hers was a uniquely female schizophrenic complex fixed between two archetypes: the Madonna and the Harlot. Barbara was plagued by voices that accused her of being a whore.

The first time I met her they came to my school play in the church basement of the Free School, where I had returned after a year in public school. She wore a seventies style polyester dress that hugged her voluptuous hips and breasts as she bounced down the aisle in high-heeled wooden platform shoes.

"Hi, I'm Natasha, Frank's daughter," I said, reaching out my hand. She shook it vigorously.

"I'm Barbara," she laughed, and looked to my father for reassurance as if she wasn't accustomed to being known. I watched them through the curtain before the show as she swatted his arm for making her laugh. She seemed like she could be the nurturing type and I was determined to make a good impression.

I was Dorothy in the play, despite being a head shorter than the Munchkins. When my best friend who played the Wicked

Witch of the West missed her cue, I yelled from the stage for her to come out. She was crying when she did, but I didn't care. I wanted the play to be good and Jenny was ruining it. But Dad and Barbara left before the play was over. Barbara didn't do well in the public eye. She imagined the voices she heard were people talking about her. I would learn later that's why he had taken her home.

She moved in with Dad and kept the coffee pot full and the ashtrays emptied. Her child-like enthusiasm was endearing. When I came to visit, she and I painted each other's nails and put makeup on in the bathroom. "We're gorgeous!" she announced like we were sisters. We cleaned the house together, and I could hear her singing, while she scrubbed the toilet, *"Whistle while you work... da de dadadadada,"* as if she were a character in *South Pacific*. I, too, modeled my life after Hollywood movies and loved to sing, and I appreciated that about Barbara. But her best trait was she gave Dad someone to take care of. She needed salvation, and my father was her own personal savior.

Barbara adored my father. Bounding from the kitchen to deliver a cup of coffee when he finally got out of bed, she would plunk herself onto his lap and kiss him with a loud "Mmmmah," pulling her head back to get a better view. They used the embers from one another's cigarette to light the next smoke, and drank coffee day and night. They also had an active sex life which I could hear from their downstairs bedroom. I walked in on them having sex once. He was on top of her, her legs spread wide. Nothing said before I shut the door again, relieved to see naked bodies that weren't fighting.

One afternoon Barbara came waltzing out of the back bedroom. She wore a thin polyester robe and high-heeled slippers with pink feathers glued to the strap. Her hair was in a beehive at the top of her head and the flimsy wrap was loosely tied at her bust. She reminded me of our very own *I Dream of Jeannie*. My father was sitting at the table with me when she swooped into the room, took me into her arms, and spun me around. Then she set me down wordlessly and plopped down into a chair across from me, tapping on a pack of cigarettes. She lit one, inhaled deeply, exhaled, and looked at me skeptically, as if trying to decide whether to say something. In the blink of an eye she transformed, hurt and resignation flashed in her eyes, as she pushed herself up from the table, and looked me in the eye.

"Just because you're better than me, doesn't mean you have to call me a whore," she yelled and rushed into the safety of their shared bedroom.

"No one thinks you're a whore, baby," Dad said, in his most shielding tones, as he went to soothe her. "Did you take your meds today?"

Usually she would take them, like a good devotee, but they didn't stop the voices. I knew it was her illness but I resented her fragility. Mostly, though, I hated the way it made me feel guilty for having the power to hurt her. She became another person I had to protect from something inside me.

NOBLESSE OBLIGE

In keeping with his delusions of grandeur, my father considered siring children as a way of spreading his Messianic seed. Despite the families urging, he and Barbara shunned birth control and all the ways it took the pleasure and purpose from the act of procreation. Over the years they had five children together.

Barbara rejected her meds during the pregnancy, in part to protect the developing fetus and in part because the hormones of pregnancy were a balm to her psyche. Plus, she wanted to protect the baby from her medication when she breastfed. They named their first-born child Ulysses, after the legendary Greek king famed for his intellect and cunning.

But, just after Ulysses was born, my father woke up to Barbara standing over him with a knife. He had no explanation for her bizarre behavior, didn't know if she understood it herself. Could it have been voices that warned her against the most primal of mother's fears, filial patricide or how my father may have seemed dangerously out of touch with their infant's needs?

Barbara was committed to the hospital and my father was left caring for the new baby. It was one of Barbara's sisters who came to visit and discovered the baby covered in his own feces. My father didn't see a problem with a "little shit on a child!" he said in the throes of his own mania. Barbara's sister and even Grandma felt the child needed to be taken away but what would they do with Ulysses?

In the end, Barbara's sister volunteered to take the baby. Neither Barbara's brother or sister had children of their own. She would keep him until Barbara was released from the hospital, and on this front both families agreed.

When Barbara was released months later, Ulysses was returned to Barbara and Frank. But Barbara continued hearing voices—*whore, harlot, bad woman*—voices that drowned out her ability to meet the baby's needs. At the age of almost two the boy wasn't speaking and the family was concerned.

Frank and Barbara fought about giving Ulysses up. My father lobbied to keep his child close, but Barbara understood somewhere inside that the boy needed support they couldn't give him. So, he went back to Barbara's sister.

Susan and her husband renamed the boy Elias and provided therapy and the home life he needed to begin speaking and interacting. On Elias's second birthday, Frank and Barbara were invited to the party. I have a photo. Elias is sitting on a couch fingering a small toy in his hand. I was ten years older than him and not particularly interested in my shy half brother, a blond boy in a beige turtleneck sweater. When it was time to leave, my father started demanding they take their son home. "I'm his father for God's sake—you can't keep him from me!" It was Elsie's husband who convinced my father to stand down.

"We're his parents now, Frank. We want to adopt him. You've done enough damage, don't you think?" I wonder now if my father gave up because he didn't know how to get him back or because he realized how unprepared they were to parent? Could he see the way his son, who had not spoken under their care, was now calling these parents Mommy and Daddy by name?

WITH ME OR AGAINST ME

Being his child made me unassailable in his eyes. While other members of the family became the object of my father's paranoia, even in his madness, even when he worried I was possessed by demons, his instinct was to care for me. My grandmother recognized this bond, and partly because we were so united in his care, I was her prized grandchild. Evan after my parents split up, my grandmother, Florrie, stayed in touch with my mother's mother, Annabelle, and the two of them were my biggest advocates.

Florrie wrote to Annie, *"Tash is always just what the doctor ordered and she helps us... to believe in joy and reality—a rare quality because most of us see them as opposites. I hope to live long enough to see what she makes of her life."*

But Florrie took hostages to protect and care for her son. In her efforts to get him to voluntarily go into the hospital rather than having to commit him, she called on friends and family to intercede even when it put others at risk. On this occasion she called his old friend, Don Newlove, and asked, "Do you think you could come over to talk to him? Convince him to commit himself? He respects you so much."

Evan though his wife forbade him to see Frank after the visit when Don relapsed to drinking again, he came out from the city to see to his old friend. They sat reminiscing about the early days in the Lower East Side, Gypsy and her daughter, and the alcohol/marijuana haze they reveled in back in the days.

"You know this family is full of spies?" Frank told his friend. "First, they take my children, and then they put Barbara away. It's all a scheme to take the children. You know I have an obligation, *a noblesse oblige* to sire those children? They are children of God."

"Well, Frank, this is all sounding a little crazy. Maybe you are in need of some time in the hospital, my friend?"

"You want me to consider hospitalization, Don? Well, well—I didn't realize you were in cahoots with the devil too, my good man. How about we both confront our demons and you go home to your wife?" he said, convinced that he was disarming a foe with his cutting insights.

When my grandmother walked in from her night shift at the local hospital, my father shouted for her to hear, "They're trying to frame me, Don. My family and friends are in on it, as you well know! But do you know who you're dealing with?" Don gave up and went home.

At her wits' end, the next morning Grandma called me. I was eleven years old.

"Your father refuses to take his medication and won't go into the hospital. You more than anyone understand his suffering and know better than to blame him for it. Will you come see if he will listen to you?" she asked, feeding a feeling of invincibility in me.

Filled with purpose and old enough at twelve years old to take public transport, I took the ferry to the subway to the Long Island Railroad to Hempstead. I gave the cab the address to Grandma's house.

I entered through the back door, closest to the kitchen, the way I always did. There he was, sitting at the table cloaked in a blanket of cigarette smoke and indifference that hung around his shoulders like a shroud. Even dappled in the warm afternoon sun, there was a chill emanating from him. I walked over and wrapped my arms around his shoulders. But he sat unresponsive, his arms limply held at his sides, looking defiantly away from where I stood.

"Dad!" I said, looking into his steely cold gaze, trying to call him to me.

"So, are you with me or against me, my dear?" he asked, his eyes filling with suspicion somehow knowing I was there to talk him into the hospital. I had never been on the other side of my father's mistrust. I didn't even have to say anything for him to know I had been made a turncoat.

"Dad, I love you, you know?" I said, looking for his warm gaze to fix me in the world, like he always did. He sat stoically averting his eyes from mine.

"We'll see," he said, biting like a wounded dog breaks skin when they feel cornered, his love for me feeling conditional for the first time. I ran out of the kitchen into the bathroom, shut the door behind me, out of view of his accusing eyes.

My Uncle John Paul overheard my panicked sobs, and let himself into the bathroom.

"He hates me," I cried, my throat choked with grief.

"He just doesn't know who you are to him. You did your best," he offered, knowing first-hand the radioactive fallout from schizophrenia, the way it settles contaminating those closest to the core. "It's all you can do."

That afternoon my grandmother called the hospital and reported him as a danger to himself and the family. The ambulance arrived. The EMTs were literally dressed in white suits with white patent leather shoes. When my father wouldn't go with them, they wrestled him to the ground and wrapped him in a straitjacket. Suddenly calm, like a wild animal that innately understands the rules of captivity, he lay quietly as two men carried him to the ambulance. I felt a desperate loneliness and wanted to run to him. My uncle stood in the doorway and wiped an escaped tear off his cheek. My grandmother sat at the kitchen table drawing so deeply at her cigarette that it looked like it hurt.

SOS

My father, Francis Xavier Williams, had his first serious breakdown early in his life before he met my mother and long before I was born. The family didn't talk openly about his illness, preferring instead to make sense of their lives separate from him. It wasn't until I started writing this story that my aunts and uncles began to recount the day for me. It came out in bits and pieces, the way memories of a trauma might, more time spent trying to make sense of their memories or contemplating answers than actually telling the story.

"Frankie," as his siblings called him, went to Fredonia State Teachers' College in 1956 to study history and music. He found camaraderie with a group of jazz musicians and his mentor, Don ("Red") Menza. Back then, only certain kinds of music were allowed, so signs on the practice rooms on campus read: "No jazz playing." They actually banned it. So, these "cats," as my father referred to his fellow musicians, jammed at all hours of the night off campus. During these renegade music sessions, he started smoking marijuana and experimenting with LSD, but never heroin according to him. He must have been doing enough drugs to make Red pull him aside one day to warn him, "Don't ever shoot. There's no coming back from that!" Dad took that warning to heart, but he smoked a lot of grass and probably did a lot of other drugs too. I can picture my father playing piano, with a joint dangling between his thick lips, riffing on tunes and feeling part of something bigger, something more important, something verging on devotional in those rooms.

Spring of 1960, two weeks before graduation, Red Menza, as they called Don because of his red hair, was invited by Maynard Ferguson to join the band. He was on a bus for New York the next morning and my father was left to finish out his final year having lost his mentor. Was it that loss, the drug use, or the uncertainty of what was to come after college that triggered my father's unraveling at the graduation ceremony? Or, was it a predisposition that sat in wait, which would have visited him at the next juncture in life, if not this one?

From pictures, I know his mother, Florrie, wore a green dress and her chestnut-colored hair was curled chin length for the occasion. The three younger siblings—Irene, seventeen; Gregory, twelve; and John Paul, seven—were in their Sunday best. His father, John, a handsome man of average height, wore his only suit, black single-breasted wool, too hot for the early summer day. Grandpa was a hard-working man who supported his family with not one but three jobs, but his fedora told an old story of his early years as a hoodlum in Hell's Kitchen.

On the day of his graduation, the furthest thing from my father's mind was the ceremony. Eyes slit red from the pot he smoked earlier, and wildly paranoid, he was sure that government spies were in the audience. He imagined his activities were somehow broadcasted to the powers that be, probably the mob, and today was the day they would move in on him.

Could his family feel Frank's agitation as he walked urgently over to meet them? I picture his graduation gown billowing open, superhero-like, exposing an untucked and wrinkled shirt.

"I've gotten into some trouble, something big," he said, looking down at the ground where the story was unraveling at his feet.

"See that guy over there, he's the mob. They're fucking trying to frame me; I think they planted drugs in my turntable. Don't talk to anyone!" he warned.

Did my grandmother's normally commanding steely gray eyes waver in disbelief or was the day too grand to admit doubt. Had she registered the glimmers of paranoid thinking earlier, like the time he came home sure that Sister Mary Josephina was out to get him, or when he stood up his senior prom date, convinced she was planning to poison him? Or did my grandmother decide these were just moments of insecurity in her otherwise brilliant firstborn? It was, after all, a great day, the day of the first college graduation in the family. My uncle tells me their parents *believed* the mob was a real threat. While the class walked on stage to receive their diplomas, Florrie and John were scribbling notes back and forth on the program, deciding if they had time to get his stuff or if they should simply go to the police.

Meanwhile my father, handsome in his cap and gown, with strong features and thick eyebrows that accentuated his dark blue eyes, sat among the graduating class. His penetrating gaze was trained up and to the left, avoiding eye contact with his pursuer, suspicious of a man in a black suit in the front row whose eyes had briefly locked onto his.

My grandfather, not usually the one to take control, decided they should take this problem to the authorities closer to home. They would leave after the ceremony and drive directly to the police precinct in Hempstead, Long Island to deliver the drugs and turntable into the hands of the police.

"I'm not sure that's a good idea, John," Florrie whispered into his ear, likely tapping her long nicotine-stained nails painted pink on the graduation program, a habit that let you know she was thinking. Her eldest son, the chosen one, was to be their salvation from the working-class grind of their immigrant family. Turning her son into the police was never what she imagined for him. But in this crisis, John prevailed.

After the ceremony they went to Frank's dormitory room, quickly packed his belongings into the car, and left for Long Island. My uncles recall the warm day had turned chilly by the time they got on the road, and the fog was dense. "You couldn't see two feet in front of you," John Paul said. For twelve hours they hugged tight to the rear headlights of a sixteen-wheeler as they traveled downstate. The whole time Frank kept an eye trained out the back window.

"See that car behind us?" he warned his parents from the rear seat. "They've been trailing us since we left the college!" he practically shouted, annoyed at them for not appreciating the peril they were in. John drove faster. Florrie pulled out the graduation booklet, and in her elegant script, as if inscribing a keepsake on the back, she wrote: *If we are found dead it was the mob.*

My Uncle Greg wasn't buying the story for a minute. "It's not the same car following us! You're going to kill us driving so close to that truck!" he yelled. He was the middle son and the one most likely to call bullshit when the family wasn't making sense. When they reached Long Island, the younger siblings were dropped off at home with Irene instructed to get the younger boys in bed. Florence and John brought their son and his turntable with the drugs planted in it directly to the police. They arrived at the station with a tale of espionage and mobster involvement, which in the telling, might have started to sound implausible, even to their ears.

The police took the turntable apart, unscrewing the metal cover and looking at the machine's insides with a flashlight for drugs that might have been lodged between the component parts, but found nothing.

Frankie got more and more agitated: pacing the floor at the station, raising his voice at their incompetence. "For Chrissake, I know it's in there! They've been planning to frame me for weeks now."

"Who are *they*?" the officer asked.

Sure that the police could turn the situation against him and his friends, Frank felt a welling up of hatred for his father who apparently had set the whole family against him.

"I know who my enemies are now!" he ranted, glaring at his father as he paced the floor and tried to figure out how to get out of this mess, unaware of just how manic and suspect this internal rumination looked to the others.

With the insight of an outsider, the police officer realized that the young man was not well. *Was he a kind officer?* I wonder. Did he take Florrie and John aside and speak gently about the possibility that their son was suffering from delusions? Or, did he summarily dismiss the family from wasting any more of his time? That detail is lost. Either way, the three of them left the police station with a dawning awareness that my father wasn't well, that on the occasion of his commencement, my father's brilliant mind had betrayed them all.

There are variations of the story of my father's first breakdown. I've pieced the whole together from the points of view of my father and his siblings. My father's version has at times included the make and model of the car he thought was following them: "It was a black Ford Victoria." Always there is the inevitable return home, their family facing the impossibility of their first-born doomed to a life of delusions and mental breakdowns.

I can picture my grandmother, Florrie, endlessly smoking at the kitchen table trying to reconcile her son's delusions with the promise of the day. *It was the stress that had gotten to him. He would*

115

be better now that he was home.

After my grandmother went to bed, my father, only twenty-one, paced the floor of his parents' house like a caged lion, moving to the dining room windows to peer through the curtains, then back into the privacy of the kitchen, where his brooding will wear a darkened path in the mustard yellow of the kitchen linoleum. He's sure he's being watched and suspicious that the family is in on it. He, alone, is receiving messages in words and symbols that only he can decipher. They come to him through the radio he leaves on all night. They tell him about his role in something bigger and more important than his family can contain.

* * *

Over the next few days, my father's breakdown worsened. In response to questions about his plans for the future, he declared with an unfamiliar arrogance, "As the Son of God, the chosen one, I'm sure the plan will be communicated to me in due time! I am in direct communication with God, you know. Those of you who doubt, who have forsaken the lord to do the devil's works, will be cast out." He spoke to a family whose lack of recognition of him as the Messiah was further proof to him that they were in collusion with the forces of evil. He avoided making eye contact, afraid they could read his thoughts, as he was able to read theirs.

Eventually the police were called and my father was taken from the house, hands strapped together over his chest, in forced repose, headed for Pilgrim State Psychiatric Hospital thirty minutes away. His sister, Irene, stood in her nightgown at the foot of the stairs shouting at the ambulance workers, "Leave him alone!" while my grandparents stood silently in the shadow of her rage. Surely, they agonized over his treatments and over sending their son into the forced care of strangers, but his madness was a pain they shouldered privately.

Before they knew what a hospital visit would be like, the family made an outing to visit Frank at Pilgrim State during his first hospitalization. They brought a picnic to have on the lawn of the grounds. They arrived to find my father locked in a small, padded room in a hallway of similar rooms with small square windows in the door. On my father's window was a layer of slick that Irene asked about. "What's on the window?" she asked, disgusted by the slime.

"Semen," Frank said, in a taunting voice. They sat outside, near other visiting families, while patients less fortunate screamed through the narrow-gated windows for release. It was the first and last visit the whole family made to the psychiatric ward. I imagine my grandmother made other visits on her own. I can see her eyes stowing the pain behind a shield of endurance as she faced his heartless mania and anger by herself. I assume she visited, rather than leave her son alone in a ward not fit for a family visit but considered restorative for the patient.

He was diagnosed with paranoid schizophrenia with a Messiah complex, and after months of treatment and medication was released to his parents' care, parents who would for the rest of their lives be responsible to keep him sheltered and safe. He returned to them medicated on Thorazine and Prolixin, two early psychotropic drugs that treated what they ironically call the *positive* symptoms of his schizophrenia: the hallucinations, paranoia, and thought disorders. He says it was the first time he felt he could think straight—but the drugs had little effect on the negative symptoms of his illness: the apathy, lethargy, and social withdrawal, which would plague him his whole life. His mania and purpose stifled by the drugs, he would sit and ruminate, his forefinger and thumb rubbing together in perpetual motion, as if to keep tempo with the way he chewed on his thoughts. As if his impulses moved through cotton batting, his movements were slow and unresponsive, from bed to table, to coffee pot, to smoke and smoke and smoke as if sending an SOS to the gods.

ANOTHER BREAK IN THE WALL

So often things happen in life that have unintended consequences, which in hindsight feel destined. July 4th, 1976, the New York City Bicentennial Gala was one of those turning points. Hundreds of tall ships collected in the harbor in celebration of our country's birthday. Sails fluttered against blue skies, boats from all over the world circled around Lady Liberty. Neighbors gathered on our apartment rooftop overlooking the New York Bay to watch the parade of ships, eating spoons of spiked watermelon to toast our independence. I watched on the television from my grandparents' cottage in Canada unaware that day would be our last summer there.

Months before, Ted had reported a dangerous crack in the side of our building, a result of the pounding from ongoing sewer repairs. The city sent inspectors but nothing happened until, a month later, the Friday before the fourth of July, each family in each apartment received eviction notices. The building was unsound; we had forty-eight hours to evacuate. My mother recalls, "They were supposed to have notified us earlier, but someone went on vacation without sending the notices." She called me at the cottage. "You better get down here, we have to move out!" she said, leaving it to my grandparents to make the drive from Canada to Staten Island.

When we pulled up at the curb, I ran into my bedroom to grab my most important keepsakes: my trusted Barbie and her pink jeep with white wheels for quick getaways, a favorite foreign coin, and the Beatles *White Album*. I agonized over leaving the huge stuffed giraffe my father had bought me, but we didn't have room in the car. I sat on the rungs of the ladder of my loft bed, not understanding this would also mean the end of a community of people who I counted on for care. Ofelia and her family and most of the building would disperse to nearby neighborhoods and we would move far away.

At the appointed hour, the police started knocking on the doors to each apartment to enforce the eviction. Ted argued with the police, "You can't kick us out with no notice, we're not going anywhere!" My sister, who was about two and a half at the time, remembers hiding with her dad behind the crib in her bedroom, easy to do with so many of our belongings left behind. Ted wasn't coming out with her until he was ready. She stood with her father crouched out of sight while the police made their second round to check that all the apartments were empty. They did eventually leave the building, but my mother, sister, and I left Staten Island without Ted. It took a crack in the foundation on Independence Day to break her free, but she finally left Ted. We moved out of state and lived without a man in rural northwestern Pennsylvania.

* * *

We spent two years living close to our friends' commune like farm in the beautiful endless mountains of Pennsylvania. They, too, had left Staten Island for bigger pastures: to garden and make pottery. My mother, toddler sister, and I spent two quiet, even lonely, years in a two-bedroom asbestos shingle farmhouse nearby.

My first day in public school I wore a polyester pants and suit jacket to help me fit into a country school. I was petite, well under five feet tall with thin light brown hair below my shoulders and a brightness in my hazel eyes that invited connection with my new teachers and peers. I spent the balance of the day explaining to friendly kids in jeans and T-shirts, "This is how I thought you dressed in the country."

My mother cleaned houses and collected welfare to pay the bills. On weekdays I returned home on the school bus, where my mother was often sitting in the living room reading. It was a two-bedroom, small house. My sister Laura slept in my mother's room, and I had my own room with a Kiss poster above my bed. I had figured out what country kids liked: Kiss, jeans, and T-shirts with Adidas—not converse—sneakers. Alone in the bathtub I found my first pubic hairs, and had an unspoken and powerful crush on a boy at school who was albino-like with white hair and light, light blue eyes. I still remember the inexplicable but unspoken connection I felt between us.

* * *

After two years of weekends with our family friends and alone with my mother and sister during the week, I missed the city. At fifteen, I declared I was moving back; my mother could either come or I was going to move in with Dad for the start of junior high school. I imagine she was lonely too, and she agreed to the move. In fact, she took a job on Long Island cooking for a boat crew before the school year ended. She arranged for me to live with a family from my sister's school, a family who didn't know me, while she took my younger sister and started a new job.

My temporary family had a lovely country home with horses and they taught me how to ride a horse English style. I was grateful for their generosity and even enjoyed pretending this was my beautiful farmhouse and my family. It was so like my mother to be the one who left first.

A LIGHT PUERTO RICAN

1978

We moved back to Stapleton, Staten Island, and shared a house with friends of friends. It was a Victorian era brownstone with turrets and lead arched windows on the third floor. The front door opened into a closed hallway with stairs on the right and a living room to the left of the hallway. The kitchen was in the back, smaller than the other rooms, and the only room besides my bedroom I spent time in. My bedroom was on the top floor, the small room with the turreted window. My loft bed stood near the top of that window where I could watch the birds in the tree out front.

When our Albanian landlord defaulted on payments for the brownstone, my mother went to the auction and purchased the property. She turned it into a boarding house to make the payments, and I came and went like any other boarder. My mother asked for no explanations about my comings and goings, and I gave her none.

One of our friends had just started a magnet junior high school in Harlem, and they invited me to come to the school. I would be the token white kid, which got the school more Title I funding with me as the diversity. From age thirteen to fifteen I traveled to East Harlem. I took the bus to the Staten Island Ferry, to the subway uptown. I took up smoking and became friendly with a group of early morning commuters. We sat on the lower deck drinking tea and coffee and smoking cigarettes with the Statue of Liberty in our wake.

Over time I developed a Hispanic accent and permed my hair. I imagined people might see me as a light-skinned Puerto Rican with my brown-maroon lipstick, permanent waved hair in cornrows, and new accent to match. Like a chameleon employs tiny nanocrystals to reflect light and change color, I tried to look and sound Latino to fit in. I rode the graffiti-tagged subway cars on the Lexington Avenue line of the late seventies of New York City and carried a boom box to play my music out on the street. I walked from the subway to the school on 103rd Street, with the large radio, a third my size, on my shoulder, blasting "Got to be Real" through the streets of Spanish Harlem. "Hey, mamacita," the older men on the street corners called out, and I smiled with the beat of the music in my stride, feeling invincible.

The school's mission was to bring communication and health to an uptown neighborhood, which translated to students selling tuna fish on whole wheat pita bread with sprouts to anyone who would buy them out of a food truck. Not many people on 103rd and Madison were interested; I, too, preferred a ham and cheese sub for a dollar from the corner bodega.

* * *

To pay for the pot I had started smoking, I stood at the downstairs entrance of the ferry dealing loose joints during my morning commute and again at lunchtime outside the school. That's how I met Freddie, a short, flamboyant Hispanic man dressed in all white, a twenty-something party boy who drew me into his Staten Island crowd. His sister, Sugar, a squat woman with spiked blonde hair, became my partner in crime. Her bigger than life almond-shaped eyes and wide full lips made her look like a caricature of herself, like a current day Blyth doll with a head too large for her body. But when Sugar arrived, the volume always went up. "Now the party can get started," she announced when she entered the room. I sat on the sidelines, in tight Jordache jeans and silk blouses that hinted at the sex I was almost old enough to have. Skilled at feeling out a crowd, smoking was my shield and armor. At sixteen, with all the freedom of a young adult, I was determined to seem composed and in control.

Sugar was my counterpart, wild and crazy and out for a good time. We took Quaaludes and amphetamines. She drank rum and coke to my whisky or cognac neat. At times I passed out in their bathtub, woke up, and stumbled onto well-placed piles of garbage bags on my way home. Other nights, Sugar and I stood on line outside discos and bars in Manhattan where bouncers would regularly let us in despite my being underage.

One night Sugar and I sat at a table in the dark balcony of the Roseland discotheque while the music and lights thundered downstairs. Like so many of my memories, there is little or no conversation, as if my psyche only remembers what wasn't said. A small-framed Hispanic man asked if I wanted to dance. Our chemistry was strong on the dance floor. His hips and feet found my rhythm easily and we danced into the night. Then, when Sugar was nowhere to be found and he asked me back to his place, it seemed like a good idea. It was too late to travel home alone.

My age was always a question. I was less than five feet tall but I talked a good talk; I knew how to shift the attention from myself to the other person. Bent on concealing the girl inside, I was always trying to pass for older. I have two conflicting memories: one version that he asked me my age before asking me to come home with him, and the other that he never asked. One way or another I agreed to go home with him and we traveled by subway to a large apartment complex somewhere uptown. Tall buildings surrounded by trees in a neighborhood I had never been to before, far from midtown, maybe Morningside Heights?

After hours of more drinking, Quaaludes, and heavy petting, he wanted sex. "Come on, baby," he begged. I was embarrassed to admit I was a virgin and ashamed of myself for landing in some stranger's apartment who might not care that it was my first time.

"Do you have a condom?" I managed to ask, and we had uncomfortable intercourse with him holding my arms at my sides. I lay in his bed before I fell asleep, my pride hurt to have slept with a grown man, a man who didn't know me well enough to know how old I wasn't. In the morning, I remember looking to find a small trace of my virginity, fluid slightly tainted with my blood on the gray sheets, a trace I either hoped would or wouldn't give me away. That morning, he rode with me downtown on the subway. We sat next to each other with nothing to say, a girl and a grown man. At the South Ferry stop, I stepped off the train feeling ashamed that I had given something to someone without even naming it.

The next week I went to the Planned Parenthood office near school. I sat by myself in the waiting room with other girls and women, waiting for the free birth control we could get with limited explanation.

A BIG DEATH

1980

Early fall of my first year of high school, my grandmother, Florrie, died. She collapsed on the toilet from a burst aortic aneurysm. She died before she got to the hospital. My father's siblings flew in from the Netherlands, Boston, and the far regions of upstate New York to make arrangements.

Florrie's two brothers and sister, my aunt and uncles and cousins all stood in the funeral parlor like a crime family without its kingpin. Grandma had orchestrated allegiances and maintained control of my father's life at great cost. Without her, the looming question that no one dared to articulate yet was: What would happen to my father? The adults held whisky glasses tight and stood pensive in the vacuum she left behind. My father avoided looking me in the eyes, and he wouldn't look in the casket either, as if he could avoid acknowledging her death if he didn't see her. He stood back from the coffin emotionless in the wake of our loss. My grandmother's artificially put together corpse—the unnatural dense flesh color of the foundation on her face and her thin perfectly pink lips offended me. But it was her closed eyes, a repose she wouldn't be caught dead in with people in the room, that made it hard to stand by her dead body. That, along with my father's detachment, sent me howling out of the funeral parlor, trying to jog his heart with my outburst or seeing myself in my grandmother's corpse as the heir apparent, your pick.

The family drank and reminisced, telling stories and

remembering the best parts of her, while my father and I stood outside my grandmother's influence and protection for the first time, numb to what it might mean. I had a dream after Grandma died that she was a large serpent-like beast that resided in my father's head. She exploded out of him, octopus-like with many tentacle arms. It wasn't until her death that I realized she possessed us all, monster-like in her mission to protect my father.

After the funeral we sat around the dining room table of Grandma's house to discuss what was to happen to my father. What did I think about Frank coming to live on Staten Island, if the family were to use his inheritance to buy him a home there? Although in my teen years I had less to do with my father, my position in the family was clear; I had been groomed in this family for this moment. There was really nowhere else for him to go.

* * *

At the time Frank and Barbara, who were living in an upstairs apartment of Grandma's house, were pregnant with their second child, a fact that either no one knew because it was early in the pregnancy or everyone ignored. But Barbara's siblings were aware and they were fed up with Frank getting Barbara pregnant. Late the night after Grandma's funeral, Barbara's mother and sister showed up at the house. They banged on the door and shouted in guttural drunken German accents.

"Vee vant to see Fronk!" they called from outside as they banged on the door. My father's youngest brother opened the door.

"Let us in," they cried. "Vee 'ave come to take off his thing! So he can't make any more babies. Vere is he? Vee're going to castrate him vonce and vor all!" they yelled.

My aunts and uncles were sleeping in all the spare beds. I lay under the dining room table on a pad made of extra blankets, listening to their calls. "Come down, you coward" they yelled to my father, who either didn't hear them or ignored their shouts. My young uncle, John Paul, stood at the door between them and the dining room floor where I stayed hidden.

"It's time he stops siring children he can't provide for!" they said, pointer finger to his chest. On this point, we all agreed, and perhaps it was this common ground that John Paul used to convince them to leave. The rest of the conversation was lost on the other side of the door and my memory.

After my grandmother's death, the family purchased a house on Staten Island and Barbara, who was visibly pregnant by then, stayed on Long Island with her family. Five years after the birth of their first son, Barbara gave birth to their second child, Katarina. Barbara's sister Elsie convinced Barbara to put "father unknown" on the birth certificate and let her begin adoption of the second child from the hospital.

After Grandma died, things changed between my father and me. I felt his eyes on me differently. I remember standing in my dead grandmother's living room, crossing my arms over my chest to protect myself from his glances. "Stop looking at me like that," I yelled and he flashed me a look, as if my need for boundaries was an affront. As if, above being a father, he was a man looking for connection and safety after the loss of his mother. My father's new house on Staten Island, five blocks from my mother's brownstone, was a little too close for comfort. I rarely visited my father in those years.

Two years later, Barbara had moved in with Frank and they had gotten pregnant again. It was in that house that Dad and Barbara had their third child, Jacqueline. Jackie, as she was called, was born at home, without social services knowing. That's how they were able to keep the child, while the balance of the family, living far away, weren't paying attention.

CALEB

Meanwhile, I had tested into and was unhappy at Brooklyn Technical High School. I had hoped to get into Stuyvesant High School, the top science school in the city. Brooklyn Tech was too large and impersonal. After Florrie's death, I felt very much at sea, swept up in the school's industrial halls by aspiring engineers and teachers who had no clue about the profound loss of my grandmother as caregiver. In my first year of high school I transferred to an alternative high school in the West Village, called City As School, where internships earned high school credits.

I worked and went to school in Manhattan and had very little to do with either of my parents. By day I went to various high school placements, testing my aptitude for politics in the borough president's office, dabbling in acting at a socialist labor theater company in Chelsea, and building my activist chops assisting the director of the Religious Coalition for Reproductive Choice and demonstrating on the streets. When I wasn't in school, I worked as a server at a Mediterranean restaurant on Chambers Street in Lower Manhattan. It was run by a beautiful young woman of Chinese descent named Helen and her scrawny white pothead husband. She ran the front end and he prepared the food. My job, as I saw it, was to serve the food as it was ordered and make sure my fellow line workers were doing the same. Sometimes Helen had to pull me aside. "Give them a break," she coached me, and I felt misunderstood but loyal to her cause.

I took myself to museums and sustained a couple of friendships through school. But at night I was drawn to other lost souls, to partying and drinking and proving I could match any of the adults in the crowd.

It was at a party at Freddie's house that I met Caleb. He stopped in to deliver cocaine and stayed for a drink. I was immediately attracted to his perfect height and Romanesque face. He had thick, curly dark hair you wanted to run your hands through, lovely brown eyes, and lush lips; he was gorgeous. He dealt in rocks—cocaine at night and gems in the diamond district by day—and was in his early twenties; I was sixteen. We sat and talked for hours. Mostly he talked and I listened. I was hungry to understand how other people thought, in part because I didn't know myself; listening was safer than exposing what I didn't know. Caleb offered to walk me home and we stumbled back to my room on the third floor and had sex. He left that night.

It was the beginning of a clandestine relationship that lasted through high school. He visited me on Fridays, never in the company of friends. He came to my door at the appointed hour, and we walked up the creaking Victorian brownstone stairs to my bedroom on the top floor with the arched leaded window. It was a tiny room. Under my loft bed was a dresser on one side and a small sitting area: two bean bag chairs with a small table lit by a lamp with a red light bulb that made everyone look better than they did.

Most Fridays, my diaphragm in place, we sat in my room and he told me about his week, his diamond and cocaine dealings, and the parties he went to on Fire Island, parties I was never invited to and never imagined attending. We snorted lines of cocaine and climbed up to my loft bed to have sex that always hurt me. In the years we saw each other, Caleb never met my mother or set foot in the rest of the house, except for the bathroom. He always left before morning.

At the time, I felt lucky. I absorbed his good looks and Latin sensibility, just the two of us. The rest of the week our lives were separate; jewelry appraiser by day and bisexual Fire Island playboy on the weekends with me, his girl Friday. We continued this way until the summer before college. I returned from my grandparents' cottage, tan, well fed, and ready to move on and get away. He wanted to introduce me to his family. He took me home and told me he loved me, as if by leaving I became something to acquire, like a precious stone. It was an attempt to make us into something we never were and that dishonesty made me question him more than all the years of being kept hidden.

The following year I will learn he became sick with pneumonia. I will worry about the bisexual escapades he was having on Fire Island and get myself an anonymous HIV test that will be negative. I will never see or hear from him again. For now, I was heading off to college and he was staying on Staten Island.

WORLDS APART

I was seventeen when I left for Hampshire College, a small liberal arts school nestled in the Berkshires of Western Massachusetts. I brought all my belongings from my mother's house, intending a clean break. Outside my dormitory window there was a blooming cherry tree with powder pink petals, very much like the flowering tree on my grandmother's lawn that promised this American dream: an education and social mobility, a dream my father's insanity took hostage. I felt out of place. I watched how the affluent students banded together while I brooded behind reflective glass from my dorm room. I missed our brick tenement, its forest green metal door, dented from some unknown trauma, and *Black is Beautiful* tagged like a zip code.

Is there a word for what gets said without language, how we carry the weight of the lives that come before us? Even now, I am searching for a way to convey the power of my father's love, the implicit nature of his psychosis, and how that made making friends and feeling at home in a normal world impossible. The way college became not just a challenge but a question of my merit; a lonely room piled high with books, a wake of emotions that swept up words and dashed them like sea foam ideas I couldn't hold on to.

I have a picture from *Life Magazine* of a young man at Pilgrim State Hospital where my father was frequently taken after his first breakdown in college. The man looks very much like Dad: young, dark haired, trapped. His hands are strapped around his waist, and he looks directly into the camera with a defiant stare. He's sitting with two other men also in straitjackets, in a cluster of chairs that look like school desks.

I, too, felt trapped by the voices in my head that guarded against failure and exposed weakness. My professors critiqued my analysis and, challenged my ideas, and I felt irretrievably deficient. Instead of schoolwork, I found refuge in the powerful voices of James Baldwin, Toni Morrison, and Zora Neal Hurston, looking for myself in the power of their words. In a letter my father wrote to his sister from the psych ward in 1961, he reminisces about his time in college: "There are more mental challenges in the school world, yet reality forces you to take a close look at the workings of the real you. It is the blood-drawing element that makes you sweat. School is a delightful time of your life." But I was floundering.

Picture me in a dorm room with antique bottles I dug from the backyard as a child, bottles that reflect the sun, in green and sepia tones like my grandparents' dreams standing in the window. The poster above my bed is of the fifteenth-century tapestry of the Unicorn in Captivity. A wounded unicorn sits in a garden surrounded by a circular fence that's low enough to escape, and yet it stays. An allegorical interpretation is that the unicorn, with all its implied magical powers, is the wild tamed. I can't help but think of a line from Mary Febose: "Imagine Persephone loving Hades... Is it so impossible?... We often love the things that abduct us, that abscond with part of ourselves."

In this story, my father and I are both captives of the schizophrenia and the symbolic nonverbal world that felt more real than what we had to say, more real than the fence. How do you explain what you know but don't understand? For Lacan, the French psychoanalyst and philosopher, language allows us to distinguish between the way we construct the world and what is *real* beyond language and construction. But in my twenties, I don't know I'm trapped in the symbolic nonverbal world of allegory with my father. I only know I can't separate one idea from how I feel about it. I resent the necessity for evidence and feel ashamed that I can't find it.

In another picture, my father sits in a chair. He's stoned, his eyes are slits, his lips are parted as if smiling inside, and his hands sit squarely on his knees, Buddha-like. If I let my eyes soften and lose focus, my father's face disappears, I see only an outline, a skeleton of a man like a frightening clown. I'm crying now. It's how my father once painted himself: like a child in primary colors, a red circle with two eyes, a wide smile and a yellow upside-down triangle hat. He's a clown face in a house of cards. Could I tell he felt like a caricature of a man, a lost clown? How hard it must have been to be a father, to be a son, to be the Son of God. If, as Socrates says, language is a conversation with the soul, what happened when his soul stopped making sense? How does a child form identity in the face of a parent unraveling?

* * *

When I was three, after my mother left my broken father, there were years before her next live-in lover. "What was that time like?" I ask, looking for a window of time when we might have bonded. The way your children can become your most precious *other*. Maybe we just forgot? She reminds me we went to New Mexico so she could be part of an open relationship. The couple and their kids went out ahead to find a place to stay. We joined them, but by the time we arrived their New Mexico friends had convinced them it was a bad idea.

"They would barely let me in the house," my mother remembers. "I took you for walks every day in the stroller; we just walked the streets." She was a young twenty-seven at the time. She walked a baby when she was still a child.

"What was it like, just the two of us?"

"I was your mother, and you were my daughter. That's all. I didn't know how to be a parent. I didn't know what you needed. But you fit right in; you were able to carry on conversations with any adult, you were three going on thirty." It's true my mother always felt more like a sibling; we competed for attention, and I was winning and losing at the same time.

"I was a mother, you were my child," she says, "nothing more, nothing less." She has no idea I'm looking for a picture of our young love together, pushing me in the stroller every day. *Did you love me?* I think but don't ask. How *do* parents learn what love sounds like?

My father was the warmth I craved. Like a lion, he slept in his sun-drenched bed in wait for the adventures his mania promised. When the metaphysical world came alive for him, the moon and sun were of special interest. "Pure ideas" were the language my father spoke: light beams and how they could power the world; sound and how its resonance could be heard at a soul level; understanding without explanation. In my father's world there was no distinction between what he thought and what was real. Many years later I will be married and visiting him in the nursing home. I'm smiling at the heartfelt guitar player. My father leans into my face, "You're in love, aren't you?" and in that moment I am back in that space where there were no boundaries with my father, where he thought he could read my mind, and was sure his thoughts were true.

* * *

In my first semester of college, I took courses on global poverty and Latin American fiction. I learned about law and mental illness and was confronted for the first time with the way my father's psychiatric care was less than humane. I had no memoires of visiting him in the psych ward. I hadn't considered how once he was committed, he couldn't say *no*, was strapped down to his bed, shocked with electric currents. I only knew he was silenced by his medication. No longer inspired, I understood but couldn't develop a thesis for a paper with our dissonant history and future looming in the foreground.

I have a letter my father wrote his sister from Fort Dix in 1961, four years before I was born. It would have been after college and after his second or third breakdown, when his father encouraged him to join the Army, hoping it might give his son rules to follow and structure for his ailing mind. Dad tells his sister he's been transferred from boot camp to a special Morse code training. At first, I think it's the perfect job for a man practiced at hearing messages until I realize it must be a figment of his imagination.

"They told me I must learn the Morse code. This entails sitting in one spot with earphones on while they send Morse code through your brain. So, I said to myself, this nonsense must stop... the army was a complete act of insanity... I will advise you when I have completed my separation... There is only one certainty in my life—that once I find the art form I can master, this is where I will devote most of my energies. I hope to get into the Sun as soon as I can—*Frank*"

I'm struck by how fluid the line is between his philosophy and his insanity. Moved by how he's trying to make sense of his life, the striving and truth seeking, the drive toward the sun's baptismal fire.

My own disjointed letters resonate with a similar struggle to find meaning, letters written to friends and lovers in college. Letters I apparently never sent. *"If we don't believe we are all pieces of one dream we are left alone to possibly fail. Freedom seems to have become an internal event...* " I hear his voice, similar questions but also our shared vulnerability: *"I sit here feeling a little frightened. My distaste for the way I speak, the way my mouth tells of all my inner thoughts while talking to others. What a nasty mouth to tell my secrets... well mouth now I know also, so you can quit playing games with my social affairs I'll deal with it as I can."*

    I sound crazy in my self-talk, paranoid even, of my inner child. Afraid her needs will frighten everyone away, desperately trying to be a person people wanted to be around. But when I move out of self-loathing I can see how, like my father, I am corresponding to keep my own counsel, advising my inner child to keep her thoughts and needs to herself. My yearning for connection was a softer side of myself that terrified me.

* * *

    I briefly had a thing with a strange boy, a linguistics major whose hobby was investing in mutual funds. Like me, he was out of place and out of step, too young to be so excited about investments and too weird to have many friends. He also had a penchant for sadomasochism. He wanted to handcuff me. I let him try, then panicked in his custody and demanded he take them off *now*. That Thanksgiving, I gave him a ride home to New Jersey on my way to Staten Island. I came in to use the bathroom, and he took me to his bedroom in his parents' finished basement. In the center of the room sat a mattress with chains and cuffs at each corner. It took the permanence of the chains for me to realize we had nothing in common; I was really not into bondage and had very little money to invest.

CLOISTERED INSANITY

Like a last supper gone wrong, I sat in the basement kitchen of my father's time-worn home on Staten Island for Thanksgiving dinner. When I called the week before about coming home for school vacation, Dad lit up, "Why don't you come by my house for the holiday, baby?" I came out of obligation to a father whose drive to be a father to his children had always moved me, but I could barely stand to be with him now.

He presided at the head of a large oak table that stood on a dirt floor; a handsome dark Irishman in his youth, my father weighed nearly three hundred pounds now, his large belly distended over the waist of his pants. His thick head of grey hair was tinted yellow by the tar from chain smoking, as were his thick, stained brown fingers.

Our neighbor and local pot dealer, Bashkum, a large chubby-faced Albanian, sat on one side. Barbara sat on the other. Her blonde hair was pulled up in a bun, she wore pink lipstick, and the empty space from a missing front tooth was filled with dental gum. She grasped her fork in her hand, like a child waiting for food. Next to her sat their two-year-old daughter, Jackie, whose pale skin showed translucent blue veins just below the surface. Struck quiet by visitors, Jackie pressed her hands against the table that constrained her to her chair, her watchful eyes glued to her plate. Then she wordlessly slid off her seat and hid under the table. I felt her on the floor vulnerable and rodent-like; I imagined the safety of being out of view in the sheltered space below. I wanted to slip away, too, but also to make her come out and sit down. My father stood over the sizable turkey with a large dull knife. He wore a coffee-stained T-shirt, and his hands were greasy from the meat he was sawing off in big hunks to match his appetite. He alternately shoved a piece in his mouth and then unceremoniously put the next on each person's plate.

"Here." He pulled a leg off the carcass and thrust it in my direction. "Have some turkey. It's Thanksgiving, for God's sake," he said.

"I'm not eating meat, Dad; I'll eat potato and stuffing."

"Suit yourself," he said with disappointment on his face. "I don't know why you won't eat the meal I cooked."

"I'm eating, Dad." I took a baked potato from the sauce pot they were served in, and asked Bashkum, who was helping himself to stuffing and potatoes, to pass the butter.

"Here you go, Tasha," he said, making himself more familiar than we were. Why wasn't he with his own family for Thanksgiving and what was he doing at my father's table for the holiday?

The house smelled of stale cigarettes and cooked on grease; it was a home seeped with my father's frustrated desire to provide for those he loved. I pictured the upstairs apartment, their bedroom draped with dark green sheets, two bare mattresses, and a portable crib. The surfaces of their home cluttered with crack pipes, empty baggies, and overfull ashtrays. I hated him at that moment for the company he kept, the dealers and prostitutes he frequented, the way mental illness isolated him and made him a mark. I hated him for naming Jacqueline after a saint and a president's wife and then failing to provide what a child needs to develop language or stay at the table. I hated the translucent-skinned child hiding under the table like prey, who I instinctively distanced myself from. Children know when they're at risk—the way an animal senses danger when the herd disperses.

With nothing to talk about, we all ate in silence. Dad slurped up gravy from his now empty plate and Bashkum helped himself to a glass of the wine I brought. Jackie crawled out from under the table and stood at the door looking out into the fenced in backyard with uncut grass that was taller than she was. Was she trying to get out?

"That was delicious!" Dad said, relishing a good meal and watching Jackie standing at the door. "Did you see the pot plant I'm growing out there?"

"No, I didn't"

"Actually, it was me who planted it," Bashkum announced importantly.

"Yes, that's true," my father admitted.

Jackie walked to her mother and pulled at her arm. *Did they ever take her out?* I wondered. Had they been back to the playground my father had been thrown out of months before when the weather was warm, looking like a vagrant sitting on the bench in his stained shirt and unshaven face?

"They kicked me out, Tasha," he would complain of their last visit.

"Sir, we're going to have to ask you to leave the park," the officer had said.

"What do you mean? I'm here with my daughter."

"Yes, and we've gotten complaints. We're going to have to ask you to leave."

"I'm watching the children, it's as close as you can get to God, man!" he would tell them, raising his voice.

"Which is why we have to ask you to leave. Which one is yours? It's time for you to go, sir."

Did Jackie notice the police? Or was she intoxicated with the fresh air on her face, the rush of the slide, and the sound of other children? Did she take his hand willingly or cling to the swing set in protest?

"Would you like me to take Jackie to the playground?" I asked, looking at my dad. It was Barbara who spoke first.

"Well! I'm going upstairs now since everyone in this room is acting like I'm a whore." Over the years I had come to understand this refrain as her version of *I don't feel safe*. She stood up and marched upstairs. Jackie shrank into herself and climbed back under the table. I could see her in the shadows. Her large blue eyes dilated from seeing too much, eyes that asked: Do you recognize this childhood? Can you see me? I remembered a different table, a different dealer. My father was more hopeful when I was a young child and my mother was more sane—sort of—but I knew this life.

Dad and I sat at the table. Dad lit a smoke.

Bashkum stood up. "I should go," he said, taking the last drink out of his glass and heading with a jaunt to his step to the stairs that led up to the front door.

Jackie came out from under the table and took my hand, looking desperately into my eyes. "Ice cream?" she begged, pulling her truant half sister toward the door.

"I'll be back," I said, taking Jackie's clammy hand and leaving my father sitting alone at the table.

She held my hand tight as we walked in the chilly November night toward the neighborhood store. The dealers on the corner called out, "Five dolla bag, three dolla vial," and I felt the threat of the street. I had played in the projects down the street as a child and walked these streets but in safer times—when methadone clinics treated addicts, when the war on drugs hadn't yet been declared. The neighborhood felt desperate now. I knew enough to keep my eyes to the ground, to hide our vulnerability. The trick was to project an air of not caring, to show you knew the way. Jackie walked slowly like she wanted our outing to last longer, which made me feel impatient. I chose for her and, ice cream pop in hand, we walked back to the house in silence. Jackie held her still wrapped ice cream tightly in her other hand.

I have a picture of her from that day, standing outside in the street light, holding a large cone between two small hands, licking from the bottom up. She was wearing a light purple jacket, nearly the same hue as her skin. Her thin hair was uncombed and her cheeks were streaked with tears.

She pulled me back into the house to the bedroom at the end of a long dark hall where her dolls lay askew with missing limbs and chopped off hair. I sat awkwardly on the bed. Jackie sat on the floor, a pencil in hand, scribbling onto a napkin. When I couldn't stand it any longer, I reached down and rubbed her back, like a dog I couldn't take home.

"Jackie, I have to go now," I said and she said nothing. I walked toward the door, leaving her sitting on the floor, the sound of her pencil scratching out a sinus rhythm of distress that I couldn't bear. It was the last time I saw her alive.

AT RISK

My second year at Hampshire, I lived in a house of seniors—women engaged in a high level of academic critique. One was writing her thesis on Nazi representation of Jews during the war. Another focused on feminist conceptions of labor. I became interested in the ways social attitudes are communicated and translated into family systems, the way Protestant mores of sixteenth century European families influenced child rearing. The central idea was the concept of original sin, the idea that children came into the world needing to be reformed, physically bound to constrain their impulses. I, too, felt dangerous, angry, and in need of restoration.

James Baldwin came to campus as a visiting professor that year and delivered the welcome speech to the incoming class of 1984: "White as a Metaphor for Safety." I sat in a room of white, affluent families as he challenged the audience to consider the safety we were afforded based simply on the color of our skin. One evening, I saw Baldwin in the pillowed quiet of the backwoods of the campus. He held a glass of wine and stumbled over the protruding roots of the large white pines. His prominent eyes were glazed with cataracts, the pain and alienation of his prose indelibly mirrored on his face. I imagined he, too was accustomed to an urban sidewalk where roots were bound under concrete. I watched him from a distance, hoping by proximity to learn how to articulate what it felt like to be an outsider.

Separated by class and a family I couldn't make sense of, my sarcasm and wisecracks fell flat, as if I were picking a fight at a Quaker meeting. I recently heard a second-generation immigrant speak about how her Sephardic family moved from Southeastern Europe to Cuba in order to be able to speak Ladino, or Judeo-Spanish—a language she still speaks with *her* children. "Sometimes language is the only thing an immigrant can take with them," she said.

Often, our native language doesn't translate.

From the psych ward, my father writes his sister: "Let me tell you now—I am beginning to find the more real parts of life, the parts that sear and burn instead of lightly brushing past are the blessings of reality... I intend to get my paints back from the other ward and do some work. That will give me my first composition in the insane asylum. It will be a group of brightly colored teardrop-shaped figures traveling in various directions. This will, I hope, give strong movement to the canvas..." My father's metaphysical melancholy, lyrical as Chopin or Coltrane, was the latent language I yearned for like a purple velvet cloak to make me invisible, royal even. My father's psychosis was a silent liturgy that summoned reverence and devotion in me. I felt a deep ambivalence toward academia because it seemed devoid of the feelings and instincts I had come to rely on.

When my father's younger brothers came home from college, Frank was there. Summer afternoons he played his saxophone with his youngest brother JP, a guitar player. "He was pretty good," says John Paul. "He could follow the chord progressions very closely, I was impressed," and then he goes quiet. "I'll never forget one morning Frank and I were sitting around the kitchen talking about politics and really enjoying each other. Then it was like a switch flipped. He walked up to my face and said remorsefully, 'It's time to fly to the moon, man' and left the room." My uncle is crying now, gulping air quietly to keep the sobs from escaping out of his big belly where grief and fat are on reserve. He flicks the tears away that fall down his cheeks. He was a twenty-something forestry student, faced with the impossibility of his brother's break. We all stood witness to my father's departures, the way he let you know he was going, as if he wished we could join him but also knew we couldn't, the yank of his soul, a chemical fucked up cosmic mystery to us all.

My last semester, I took a course on the Old Testament, trying to understand religious history, to know the book that informed my grandmother's identity as Jew turned Catholic. My proposed thesis was to explore the question of whether God felt betrayed by individual will. My professor, who had asked me to his office to discuss my topic, sat at his dark mahogany desk with a wall of leather-bound books shelved behind him. He looked at me over his bifocals like I was hard to see, and said, "I don't imagine you'll be able to support this thesis from the text."

"But don't you think God must feel conflicted by the free will of beings he created with a purpose?" I challenged my professor, grappling with my particular problem with authority, searching to understand free agency and betrayal. Francis Martin's *The Spiritual Sense* discusses ways of understanding symbolic or allegorical texts, the idea of Sensus Spiritualis: *Sensus* the Greek term for the power of perceiving, coming into contact with the reality mediated by sacred texts. I was interested in the way allegories contained hidden messages and felt ideas.

"But where is the evidence for your argument?" the professor challenged me in return. I didn't have the answers to his questions and he didn't understand mine. I had imagined the Bible could teach me something about capricious gods and the cost of fealty. Instead, I packed my bag and left his office quietly raging at him for confining me to the text, for insisting on evidence for the enduring mystery of life's injustices. For not understanding how language failed to convey the ephemeral nature of devotion.

The existential psychologist Rolla May describes guilt and anxiety as the experience of forfeiting one's own potentialities—guilt as self-betrayal. At the end of my third semester of college, I took a leave of absence. I was failing, and leaving was the only act of volition I could manage.

* * *

I moved to a shared apartment in Northampton, Massachusetts and got a job. My roommate was a girlfriend who was finishing her thesis. Jill was one of my few close friends at Hampshire. We met in the cafeteria one afternoon and were instantly attracted to each other. We were opposites in how we didn't fit in; she was nurturing and calm, and I was brash and brooding. Both of us felt out of step on campus and decided to get an apartment together.

Jill worked on her thesis and I got a job preparing food—if you could call it that—for a woman who couldn't leave her house. The woman I worked for believed she had allergies to just about everything and never left her home. She had the ingredients for her recovery regimen delivered to the house and I spent the day preparing her a diet of juices made out of raw liver and vegetables. It was unappetizing at best but there was something remarkable about her commitment to treating her somatic needs. She was captive in her home, but at the end of the day, I got to leave. In hindsight, practicing the act of leaving people who couldn't function in the world.

After work, I regularly trekked up the hill to the music rooms on the Smith College campus. I spent hours at the piano alone in one of the small white fluorescent-lit rooms. I improvised tunes, driven to find my center. Was this something my father did in college? Was jazz a balm to the psychic upheaval that preceded his first psychotic break? Jill complained that I was never around, and she was right. I couldn't bear to be seen, couldn't stand being in my own skin. I wanted her nurturing but was desperate not to be caught needing it.

At the end of the spring semester, Jill finished her thesis and moved to California. I couldn't afford to stay in school not completing work. I rationalized that school was out of touch with the real world and I wasn't cut out for the impartial thinking of academia. I felt drawn back to the comfort of what was familiar: the working-class conditions of my family and the city I grew up in. I withdrew from school.

ANOTHER SISTER AT RISK

I returned to an available room in my mother's boarding house where she continued to rent rooms to pay the mortgage. She generally had three or four boarders that commuted to and from Manhattan on the ferry, like I had as a teen. I worked as a server at that same downtown restaurant I worked at in high school and felt the relief of being back where my grit measured my worth.

During that time, I watched my now twelve-year-old sister Laura struggle to get up in the morning, and in the afternoon slip back into her bed piled high with clothes, as if she didn't want to be found. My mother took her to chiropractors and doctors, but no one could diagnose her overwhelming fatigue. I didn't know her well enough to know it was an early sign of depression and possibly an unconscious effort not to be found by a father who wanted his daughter to himself. After Ted and my mother separated, he became more and more antisocial and more and more attached to his daughter.

When Laura was seven years old and I was still in high school, Ted came to our door at the end of a weekend visit to get Laura's belongings. "Let me in, Judy! I'm here to get her stuff. I'm keeping Laura with me now," he said, holding his daughter still, ready to fight an informal custody battle.

"You can't just keep her!"

His sickening reply was clear for me to hear in the living room. "She's all I have! You have friends; I just have her! Let me in," he said, trying to push past her.

"You're not coming in this house, Ted. I'll call the police!" she said, blocking the doorway to the front hall, and this time he didn't overpower her, didn't push her aside. Instead, he turned on his heels and started running away with Laura in his arms.

"Help me. Stop him," my mother yelled, and our neighbor Bashkum—the same boy turned young man who was now Dad's dealer—a teen at the time he heard her calls and came running down the street. He put his large adolescent body in front of Ted.

"Now, Ted, give her back," Bashkum coached. My mother grabbed for Laura and, with Bashkum on her side, won her back. Like they were fighting for a turn with a toy, my mother ran into the house. Hustling my confused sister away from a father who made her feel like he couldn't do without her.

"I'll be back!" he threatened, and my mother, who should have wondered why he wanted his daughter so badly, simply shut the door against him. For future visits, she took to picking my sister up to get her back from his lonely house next to the paint factory.

"Why do you even let her see him?" I asked her. "People don't even let him in their house anymore."

"It's her choice. I don't want to be one of those mothers who turns their children against their fathers. I don't want either of you to hate me the way I hated my parents." But I did hate her, had decided she was useless to me long ago, and now she was failing to protect Laura from her troubled father.

In years to come, he will be held up at gunpoint and refuse to give his wallet. He will be shot in the throat, left having to push a button to simulate his vocal cords. I had been wrong as a child; not even a gun made him do what you wanted. Watching Laura and

Jackie's predicament helped me see how unprotected our childhoods had always been and I had no idea how to move forward, let alone help either of them.

I once asked our close neighbor, Ofelia if she worried about me as a child. She said, "When I met you at three years old, you knew exactly who you were and what you wanted." Is that possible? Didn't my role as my father's keeper, his significant other, need to be questioned?

It was my mother's mother who provided some of those boundaries for me. One of my last summer visits to the cottage, before smoking and boys meant more than grandparents, my grandmother Annabelle asked me, "Where do you sleep when you're at Franks?" I must have been around 13, but the truth was I still depended on my father for comfort.

"In Dad's room, where I always have."

"That's not right, Tash, a girl your age shouldn't be sleeping with her father," she said.

"You have a filthy mind!" I yelled, storming out of the room and not speaking to her for the rest of the day. I didn't feel at risk in his care. I felt sheltered by his large protective mass on the outside of the bed; the familiar smell of tobacco and the rumble of his snores were soothing to me. But she was right. I was too old to be in his bed.

Grandma was the one who upheld the social constraints my mother and father both rejected. The one who made me confess and return the items I shoplifted from Woolworths, the one who taught me to say thank you and you're welcome, the one who saw me as a child who needed rearing.

Now, as a young adult back at home, watching how my mother was failing to protect Laura was more than I could stand to witness. I had to get out of that house. I found a sublet in Lower Manhattan, moved out, knowing I was leaving another sister at risk.

A LURE

My father marched to the café table where I was sitting like he was on a mission from God. His dirty T-shirt, slacks, and black dress shoes hinted at the early beatnik days when the East Village was his stomping ground. Now it was mine.

"Hey, baby, what a hassle getting here," he said, swiping his thick dark hair from his eyes. He was five eleven and nearly three hundred pounds. His shirt was wet with sweat and he smelled like cooked grease and cigarettes, an odor I associated with being poor and hemmed in.

On a warm autumn day, we sat at an outside table with an ashtray. He stubbed his cigarette out on the sole of his shoe and put it into his pocket, looking at me like we shared a silent language. "Let's have coffee and find some place to get a drink," he said, manic and agitated like he had better places to be.

"Hey, don't I know you from somewhere?" the waitress asked as she set menus at our table. We figured out we had both graduated from City As School two years earlier and she left us to decide.

"Maybe you could introduce me?" Dad said after she walked away.

"What? She's my age!" I said, like age and social mores had ever mattered to my father.

"I'm simply mentioning the woman is attractive," he said, with a tone that implied I was getting in the way of his creative pursuits. I crossed my arms, looking at the menu not at him. The Second

Avenue bus pulled up and I imagined getting on and leaving as the doors eased shut. I was not yet twenty-one, had recently dropped out of college, and was increasingly sure there was something wrong with me that could be traced back to caring for him.

When our waitress returned, I ordered a tuna on rye.

"I'll have a cup of coffee" said Dad, tilting his head with a smile, the way he did when he had the answers the rest of us were looking for. "And maybe there is something I can do for you in return? Like make you immortal, my dear?"

She laughed awkwardly, flashing me a questioning look, and left to place our order.

"What the fuck was that?"

"I'm offering the young woman a chance of a lifetime," he said, looking me in the eye with the cool arrogance his delusions fueled. I hated being with him when he was like this.

I ate my sandwich with nothing to say and he inhaled his coffee, sucking the overfull cup to cool and drink at the same time. You could smell urine on the grimy cement where our table sat. His leg shook under the table as he took the cigarette from his pocket to relight it.

"How's Barbara?" I said, trying for normalcy.

"She's crazy as a fucking bat!" he complained with none of the loyalty he previously showed his fellow schizophrenic, his partner of the past ten years, the woman with whom he'd had three children. "I really think it's affecting Jackie," he said. I pictured the way Jackie hid under the table to get away from Barbara's paranoid shouting, and felt passing guilt at never coming to visit.

After my lunch and his coffee, with nothing else to say, I asked for the check and paid, relieved to be leaving.

"I have an idea, Tasha," he brightened. "Let's go to a bar where we can meet people."

"I'm not going to a bar with you," I said harshly, imagining being the only person with him in a dark bar in the middle of the day.

"Well, suit yourself," he said and started toward the downtown bars limping on ruined knees, the effects of years of psychotropic meds. He looked so alone with his uneven gait and his imaginary powers, I wanted to join him, to call back an earlier version when he seemed gallant, even heroic. I wanted to be the daughter who stood by him even in his mania, but I couldn't bear him.

DROWNING AFTERMATH

That spring, on April 10, 1986, my father took Jackie for a drive to the piers on the bay of Stapleton, Staten Island, just two blocks from where I grew up.

"She wouldn't go to sleep so I drove her around in the car and then headed out to the piers to see the city lights while Jackie slept," he told me, explaining why they were at the docks that night. I can still picture this view, from our quiet Staten Island harbor, fifteen years before the World Trade Center would implode. The abandoned piers were across the street from the apartment I grew up in. In the dark of night, my father didn't see the caution tape and drove right into the freezing cold New York Bay. I flashed on all the pipes and empty baggies in their apartment and wondered if he had been copping crack.

My father escaped the sinking car but wasn't able to reach Jackie. Did he argue with them about being taken to the hospital for hypothermia before they got her out? Did he imagine it was already too late to save her? It would be forty minutes before divers pulled her out, not breathing, her heart not beating. Miraculously they were able to resuscitate her, her brain and vital systems had been suspended by the cold. Jackie was alive by the time she reached the hospital. She survived, but there was significant brain damage, and she needed to stay in the hospital.

She lay on a respirator in the intensive care unit, her muscles spastic from the disrupted signals from her brain. Her little body curled into an ungodly shape. Her hands wrapped together and twisted upwards like a praying mantis. Her knees pressed into her chest and her feet pointed down. When my father saw her little body in this contorted state, the way she didn't seem to inhabit her body, he became convinced that she was possessed by the devil. Like we all have stories we tell to make sense of our lives, this was his recurring story. As the Messiah, his children were always at risk of possession.

So, when the doctors told him of her irreparable brain damage and posed the question of whether to take her off the respirator, he was convinced that the only way to save her soul was to pull the plug. "Yes, it's the right thing to do, doctor," he agreed. Since her chances of recovering brain function were slim to none, it must have been an easy decision for the doctors.

But she miraculously didn't die. She lived for nearly four weeks breathing on her own. I can only imagine this seemed like a sign to my father and Barbara, but sign of what I don't know. In a surprising show of empathy, it was my mother who came to Jackie's hospital bedside to try to help usher her to the other side, and, for this, Barbara thought my mother was a saint. The truth was, my mother and I shared the feeling that Jackie was better off dead than living the life ahead of her.

Two weeks after the accident, I dreamt I was with my father and Jackie. In the dream, she's showing me a photo album. Instead of pictures, there are pages covered in wrapping paper, as if marking how I managed to not look at her life even when she tried to show me. I never went to the hospital to see her.

* * *

Jackie died on May 27, 1986. A Catholic mass was held at the local Dutch Reformed Church down the street from their home. We all watched the tiny white casket move down the center aisle of the church holding her little body like a sacrificial offering. Members of both sides of the family sat in the front pews while frankincense embers were swung over her coffin like Catholic magic. My father's brothers and their wives stayed seated during the mass, which seemed like a cruel demonstration of their lack of faith.

I assumed my mother was there, but years later she tells me she wasn't. "What was the point?"

Meanwhile, Barbara's sister and brother, who were devout Catholics, brought my two remaining half siblings, whom I hadn't seen in over ten years. Outside the church, the air was crisp and the sky was blue, a day that didn't register our loss. My half siblings stood with their adoptive parents in front of the church. Both kids were blond like their mother. The boy, now eleven, wore an ironed shirt and pants, and the girl wore a Sunday dress. They stood behind the adults as if for protection. The way they kept their distance made me feel culpable, as if I could be a danger to them. But also, I felt jealous of the shelter they had with their adoptive parents.

What I didn't know at the time was before the accident, Barbara's sister who had adopted the other two children had been trying to gain custody of Jackie. She had been pleading with social services to let her have the girl and to keep the siblings together. Just one week before, their family had come to Staten Island to bring Jackie to the mall for a family picture, proof that the siblings belonged together. Someone was watching out for Jackie—it just wasn't our family.

What none of us knew was that Barbara would become pregnant again four months after Jackie's death with their fourth child.

A girl was born in June of the following year, and this time Elsie fought like mad with social services for custody. Then a year later, their last child, a second son, was born and adopted, this time by Barbara's brother.

The fact that her siblings, unable to have children of their own, were willing to take all four kids despite the complications and risks associated with having two schizophrenic parents was remarkable and curious. Elsie in particular was uncommonly dedicated to raising her sister's children. Maybe it had something to do with a story I'd heard from my father and later heard from Elsie herself?

When Barbara was seventeen, her parents were building a bike for her little sister Elsie's birthday. The sun was setting and they were trying to finish the job when they realized they had forgotten candles for the cake. Barbara offered to run out to the store to get them. On her way home in the dusk of a warm summer night, she was pulled into an alley and raped at knifepoint. She was a very devout girl and a virgin at the time, and losing her virginity in such a heinous way was earth-shattering, something she turned to religious counsel for. But when Barbara went to the priest, he insinuated that she shouldn't have been walking alone at night, that it was her beauty that made her a temptation, that she had brought it on herself. Barbara was never the same after that. Elsie believed it was the priest's betrayal that was most traumatizing. Would Barbara have had a different life if these assaults—first the rape, then the priests holding her responsible for the assault—hadn't broken something in her? I can't help but wonder if Elsie, who idolized her older sister, felt in some way responsible for the role her birthday candles played in that terrible night, may even have felt somehow responsible, the way children do. It helps me understand why Elsie kept all three children and fought for the fourth, why she made sure Frank and Barbara could see them from time to time. Even though, when they visited for birthdays and holidays, they were called Frank and Barbara, not Mom and Dad or even aunt and uncle. Still, they must have taken solace in knowing that the kids were still in the family.

As a mother, Barbara seemed to understand that it was better for the children to be raised in her sister's home. My father, on the other hand, rued the way the children were taken from him and how he missed out on the opportunity, the obligation really, to convey his paternal nobility. As a young adult, my impulse was to respect their distance, to be suspect of their gene pool. I never felt related to them, never wanted to know my half siblings. Later as an adult, I did on occasion try to find them on social media. I hoped to catch a glimpse of their adult lives, the way one slows down at a car wreck wondering what happened without any intention of stopping to help. That I was always unable to locate them left me imagining the worst.

Recently, my Aunt Irene and I were disagreeing about the number of children they had between them. "I have a list, Tash," she said and pulled out an address book on which she had written the names and birthdates of each of their children. She explained it was in case either of her children ever became romantically involved with someone with that name and birthdate, she would know. My aunt has a list.

PART 2

A RELUCTANT MANTRA

1989

Meanwhile, I had started a training to be a masseuse in the Berkshires. After I completed the two-year healing arts training and got my massage license, I found an apartment in Manhattan—in Stuyvesant Town on the East River and Twentieth Street. They say you do what you need to learn. At twenty-four years old, I threw myself into the wordless care and intimacy of massage, providing therapeutic touch to strangers. Hourly, I found where it hurt, where muscles and tendons held tight, where injury was located and I applied pressure; this circumscribed intimacy came easily to me, paid caregiving.

I returned to school at Hunter College, first as a nonmatriculated student, to see if I had it in me. I found part-time school with other working-class students a better fit. I found the study of biology, the parts and facts of life, more satisfying than the opinions of the social sciences. In molecular biology, I learned about cell signaling pathways, the way biomolecules facilitate physiological processes. Biology was a window into the complicated and beautiful mechanisms of life.

I didn't see either of my parents much during this time, but when my mother's mother was dying, she contacted me and told me she planned to leave her estate equally to my mother, my sister, and me. Her decision to leave her grandchildren the same as she left her daughter was unusual even though I understood my grandmother was looking out for us. When I mentioned to my mother that we might have to sell the cottage we loved so much because it was so far away, she rejected the idea on the spot.

"I don't want to sell the cottage, and I can't afford to buy your portion. We are going to have to work this out," she said, determined to have her way. I dreaded what I anticipated would turn into a fight, so I insisted we find a mediator. We decided to see a therapist together, someone recommended to us as the guru of relationship therapists. Even though her fee in 1990 was a whopping three hundred dollars a session, we decided we would share the expense of one session to see if she could help us.

In her Upper West Side office, we sat across from a tall African American woman with a cropped Afro and a discerning presence. We each explained our point of view. I thought we wouldn't be able to care for the property, and my mother said she didn't want to sell it. I expected the guru to put all her skills to work to help us find a way forward. Instead, she sat amidst the beautiful African masks on the wall behind her and gave us her appraisal.

"I'm sorry I can't help you. In my opinion you will never be able to reconcile these differences," she said in a cavalier way, like we weren't worth it. "That said, because I don't have anything to offer you, the session will be complimentary," she said decisively. I was shocked.

"Complimentary? You mean you aren't going to charge us?" my mother clarified.

"That's correct."

I didn't know what to say. What was wrong with her? What was wrong with us that this expert couldn't do anything to help? My mother reached out her hand and thanked the therapist for her honesty.

As we left the office that day, my mother seemed almost relieved. I couldn't look at her. I felt exhausted in my loneliness.

This failed therapy session seemed to guarantee that there would never be a time that my mother would see my needs; even the expert agreed. On the way home that day I saw a bright red ankle-length coat for sale along the Upper West Side of Broadway. It hung on a hanger, flying in the wind, and was soft and new. I felt I deserved the coat, and I bought it with the money I hadn't paid the therapist. I don't recall if my mother and I walked out together—somehow, I imagine that when I stopped for the coat, she continued to the train without me.

I have since then talked with my own therapist about that session. "How could she have taken such an easy out with us?" I complained.

"It could have been an intervention strategy; maybe she was testing to see if anyone fought for the relationship?" Neither of us did.

I called my grandmother and asked her to please leave us something discrete, so I didn't have to be linked to my mother's wishes. She changed her will at the end and left my mother the cottage, left me her house and my sister stocks. A year later, my mother sold the cottage and made substantially more than we received in the inheritance; it was so like her to want something badly and then give it up. My sister lost the most, but for me, getting less money was worth not having to fight.

* * *

Eventually, I found a therapist of my own and worked to afford the Manhattan sliding scale at her spacious loft on Prince Street. Susan was a petite, well-groomed woman with chin-length wavy brown hair and dark blue eyes that conveyed her warm intelligence. She was a cognitive and behavioral therapist with Buddhist leanings, evidenced by the photos of eastern gods on her walls and the compassion in her work. Weekly, I grappled with the way my self-esteem was tangled up in my mother's disaffection and my father's mental illness. The lonely truth was, I didn't feel entitled to the heartbreak of my childhood. I thought I should consider myself lucky, a kind of survivor's guilt.

It was around this time my father called me for help. He and Barbara had sold the house the family bought Dad and were renting now in the nearby neighborhood of Rosebank, Staten Island.

"Tasha, I need you to get my saxophones and paintings out of the apartment."

"Why do you need *me* to get them? Where's Barbara?"

"I'm in the loony bin at St. Vincent Hospital, and she went home to her parents!" he said, pausing for effect. "There was a fire in the apartment; the landlord told me I better come get my shit. Please get them out of there before someone steals the only valuables I own, baby."

Knowing the company my father kept, I wondered if the landlord had set the fire to keep him from coming back. I could picture the mess of his apartment, the scattered urine-stained laundry on the floor, the tar-coated paintings and open music cases, covered now in soot from the fire. I couldn't bear the thought of going. It was the kind of rescue I had felt compelled to do for as long as I could remember: if I cleared his ashtrays, if I stayed after the crazy roommates left, if I was the last princess standing, maybe my father could become the king.

In therapy that afternoon, in the safety of Susan's industrial size loft, with its forest green carpeting and vast floor to ceiling windows, I imagined going over to my father's decrepit apartment.

"It's not that big a deal to get his stuff—but it will need cleaning, and he probably owes the landlord money." My throat tightened against the thought and I started sobbing.

"What's happening?" Susan asked.

"I just can't be the one this time. I don't want to be the one he turns to, but how can I say no?" I asked, my throat so tight I could hardly speak.

"You *can* say no."

"He's stuck in the hospital. If I don't go, who will?" I cried.

"Does he have any friends who can do it for him?"

"Maybe? We have some friends from the old days still on Staten Island," I said, feeling the tightness in my throat relax a little.

"What if you called him and asked if there was someone else who could do it? Call and tell him. *I really wish I could do that, but I can't right now.*"

When she said it that way, it sounded so reasonable. But on my own, it seemed heartless not to help. Someone had to go, and isn't that what families do for each other? The idea of abandoning him in his confined commitment when he couldn't do it for himself felt selfish. I was a bad daughter. My worthiness felt so inexorably linked to meeting needs that were bigger and more important than my own. But his life's undercurrent was straining to take me under. I couldn't manage to take care of both of us in this instance.

Without ever going to look at his place, I called him. "I'm so sorry," I managed to say over the phone. "I wish I could help you, Dad, but I can't."

"I'm not sure why you can't do a simple thing like get my paintings and instruments for me," he said, sounding more annoyed than hurt. He was right; it was crazy not to get his stuff for him.

"I'm so sorry," I repeated, wondering what was wrong with me. "Is there someone else who can help? I wish I could, but I can't," I said, practicing what would become a reluctant mantra.

At the expense of my father's most prized possessions, a man who had so little, I was taking care of something I couldn't name, needs I had been trying to still, like an unwanted fetus that had no place in this family up until now. His cause was so familiar, so comfortable, but I had to put myself first, as selfish and irrational as it felt. I needed to separate my survival from his. My psyche begged for space with its own oxygen source and less smoke.

I recently read an article about memory and trauma and the way forgetting is often a natural trauma response, which can have lasting side effects. "Emotional blunting" is a result of forgotten trauma for some, a coping mechanism that includes: having difficulty accessing emotions, having less empathy for others or yourself, and difficulty maintaining relationships. I was not uncommon in this respect. I rarely felt close to people. I had few close friends, none of whom I confided in.

Virginia, a fellow masseuse who lived in Greenwich, Connecticut, was one of a handful of people I called friends. We shared a dark sense of humor and a love of the ocean. That summer, I visited her on Wednesday mornings to sail at the yacht club school near her home on the Long Island Sound. I saw my roommate in passing, or when we happened to find ourselves sitting on the couch to watch her old cat we called "civil war kitty" play with the other cat. I discovered a chiropractor I worked with also enjoyed singing *a cappella,* and we met in each other's living rooms to sing old gospel tunes like, "O, Mary, don't you weep, don't you mourn." But I wasn't intimate with anyone. I wasn't in the practice of endearing myself to others. I felt secretly unentitled to the friendship of people I admired, sure that if they knew I cared, they would leave.

I took long runs along the East River. I learned to light candles and cook for my own enjoyment. On my twenty-fifth birthday, I made myself a lovely meal of broiled sole with a white wine and caper sauce and went to see a movie, content to be alone. I found space for self-care where there was none before. Susan introduced me to twelve-step programs for adult children of alcoholics, or in my case, adults I had no control over. I sat in the St. Mark's rectory in the East Village with others who shared their stories and gave voice to the idea that each of us was powerless, powerless over the other's drinking, drugging, or insanity. In the company of strangers, we learned to let go of those we loved most.

I dated men who were as different as possible, dark and Mediterranean to my Irish light. There was an Indian music producer, who I met on a bus. I was reading a philosophy paper and asked, "Hey, what's the name of the guy who wrote the story of Gilgamesh?" He thought for a moment and admitted sheepishly, "I don't know, but if you give me your phone number, I'll find out." It was a very charming response, and, in my fantasies, he was going to be sexy in the ways Hindu polytheism, with their many gods of fertility and play, promised. We vacillated between him wanting me in more ways than I wanted him, and me using his adoration like a blanket when I felt lonely. Short-lived romances were the only kinds I could manage.

THE REAL KEN

I was twenty-six when I met Ken at the thirtieth birthday party of a mutual friend, who lived upstate in New Paltz, New York. It was nearly midnight, and I was overdue to leave to spend the weekend in Connecticut with a girlfriend. I had made a few friends along the way. Ken showed up in a white polyester button-down shirt and grey bellman's pants on his five-foot seven-inch frame. I overheard him talking about renovating a property, which seemed industrious. He had come from work and, in contrast to the other upstate musicians and rock climbers at the party, was well groomed. But more than anything, I was drawn to a kindness I saw in his red-rimmed eyes, as if he had been crying earlier, like a man whose feelings ran deep. (I now know the redness was due to his predisposition to blepharitis.)

We went home together that night, something I was less prone to doing in my twenties than I had been in my teens. I had dated a few age-appropriate boys and men in high school and more recently living on my own in Manhattan, but nothing serious or lasting. I lay in bed, a child of beatniks, wondering what to make of this young man's goal chart, taped to his ceiling, for making millions by the age of thirty. Early the next morning, due at a friend's house for the weekend, I dressed to leave and left my phone number on his dresser before kissing him goodbye as he slept. "Hey," he said half awake, "take my number."

"I left my number on your dresser. You can call me," I said, sure that he had to be the one who pursued me and that I would never see him again.

I was surprised when he called on Monday wondering if he could drive down to visit me the next day. "I have the day off and I thought we could go to a museum together?"

We made a plan, and he arrived wearing a Frank Zappa T-shirt and jeans with a red rose in his hand at my apartment door the next day, just as my last massage client was leaving. "Oh, I see you have company," my client said solicitously as she left. I was mortified that she made so much of his visit.

We went to the Natural History Museum, and Ken, a climber himself, wanted to watch a rock climbing film in the IMAX theater; a man for whom sport was an art.

"Hey, that's Lyn Fisher," he said during the film. "I dated her for a while."

I don't need to know that, I thought. It made me uncomfortable hearing about an ex so soon, and after fighting with myself about how unreasonable my feelings were, I told him how I felt. "I don't think sharing that at this stage is appropriate," I said defensively.

"What does that mean?"

"It means, I don't want to hear about an old flame when I'm just getting to know you." This would become an ongoing struggle to set boundaries with a man who had few of his own and who didn't like to be told what to do.

We walked along the East River near my apartment and, as we left the walkway, despite the earlier disagreement, he caught me in the turnstiles that protected the pedestrian way.

"I'm not letting you through until you say you want to see me again," he said, sensing that I was upset. This playful gesture of keeping me close, of not letting me go, moved me. We began to see each other weekly.

In fact, Ken had dated many of the women I would meet at upstate gatherings, and for some reason he often felt compelled to share. A little drunk and daring me to set more boundaries, he said, "See that woman over there, once I showed her my bad circumcision at a party."

"And you're telling me this *why*?"

"I just thought it was funny," he said in his defense. He lived a communal lifestyle and was prone to sharing. He reminded me of my father in that way, but he was sane, and attentive. I both hungered for it and felt anxious in the face of his care.

We carried on a long-distance relationship between my city apartment and the Hudson Valley. In the words of my therapist, I suffered object impermanence. When he left, I became detached; after all, I had learned that to depend on other people could be dangerous. In therapy, Susan coached me to take it one step at a time and keep it simple. I did a lot of *acting as if:* left brief notes on the bed when I left, *"Thanks for a lovely weekend."* I kept my anxiety to myself as much as I could. And in the simple way he wordlessly laid his hand between my shoulder blades when he sensed I was sad or in need of comfort, I grew to depend on him.

CALM THE BEAST

They didn't get out much, but on the occasion of Dad's fiftieth birthday, he and Barbara met me for dinner and a concert. In the aftermath of Jackie's death, I was so struck by how their delusions kept them from attaining life's milestones but couldn't shield them from the devastating reality of losing their child. I was waiting at a corner table at MaryAnn's, a popular Mexican restaurant on the Lower East Side just blocks from where my father lived as a young Beat jazz musician. I was relieved when they arrived well dressed; Dad was clean shaven in a navy blazer that brought out the blue in his eyes, and Barbara wore a form-fitting dress, pink lipstick, and gum wedged in place to hide her missing front tooth. We had tickets to hear my cousin, David, play viola in the Philadelphia Orchestra at Lincoln Center.

I imagine it was Barbara who encouraged Dad. "Wear something to make you look like my handsome prince." Despite the loss of Jackie and the two who came after, there remained something childlike in my father and Barbara's love. Barbara held my father's arm tightly as they entered the restaurant, as if bracing herself for the onslaught of name-calling she perceived in every glance and overheard comment.

"You two look so nice," I said, instinctively trying to soothe her. We ordered margaritas and I asked about their commute.

"They don't even let you smoke on the ferry anymore," my father complained as our drinks arrived. Barbara gulped hers down quickly, relaxing into the warm sense of well-being when alcohol numbed her senses and the voices in her head were temporarily muffled. When the waitress returned, Barbara asked for another. "Would you like to place your food order?" the waitress asked. And in the blink of an eye, Barbara was defending herself from some disembodied assault, transfigured back to the fixed trauma of her schizophrenia.

"Just because you think you're better than me, doesn't mean you have to call me a whore!" Barbara blurted, raising her eyes to the waitresses like an assailant. I expected our waitress had seen it all, we were in New York City after all. But she didn't make nice or even excuse herself. She just turned on her heels and walked away.

"Barbara, she didn't say anything," I scolded, hoping my anger would regulate her. I assumed my father understood what went on in her head, that he might soothe her the way he soothed my existential angst as a child. But he looked lost, as if her insanity was as confusing to him as it was to me.

"I'm going to find the waitress to apologize," I snapped and stood up from the table. I found her by the kitchen, a slight, amber-skinned woman my age. "Hey, I'm sorry. My stepmother has schizophrenia," I said, making Barbara my family.

I expected the waitress to be sympathetic. Instead, she said coolly, "So is my mother. You don't have to tell me," and she walked away as if she couldn't care less, as if we didn't have anything in common. I returned to the table, ready for a second drink myself. I recognized myself in her defensive callousness, but I also felt shunned.

I wanted to shout at her when she came back to wait on us, "Just because your mother's schizophrenic doesn't mean you have to act like a bitch." But it was a different waitress who took our order.

When we finished, I paid the bill and looked Barbara in the eye. "If you can't act reasonably at the concert, I will put you in a cab for the ferry *now*. Your call," I said, hoping she could pull it together.

"No, I don't want to go home. I want to come," she said, taking Frank's arm. We left the restaurant together, relieved for the fresh air and momentary anonymity of the street. I put my hand up to hail a cab. I felt a mixed sense of dread for how difficult it was for them to be in the world and excitement over being out, they so wanted to be part of something bigger than their lives allowed. Being with my father often elicited a confusing mix of empathy and anger in me.

We had third row orchestra seats at Lincoln Center set aside by my cousin. Dad headed off in search of his seat while Barbara and I went to find the ladies room to freshen up. "Barbara, you look lovely," I said, looking at her reflection in the mirror. Some of our best moments had been spent putting makeup on each other and painting our nails in the bathroom of Dad's family home when I was young.

"Really? Oh, you're just saying that," she said, swatting my arm like a child while ladies in floor-length gowns and rhinestones washed their hands, keeping their eyes to the sink.

I took her elbow, and we walked arm in arm to find my father. Self-conscious about Barbara's broad smile with her missing front tooth, no longer filled in with gum, I worried that she would feel the need to defend her honor again as people watched us walk down the red-carpeted aisle. But we made it to our seats without incident. There was no yelling, no storming out onto the street, no need to convince her the voices she heard weren't real.

They played a heartrending Chopin piano concerto that was bold and beautiful and lifted us out of the insecurity of our lives into the transcendent space of the music. At the end of the first movement, out of the pin drop silence when you can hear every crinkled program and muffled cough, Barbara exclaimed loudly, "That was beautiful! Everybody in the world should listen to music like this; it calms the beast inside." My father looked at her the way he did when people appreciate good art, like she was the best thing since sliced bread or raw hamburger meat. Then he put his thick fingers to his lips and shushed her gently, sh- sh- sh-, like you would calm a baby.

There are studies on the effects of music on hallucinations in schizophrenics. Through magnetic resonance, they have shown that music therapy increases the connectivity of the insular cortex, ironically known as the "Isle of Reil," resulting in reduced hallucinations. Many interventions used classical music, but in Turkey, traditional music has been prescribed since the time of the Ottoman Empire. I wonder if any studies have used jazz, which was my father's favorite refuge. Relieved it was the music and not voices she was hearing, I sat next to my father and wondered if the musicians could hear us too, if David heard her call out. I was embarrassed, but I also appreciated the power of their unfettered love.

When the piece was over, my father clapped louder and longer than anyone. He stood, calling, "Bravo, bravo!" and I basked in the way he could always celebrate another's accomplishments despite the magnitude of his losses. I imagined David's wide smile was in response to his uncle's applause. These were my people. Barbara was right; we had found refuge in the music. Liberated from what separates us, we felt, for a moment, the way lyrical melodies were thought to have created the world and healed the ailing.

A LIFE OF OUR OWN

For two years, Ken and I carried on a long-distance relationship. He joined me in the city weekly in my spacious Stuyvesant Town sublet, a coveted housing complex that Metropolitan Life Insurance Company built in the forties to provide homes for veterans. One hundred ten red brick cruciform buildings that look like a Red Cross symbol from the sky, which surrounded a central fountain with tree-lined walkways throughout.

I supported myself with a part-time massage practice and worked to complete my undergraduate degree in molecular biology at Hunter College. My college advisor took me into his lab where he was trying to elucidate the cell-signaling pathway of apoptosis, a molecular process of cell suicide that had implications for cancer treatments. They were trying to isolate and mimic protein signals that induce cell death in cancerous cells. The scientific study of cell signaling and self-organization satisfied my need for verifiable facts and evidence. He suggested I could do research if I continued with a master's degree. I could contribute to a body of work that was well funded and had real applications for clinical treatments. Like my father, I was moved by the quest to understand our basis as part of an intelligent but fallible design.

Working from home, I saw massage clients in my apartment and enjoyed the city that had always been my home. Judith had sold her boarding house and now lived around the corner in a shared apartment on 21st Street. On occasion we met for lunch on a park bench for a sandwich to compare living situations and roommates. Now in my early twenties we managed a casual friendship. She mostly talked about her work at Beth Israel Hospital, where she had a real job coordinating the volunteer hospice program. I kept the more intimate details of my life to myself. My sister, eight years my junior, had graduated from high school, and was living on Staten Island with her auto mechanic boyfriend. I rarely saw her, but I worried about her. Eight years her senior, I had been the one to pull her out of her crib crying when my mother wasn't to be found. Even though I wasn't in her life, I still felt like I should be.

I traveled upstate on the weekends to New Paltz where Ken lived in a house he purchased and shared with friends. His ex-girlfriend, Amy, had cosigned for the loan in part to build her credit and so the bank would lend him the money. Not that I knew that at the time.

Ken worked at Mohonk Mountain House, a beautiful four-thousand-acre resort in the Shawangunk Mountains, where he was a bellhop. Mohonk Mountain House became my own personal retreat on the weekends. I sat in the well-appointed library with its camel hair shaker chairs and dark oak bookshelves, in the company of the old-world leather-bound books that had intimidated me at Smith College. While Ken worked, I read journal articles on mitochondrial cell signaling and their secondary messengers; I sat for hours in the dappled light as the sun moved across the afternoon sky. I soaked in the heat of the fireplaces, fell asleep on the shores of the lake sheltered by Shawangunk cliffs, and started to feel the promise of my own life.

During the week Ken joined me in the city. His investment houses in a crack neighborhood that never managed to gentrify were hard to keep rented. He decided to get out from under and pursue his dream of becoming a doctor and started to use his time in the city at the Hunter College library to study for the Medical College Admission Test. In the mornings, Ken and I shared bagels at my small oak table with mismatched chairs. I took classes, did research, and saw clients, and he studied for the exam. We walked the tree-lined paths, arm in arm, knitting each other into our plans the way one does when you can imagine a future together.

One afternoon in the city, Ken told me that Amy had finally signed papers taking her name off his house deed. "I didn't know you had that arrangement with her. When did she sign the papers?" I asked, knowing he had only been upstate for one night.

"I left them on my dresser, and she must have signed them while I was still asleep."

"Why would you leave them in your bedroom and not downstairs?" I asked.

"I don't know; that's just where I left them."

"Seriously, Ken, you set it up so she's walking into your bedroom while you're lying naked in your bed. It's such fucking bad boundaries."

"Well, I didn't see any problem with it. It's not like we did anything. I didn't even see her. I'm not fighting with you about this, I'm out of here," he threatened and started to walk out.

"Don't walk out in the middle of a fight."

"Fuck you!" he said and continued toward the door.

Before I thought about what I was doing, I grabbed him by the shirt and tried to tear it off his back. His *fuck you* infuriated me. I wanted to hurt him, wanted to stop him from leaving. But he wasn't fighting back and when I stopped struggling, I saw a mixture of compassion and contempt on his face that scared me.

"Don't ever do that again!" he said and walked out.

I was mortified at how much the pushing and pulling reminded me of battles with my mother and her battles with Ted. I had no idea how to navigate a functional relationship. Neither did he. The assault was almost more than he would stand, but he came back and it was his turn to set a boundary with me. He told me that if I ever put my hands on him again, we would be over. We were early in our relationship. I didn't know his history yet, how being seventh in an unsupervised childhood, with an older brother prone to violence, made my assault untenable. He didn't know about the violence and mental illness in my family.

In many ways we complemented each other, but our relationship was tempestuous. He was an adventurous athlete who was happiest in a crowd. He loved when friends stopped by. I preferred planned visits. But when he left during the week, I imagined him having second thoughts. A distracted tone when he asked, "How was your week?" could easily shake my confidence.

"I'm fine, busy with school, how about you?" I responded, trying for confident and sounding aloof, sure he had stopped caring about me or my week. I reminded myself of my mother in my neediness and my defensiveness. I lost ten pounds that year feeling anxious. *You look great*, friends told me, but at ninety-five pounds, I felt insubstantial and sick to my stomach a lot of the time. I worked hard in therapy to find ways to keep from acting out with Ken and to manage my anxiety. Susan reassured me it was okay to count on him and to negotiate the ways I needed him to make me a priority.

But we had a shared desire to work things out. We decided to start couples' counseling. We saw an older male therapist my therapist recommended. We hated the art on his wall but loved the fact that it was his wife's art, displayed like an act of devotion. He had a particular linguistic approach to couples' work. It was based on the idea that in order to get in touch with the primal needs in a relationship we had to make our communication as basic as we could; to speak privately without articles or even conjugating words. *Me want you. Me need time. You come?* It was humiliating and embarrassing but there was a simple truth to not being too smart with our emotions. It reminds me even now of how I can use language, like *fragile* or *complicated* to avoid the raw feeling of being afraid. Plus, *I'm afraid* is so much easier to respond to from a loved one. Did I mention that we also had to take each other's hand and, with ape-like antics, bring each other into the bedroom? It was ridiculous but it had the intended effect. We began to let each other see our soft bellies. We both wanted to make it work. We began to talk about commitment and our future.

"I want to have children sometime in the not-too-distant future," I said during one of our sessions, realizing it for the first time myself. I wanted children of my own, wanted to make a family and hold and protect them in the ways I had yearned for as a child. I was sure of this.

"I don't know if I want children," Ken said.

"Well, if after a year or so you decide you don't, we may have to move on," I said, surprising myself with my surety.

We decided to try living together; I sublet my apartment in NYC, and he had to ask his friends to move out of his house. I expected living together to be hard, but it wasn't. Domestically, we were a good fit. I discovered that I could maintain my autonomy in the company of others, and he found that his friends forgave us for asking them to find their own place. Midweek I commuted to New York for massage clients and school, and long weekends were spent enjoying hikes in the woods, dinner with new friends, and the strong sense of community that he had built in the Hudson Valley.

On Ken's thirtieth birthday I invited his family for a surprise birthday brunch at an upstate cafe. After brunch, we sat with our company in the living room of his country house. I was wearing a red paisley vintage dress and sitting on a cardboard box in our sparsely furnished home, when Ken moved to his knee and took my hand. "Natasha, will you marry me?" he asked, looking vulnerable, kneeling at my feet in the presence of our closest friends and family.

"What are you doing?" I said, sure he hadn't thought this through. He didn't have a ring, which seemed impulsive to me. What if he didn't really mean it? I worried, gently begging, "Not now," and then to reassure him, I whispered into his ear, "Yes, I will marry you." I was too self-conscious to notice that no one else heard my answer! The family didn't know I had said yes, and no one asked. His sister and brother-in-law chatted with his parents about the weather and the drive home, things well-behaved adults talk about when they're skirting confrontation, and I wondered why everyone was being so blasé. Maybe they didn't trust the spontaneity of the moment either?

The next day one of his sisters called Ken. "How are you?" they said, tiptoeing around the possibility that I'd said no. "We couldn't tell; did she say yes?" she asked privately, not wanting to embarrass anyone. That was how his family was, gracious and polite, which I found charming. In my family, someone would have yelled, "Well, is she gonna marry you or not?"

THE PROMISE

That spring, Ken was accepted to the New York College of Osteopathic Medicine, and we moved back to my sublet in Stuyvesant Town. Ken made it a point to ask my father for his blessing.

We met at a bar we had never set foot in before, a dimly lit Irish pub on First Avenue across from our building. I was relieved when Dad arrived in reasonably clean clothes. I wonder now if I chose to meet somewhere we wouldn't be seen. It was a desperate time for my father; mental illness and poverty were taking a toll. It was common for him to call me at the end of the month when his funds ran low or when he imagined the mafia were out to get him. Which they probably were since he lived in a working-class Italian neighborhood on Staten Island and was the kind of neighbor, with dealers showing up at all hours, who most good Dons might want to run out of town.

"What can I get you to drink, chief?" Ken asked, using the old school vernacular he and my father shared like a fraternity.

"How about a Manhattan?" my father answered. Ken ordered us drinks and sat on the other side of my father at the bar.

"So, Frank, Tasha and I are planning to get married, and I was hoping you would give us your blessing," he said sweetly, getting right to the point. After a moment's pause, as if it took some time to process, Dad offered his hand.

"Congratulations, man," he said, not even looking at me. I felt displaced in the tradition of being passed from father to husband, joining generations of women handed off from one man to another. But even more, telling my father we were getting married felt like a betrayal, as if I was reneging on an unspoken promise to remain the last princess standing. He still didn't look at me. In the absence of conversation, we sat self-consciously, drinking our drinks—the ice clinking as he emptied his glass in the quiet of the bar that afternoon.

When the drinks were done and our silence grew awkward, I asked, "Are you ready to head home, Dad?"

"Yeah, I guess I am," he said, looking at the floor like he lost something. It was easy to interpret his silence as discomfort, but the reality was my father often didn't have much to say. Clinically things like lack of interest, avolition—or lack of expression— and alogia are considered negative symptoms or deficiencies of the schizophrenia syndrome. I just thought of it as who he was.

We walked along 14th Street toward the Second Avenue bus stop, on a warm weekday evening. Other people walked the streets with bags of late-night takeout dinner and groceries. When I looked back to see if the bus was coming, Dad had stepped over to the curb, unzipped his pants and proceeded to take a piss, like a dog marking his territory in clear view of Second Avenue traffic.

"Dad, you're in the middle of a city block!"

"Yeah, well I really had to piss," he said, looking me in the eye for the first time and zipping his pants up. The bus pulled up, he climbed on, and I watched him fishing for change as the bus drove away. I felt so sad. Ken reassuringly took my hand, and squeezed three times, code in his family for *I Love You*. As we walked back to the apartment, I privately worried that he might be having second thoughts about marrying into my crazy family.

***

A week earlier, I had invited my mother to lunch to meet Ken. Other than her refusal to share when we suggested ordering family style, everything went smoothly. He was his best attentive self. "Of course, you order what you want," he said easily, and she ordered what she wanted.

"I will have the grilled portabella mushroom burger, and I have to get back to work by one," she said, in a way that seemed selfish to me. But she was chatty and told him about her difficulties getting volunteers at the hospice down the block. I was surprised when she put her arm over his shoulder in the pickup truck and announced, "I like you, Ken." It may have helped that Ken had recently shaved his head and wore an earring at that time, which would have appealed to my mother.

* * *

Medical school started for Ken that fall, and we got married September 18, 1993, three years after we had met. The wedding was a small, informal affair in the Hudson Valley. The service took place in a rustic chapel on Mohonk preserve, and we had our wedding reception at a local inn. Ken had multiple best men; I chose my sister, my last roommate, and the wife of one of Ken's best men as my bridesmaids. I still had few close friends.

After the rush of last-minute arrangements—flowers to be picked up, rainy day reconfiguring for the reception—I hadn't even showered. Despite the hour, I was determined to take a moment's self-care. I sat in a tub for ten minutes before putting on my grandmother Annabelle's satin wedding dress. Even at our dear friend's home, who pinned flowers in my hair and told me what a beautiful bride I was, I felt alone. I wished Grandma could have been there to see me get married in her dress. It was a simple floor length, off-white satin dress cut on the bias with an empire waist, and a short train that could be buttoned at the waistband for dancing. Wearing it made me feel closer to her. It fit me perfectly.

Having sent my mother on to ride with our friends, I drove myself to the chapel unaware that I was thirty minutes late. Ken was standing on the porch with all his best men looking less stressed than he was, and asked "Is everything all right?"

"It's our wedding day, and I had to take care of myself for ten minutes," I only half apologized, in a whisper before we walked down the aisle. Ken has still not fully forgiven me for being late to our wedding. The last of seven kids, having spent a lifetime waiting, he is punctual to a fault. He told me later; he had been afraid I had changed my mind.

What I didn't realize was that our friends who drove my mother took a longer route to the church, so my mother walked in after the ceremony had started. In the bathroom of the inn, after the wedding, my mother said, "You know, I was hurt that you started before I got there."

"I didn't realize you weren't there till I saw you come in, Mom," I confessed.

"Oh, that makes me feel better," she said, as if she thought I had started the wedding without her on purpose.

It was my cousin Kevin who drove my father upstate for the ceremony and had to stop and buy him a clean shirt on the way. Late as I was, I also missed the scene of my uncles pushing Kevin's old Buick out of the ditch they got stuck in, when Dad asked Kevin to pull over so he could take a piss

WORST INSTINCTS

After Jackie's death, my father and Barbara's apartment was derelict in their grief. Like a rhinoceros throws shit to mark the way home, the foulness of their lives pointed right back to the loss of their daughter. Glass pipes and plastic baggies lay strewn on the surfaces of their apartment; dishes sat piled up in the sink. Their relationship was septic with the loss of their daughter. She blamed him, and he blamed himself and the world.

"I tried to save her, you know," my father lamented frequently those first years. Asleep on the couch, he would relive the accident in his dreams calling out from his sleep... *no, no, no,* tossing his head from side to side as if to escape the memory.

On one of my rare visits, during which Barbara marched in and out of the bedroom as she put herself together: blonde hair piled atop her head, platform heels, pink lipstick, and gum stuck where her front tooth was still missing, she announced, "I'm going to where the men can find me," and walked out the door.

"What did that mean?" I asked.

"She's become a streetwalker! She's gone sometimes for days."

"A streetwalker?"

"A whore," he said, as if imagining her cruising for sex hurt him more than it did her. "He has her standing on corners waiting to be picked up by local drug dealers, and then the cop busts the dealers, and takes their drugs! He pays her in crack and protects her like a pimp," he shouted at me in their dirty kitchen. I pictured her walking the neighborhood blocks, past the housing projects that loomed over Stapleton's town green, past the Off-Track Betting and methadone clinic that had been on my path to school as a child.

"Hey, baby, I'll bet on you anytime," I imagined them calling out to her, and maybe any attention was better than what my dad could offer those days. They needed money and drugs to support their habit. Even so, the thought of her prostituting herself was like a punch in my gut. How could she bear it and how could he let her? How did she manage the persecuting voices? Had it occurred to him to try to stop her? Was this all a figment of my father's paranoia? But another family friend said they had seen Barbara walking the streets. I didn't know what to believe. None of the care and tenderness my father showed her in the beginning of their shared life was evident these days. There was a callous quality to the way he hurt, like the pain was more than he could protect us from now.

* * *

Before long, I got the call from my father. "Tasha, you have to get me out of here! Barbara's disappeared, and I owe that cop money. He threatened to plant drugs in the apartment and bust me unless I pay him. I don't have that kind of money! He's gonna kill me, Tasha!"

"What happened to Barbara?" I asked.

"She just took off! I haven't seen her for weeks!" he yelled into the phone.

"I'll come as soon as I can," I promised, dreading going and afraid of what I would find.

When I arrived at their home a few days later, the front porch was strewn with their belongings. The landlord had served them an eviction notice for not paying rent, and Dad had begun dragging their stuff onto the porch. "I'm trying to sell everything," he said of their piss-stained mattresses and chairs.

"Looks like it's time to pack your bags and get you out of here," I said, seeing how close he was to being on the street. "I'll pick you up at the Staten Island Ferry on Saturday," I said, leaving without even going upstairs. I had a week to find him a place to live. I would move him upstate, to Kingston, New York. Close but not too close to where we lived in the Hudson Valley, with small city social services that would be easier to navigate.

A week later, with only the clothes on his back and one suitcase, he made his way to the Staten Island Ferry to meet me in Manhattan. He left without Barbara, and leaving her behind spoke volumes of the defeat in their lives. What I learned later, and wonder if he knew, was she was scared of *him* and had gone back to her parents on Long Island, to check herself into the psychiatric hospital. What I also didn't know was that she was pregnant with their last child.

* * *

I waited at the Manhattan side of the ferry to drive Dad upstate, but he didn't show. Almost everyone had emptied off the boat before I heard a loud scraping sound surface amid the trundle of the disembarking cars. My father emerged pushing his luggage through the boats lower-level doors. Hunched to the ground, knees bent, ass in the air, like a child pushing a toy truck, he shoved his suitcase along the ground. The case was held together with tattered rope, barely containing his clothing. His pants were cinched up with another rope for a belt. As he made his way toward me, I could smell urine and unwashed clothes—the acrid smell of grease and cigarettes. His shirt was gray and tattered, and he had no socks on. I would like to say I felt bad for him—instead his crisis sparked dread in me. What was the new landlord going to think and how long would he last?

"Well, I made it," he said, a little put out, as if I was lucky he had.

STING OF GRACE

Not long after, we moved again, this time to Albany for Ken's first residency in family practice. I started a Ph.D. Masters track in molecular biology at Albany State University of New York and my father lived a comfortable hour's drive south in Kingston, New York.

I was introduced to Casey K., the Principal Investigator (PI), in her Wadsworth New York State Institute of Health lab. Her research focused on apoptosis: the cell-signaling pathway I had become interested in during undergraduate school. The Wadsworth labs were in the basement of the Corning building next to the Capital Plaza in Albany. I finally had a badge of entry, like I had coveted as a child, when Mr. Brown, the parent teacher at the Free School, took us to visit his organic chemistry lab. I was doing the work I had been reading about, finding methods in journal articles to add to the body of research in the field. When things go wrong in the cell, like a mutation or toxic conditions, cells have a cascade of signals they use to commit suicide in order that mutations don't get transcribed into a new cell. Casey was looking to isolate a particular protein in the P53 cascade that initiates cell death. If we could understand how certain proteins in the cascade functioned, we might be able to manipulate cell suicide for treating cancer. It was a brilliant evolutionary solution to the mutations in our biology.

I got pregnant with our first daughter that September and,

although we planned on children, I didn't anticipate how the pregnancy would exhaust and unmoor me. I couldn't focus on the details of secondary and tertiary protein folding while a growing life was taking hold inside me. Not unlike my years at Hampshire College, I struggled with assignments in the psychic undertow of becoming a mother.

I also had the uncommon problem of having a teaching assistantship in a physiology lab which required piercing the central nerves of frogs. I had to put an electrical probe into the brain of preserved frogs for students to measure neurological responses. While in Casey's lab, I killed mice for cellular preparations by yanking their tails with a tiny lab spatula in their necks. With hormones meant to foster life coursing through my veins, I lost my capacity to kill lab animals. I asked my fellow TA and lab colleagues to probe my frogs and kill my mice, and seriously considered if I should continue the work.

Having a child reverberated in ways I didn't understand. I was tired all the time the first trimester, fell asleep reading texts, did poorly on tests. To stay in the program would mean twelve-hour days in the lab and our daughter in childcare, and I already knew I wanted to be home with our new baby. I decided to take a leave of absence in January, knowing I was unlikely to return.

When I was pregnant, my mother did unusually nurturing things like bringing me fiddlehead soup; the tender furled fronds tasted like manna from heaven and were supposed to be uber-nourishing. After my water broke, we all went to the hospital, where she, my sister, and Ken sat with me through labor. We laughed at *TV Bloopers* and waited all night and the next day for the baby to drop and my cervix to open. The doctor eventually prescribed Pitocin and after another twenty-four hours of contracted labor, the family was kicked out. The nurse wiped my forehead with a wet cloth and whispered like a temptress, "You should get the epidural—you need to sleep." I accepted the drugs I had planned not to use and, exhausted, I fell asleep. Finally at six that morning, my cervix opened and at last, Cora was born. We had arrived Friday night and she was born early Monday morning over 50 hours later.

Despite Ken's early ambivalence about being a father, it all changed when he had Cora in his arms. While I finally slept, he was the one who held her until it was time to nurse, refusing to let go of her except for when they had to check her vitals.

* * *

Caring for her came easily to me. Ken fully supported my desire to stay home with Cora and I relished the time with our baby. I had months of shooting pain at the start of each nursing from a painful case of mastitis, but I was determined to nurse her through her first year. I watched her in my arms, marveling at the tender beauty of our baby's lips and the flutter of her eyelashes as she ate and slept. I was content to be home with her as she grew from infant into a baby in the safety of my care. We took regular walks in the woods, with her in a front pack. "Ooh, look at the beautiful flowers," I cooed—which was her first word–*Ooooo* meant flower. Her second and third words, *Dada* and *Mama,* came in that order.

The primacy of the mother-daughter relationship was finally mine to have. Every act of loving, feeding, and keeping her safe offered me redemption from a childhood where I questioned my ability to love and be loved. Caring for our daughter was inextricably linked to what I had yearned for as a child, as if each deed of mothering was reverberating in the landscape of my own childhood.

When my mother came to visit, I wondered if she would be different as a grandmother. Would she love my daughter in a way she hadn't been able to love me? For a while, she visited regularly. She seemed attentive to her granddaughter in ways that restored my faith in my mother's ability to love.

A year later, Ken was finishing his family practice residency and vying for a second residency in dermatology. I was pregnant with our second daughter, Cali. It was the night before Thanksgiving when Ken got the call from the dermatology residency telling him he got the spot; the spot for which only twenty out of hundreds of people had even gotten an interview was his to have. Since it would be Ken's second residency, it would be unfunded for the first year, plus this new residency meant we had to make our fifth move in ten years. I started to cry.

GRANDPA FRANK

In March, when the snow was knee-high, while Cora napped and Cali grew in my belly, I packed up all but the essentials in preparation for our move to Philadelphia that June. We used the inheritance from my grandmother to put a down payment on a small twin home in the working-class Italian neighborhood of Ardmore, Pennsylvania. Ardmore had sidewalks and a sweet Hebrew preschool to send our two goyim toddlers to when they came of age. The inheritance from my grandmother gave us a cushion to live on, and Ken's parents helped out.

With two toddlers and our friend's adult daughter living with us as a mother's helper, I returned to graduate school for a Master's Degree in Educational Leadership and Curriculum Development at the University of Pennsylvania. I felt sure that when I returned to work, I would want a school schedule, home by evening and off for the summer.

But graduate school with toddlers took its toll. I thought I had it all together until someone tripped or needed time I didn't have. When Cora, at two-and-a-half years old, climbed backwards down the stairs and announced that she didn't need her afternoon nap, an afternoon nap I depended on to get my work done, I was unhinged. I forced her to climb back upstairs to rest even if she couldn't sleep. Forced naps were followed by wakeful nights that I shamed her for. "Go back to bed now, it's time for sleeping!" I worked late into the nights and suffered sleep-deprived days. I came to understand the challenges of mothering in a world where women raise children without the support of extended family. Luckily, Ken's sister and our brother-in-law lived in the area and were supportive and welcoming on weekends, but on a day-to-day basis, I was alone, like many moms raising children in isolation.

I heard very little from my father in those days. When Cora was born, I had asked him what he wanted to be called. His response, "Uncle Frank," made me laugh. Not only did it make him my sibling, it kept him from being an old man. "We're going to call you Grandpa Frank," I said, and that's what we did. In the three years we lived in Philadelphia, my mother came for a visit once—out of sight, out of mind. She came with my sister, who I trusted and had asked to make sure the kids were cared for, while Ken and I had a night to ourselves in downtown Philly.

In 2003, after three years of Ken's second residency, we returned to the Hudson Valley. Ken was a board-certified dermatologist, and our daughters, three and five, barely knew their Grandpa Frank.

SPECIMENS ARE EVERYWHERE

When I found women's clothing in his apartment and a spare mattress on the floor, I knew Dad had adapted to living upstate. She was his lady-in-waiting, he explained, who needed a place to stay for a while. I wondered how many blowjobs a week's stay on the mattress cost her.

He sat in his cramped kitchen at the battered aluminum table, layered with months of coffee spills and cigarette ash. The apartment smelled of urine and shit from soiled underpants that lay where they had been removed. I relied on house visits from his psychiatric nurse and social worker while we were in Philly, a safety net I gratefully depended on. Really, social services in this small city were a godsend, but it didn't change the fact that my father had no interest in ordering his life, sure that chaos fomented his creativity.

Still, as he aged, there was temperance to his delusions—it was his ingenuity that offered salvation now. "Tasha, regarding your research connections. I've got an idea. I've discovered a chemical compound in the urine of the cockroach. I believe it will combat the effects of radiation and provide immunity to cancer. I wondered if anyone you know might be interested in my discovery. I need a backer," he hollered at me over the kitchen table. "Lab specimens are everywhere." He smiled, as he crushed a roach crawling across the kitchen table with his wide tar-stained thumb. "They'll outlive us all," he said and dragged on his umpteenth cigarette of the day.

"Hmm," I said, more concerned with the state of his apartment and the expense of his smoking habit than his cure for cancer. "How about I sort through your mail, Dad?"

"Ehh, it's all crap."

I moved into the living room, leaving Dad sitting at the table as I dumped ashtrays and deployed plastic shopping bags like gloves to deposit his dirty laundry in a basket. I sorted through the mail, separating the offers for credit I didn't want him to have and bills that needed paying. At the bottom of the pile, I found a copy of a proposal for his Ruby Laser invention, in neat script, dated April 2nd (his birthday), 2001.

"Who wrote this cover letter?" I asked.

"Some whore helped me write it," he said offhandedly, and I involuntarily pictured her hands satisfying his needs in two acts.

Light Ship

> *I am of the considered opinion that a vessel driven by solid ruby lasers or copper- titanium lasers, producing the gas which will fill the laser, which is then fired into an extremely powerful magnetic field, that is light receptive, will produce a drive of unimagined power*—apparently, I inherited run-on sentences from my father. *The laser beam would drive the electrons out of the electromagnetic field, which would cause the core of the magnetic field that surrounds the planet to drive the ship forward ... from here the ship can go anywhere on the planet and indeed anywhere in the universe.*

I admit, I wondered if his inventions might have some basis; what if the voices most of us couldn't hear had something to impart? John Nash, the brilliant mathematician who lived with schizophrenia, described his voices as "something a little different than aliens ... maybe more like angels." Prophets and wise men hear voices. In fact, the question of whether the evangelists were mad and, concurrently, whether psychotic people could be having mystical experiences is a question debated over the course of history. Jesus himself was accused of demonic possession; the Christian apostle Paul of madness. As many as 60 percent of those with schizophrenia believe they are in communication with God or are themselves the devil, the Messiah, or a prophet.

In their paper "The Role of Psychiatric Disorders in Religious History Considered," published in 2012 in *The Journal of Neuropsychiatry*, Drs. Murry, Cunningham, and Price investigated "the basis we use to distinguish between the experiences of psychiatric patients and those of religious figures in history." They analyzed biblical passages from Abraham, Moses, Jesus, and St. Paul with the criteria in the *Diagnostic and Statistical Manual of Mental Disorders*. They identified the symptoms of schizophrenia, including auditory and visual hallucinations, grandiosity, and paranoia in a large percentage of the prophets' passages. They showed how, when paired with intelligence and strong communication skills, their delusions and grandiosity made charismatic and inspiring leaders. What the prophets didn't exhibit was the negative symptoms: the disorganized thinking, the catatonic behavior, or the lack of speech that make it hard to get your point across. They hoped their findings would translate into increased empathy and understanding for people living with mental illness; I hope the same.

Under the letter Dad sent with his invention to the United States Department of Energy was a response from the White

House. I had a flicker of hope that they would offer an acknowledgment of my father's insight, that his lifetime of believing in something beyond my comprehension would find a footing in this world. Instead, their form letter concluded, like a Dear John letter, "... in the context of the great contributions that many American citizens have made over the years to ease the burden of fellow Americans ... thank you for sending your idea."

"I see you sent your invention to the White House," I said, walking back into the kitchen with the coffee-stained response from the President's office in my hand.

"It's the answer to the country's energy needs for God's sake, and they won't even look at it!" he complained loudly.

"Dad, I'm not sure the White House heard you!" I said, trying to deflect his anger, and he half chuckled to appease me. But he didn't see any humor in it really; in his mind, their lack of recognition proved the government plot against him, was evidence that the CIA was out to thwart him still.

The fact was, to be mentally ill *had* consigned him to a life of persecution. According to Alan Frances, Chair of the American Psychiatric Association, the United States approach of exclusion and neglect makes people sicker longer. Cross-cultural studies of schizophrenia have shown that the long-term prognosis is significantly better in developing countries. Is that, in part, because of the support of extended family networks? I wondered.

Although the majority of people living with schizophrenia are not violent, the internalized voices of the mentally ill in the US are more likely to be violent toward the self or others and seen as more threatening than in other countries. In one comparative study they found the commands of the voices in India were mostly benign; they demanded hearers do things compulsively, like clean, bathe, or prepare food for instance. In Britain, more mentally ill people receive outpatient psychotherapy. The hearing voices network, a self-advocacy group that originated in Britain, has shown that engaging the voices can shift the relationship from adversarial to a more integrated awareness—think self-talk.

The United States is one of the worst places to be mentally ill, and with the push to dismantle psychiatric facilities we have an increasing population of homeless and incarcerated mentally ill people in this country. It's easy to critique psychiatric care in the US but hard to know how to make it better.

Sitting with his head in his hands, burdened with the responsibility of having answers no one was listening to, his frustration from a lifetime of unrealized aspirations was palpable in the room. How misunderstood he must have felt. Nash's colleague Harold Kuhn described Nash receiving the Nobel Prize as a turning point in his recovery: *recognition as the cure for many ills*. My father's ideas and insights had perennially gone unrecognized. Maybe with earlier intervention or in another country my father would have been a shaman, or a hero, or a prophet.

I also struggled to make my ideas understood as a graduate student, on the school board, or in my work. I have felt I had answers that no one listened to or insights that fell on deaf ears. Was I a leader with new ideas to impart or simply grandiose and out of step, like my father?

But it's this naiveté on my part, my secret wish for his success that has hardened into disappointment over time. I wanted to include him in our life, but he was hard for me to be with, plus I had other people in my life to protect.

That winter, he took a fall on the ice while we were enjoying a holiday at Ken's parents' home in suburban New Jersey. With their clan of thirty—six siblings plus Ken, their spouses, and thirteen grandchildren—the house was crowded with family. All but one of their seven children had handmade stockings with the alliteration of the letter K—Kathy, Carol, Kris, Kevin, Kim, and Ken Kircher. My stocking read Knatasha at the end of the mantle. The pile of presents dwarfed the Christmas tree, and our daughters, the youngest of thirteen grandchildren, had as close to a Waltons' Christmas as I could imagine.

Dad was home alone. He fell two days before Christmas. He was found unconscious on the street and taken by ambulance to the hospital where they treated him for a broken arm and a head contusion. It was the psychiatric nurse who called to tell me Dad was in the hospital.

When I got home to see him, he shouted from his hospital bed, "They were out to sabotage my invention, Tasha!"

"Really, Dad?" I said, weary of his mania. "Do you really think the CIA doesn't have bigger fish to fry?" In seventy years, he had failed to be the savior his mania promised, and still he held on to the idea that he was at the center of a national security effort. This inability to see one's existence self-consciously, according to the existential psychiatrist Rollo May, is characteristic of people with psychosis and severe depression. Evidently, schizophrenics haven't got the ability to see themselves in time.

MAGIC FISH

On a sunny weekend afternoon, after moving back to the Kingston area, I brought the girls and their grandfather to the Rondout River to feed the ducks. Dad shuffled on bad knees to a nearby bench. We leaned over the cresol barrier to throw our stale bread into the river when an enormous carp rose out of the murky water like a primordial beast.

"Look at these huge carp," I called, as the giant fish, easily three feet long with delicate side fins and a fanned tail, rose to the surface.

Dad made his way over to the river's edge, "Ahhh," he exclaimed, marveling at its size. "Have I ever told you the story of the magic carp?" he asked Cali, who looked up at him skeptically and shook her head no.

"Long ago, when the world was young and creatures were just coming into being, animals were learning to swim and fly, to become what they were meant to be." Dad spoke grandly, looking into Cali's eyes to make sure she was with him. The carp showed unusual perseverance, straining and leaping as high as it could, trying to reach the top of a waterfall. The carp tried for hundreds of years, until at last, a single one reached the top. With that, God smiled down in approval and transformed the exhausted fish into a shining golden dragon. Now the carp has magic powers to grant wishes, if you believe in him. Make a wish, Cali," he said with a sparkle in his eye. I wasn't sure Cali was buying my father's magic, but I did as a child.

At night, on the daybed in the dining room, before I was old enough to stay up and watch Johnny Carson with Grandma, my father would tell me bedtime stories in his masterful voice. "This was the time of flying dragons and a princess who took to the night air on a magic carpet, in search of an enchanted stone. A stone long held by the dragon in his underground lair ..." There were often dragons and gems and adventure, and I had the impression that my father's world was real and full of magic. But as I grew up, the magic wore thin and I was left with the dissolution of his dreams.

In his twenties, after his second hospitalization, my grandmother helped him get a job teaching social studies in the local high school. He knew the arc of history—the fascist leaders and heroes of democracy—but to the mostly African American students, my father was just another white man who couldn't manage a classroom or plan assignments and didn't know the least bit about their world. When he started hearing voices over the school intercom, started complaining to Grandma that *the government* was after him, he left the only position he ever held. His lack of career, lost children, and the way his oldest friends dropped away were the real story.

Later in life, he continued to use stories to make sense of his life. "You know I was born in the Bronx," he said proudly, "at *Misericordia* Hospital. You know what that name means?" he asked, pausing for effect. "*Misery of Christ*," he said suggestively, cocking his head like a dog being attentive to the signs because, of course, he is Christ. "Have I ever told you about my Nazi nurse, Tasha?" he continued. "When I was a young boy, Grandma went back to work teaching music in the local elementary school, and a German nurse, named Celia, took care of me. Well, Grandma suspected that Celia was feeding my formula to her own child. She also was suspicious of the nurse because it was wartime and she was German and she would step out to walk the Rockaway piers at night. So, Grandma fired her. The next week, we saw in the papers that she was a spy, signaling the U-boats when it was safe to refuel," he said, as if their suspicions and this fact cinched the case against her.

I knew the nurse existed because I had seen pictures of Celia sitting with him on the stairs of their Far Rockaway home when he was a young boy. But enemy ships in New York seemed made up! With some digging, I found an article in the *New York Times*, which reported U-boats off the coast of Long Island on June 13, 1942. My father would have been four years old at the time—a little old for formula. Still, the fact that spies were doing the very thing he suspected Celia of was typical of the way fact bled into his stories. When I asked his siblings about the spies, my uncle said, "The family may have read about it and joked that the nurse was a Nazi," but after a lifetime trying, he seemed uninterested in spending any more time trying to figure out the basis of his brother's delusions.

It wasn't just my father who told stories. Eyes cast down with introspective humility that contrasted sharply with the usual—*You waiting for the coffee to make itself?*—sarcasm, one member of the family or another would tell the tale of my great-grandmother Stella and her alleged affair with a Guggenheim. Sitting around the table with Entenmann's coffee cake crumbs at our elbows, the room dense with smoke, they told the recurring fairy tale. Legend had it that my great-grandmother was the daughter of a German rabbi, who had an illicit affair with a wealthy Jewish industrialist in the Guggenheim family. They got pregnant, but were either never married or divorced quickly, and the child stayed with her father in Europe. Proof of the relationship was a mysterious and much older wealthy relative of my grandmother's, Natalie. My aunt has pictures of Florence's visit with Natalie when she came to Europe late in life to visit, and with whom she corresponded periodically. Her children would have been cousins to my father but there was no contact between our families.

Even my *mother's* mother invested in our Guggenheim genealogy—she pulled me aside one summer afternoon in my early twenties to point out the family resemblance in a photograph of the Guggenheim family she found in the library. "Tell me these people don't look like the Williams, look at those noses!" she challenged.

"All my grandmother's siblings have big bulbous *schnozzes* and are Irish Catholic," I countered.

"What about the silver bowl the family received anonymously when your grandmother was born?" she asked. "Why are you so against believing you are related to the Guggenheims? Are you antisemitic?" she goaded me.

"Call me crazy," I said. "I have never seen the bowl or my illustrious relatives!"

My uncle recently shared a picture he created with Photoshop. It's a photograph of Peggy Guggenheim in a satin dress and pearls, Paris circa 1930, with my grandmother as a miniature figure standing in a bowl on the windowsill. She's wearing a housedress, her eyeglasses hanging, as always, around her neck—she's a figurine in a bowl. The Guggenheim story lingered like a residue of our imagination—our attempt to distance from our working-class normality, and make sense of dueling Irish Catholic and German Jewish origins. Grandma kept the real story hidden behind impenetrable stoic pride; untold ambitions and disappointments, little figures in a big bowl of bastard lives.

When my grandmother died, I found her diary. It had only two entries: one, a shopping list, and the other, the night of my father's birth. Apparently, uninterested in documenting the tedium of domestic life until the pain of labor set in. She wrote vehemently about not wanting to be seen in pain. Despite regular contractions, she delayed going to the hospital for as long as she could. She complained, "I can't stand listening to the pathetic moans and whimpering of the other woman in the room." My grandmother never shared her pain unless it was something to be grappled with; complaining for its own sake was and still is pathetic in our family ethos. She had a steely approach and could communicate volumes about her disappointment without saying a word; it seeped out of her, like the cigarette tar on the walls of the house, undetected unless you tried to wipe it off. To be worthy of love, you had to prove you didn't need it.

If identity is wrapped up in memory and story, I wonder if my father's delusions of being the Messiah were the ultimate story of self-reliance? Was his illness an ancestral relic of the importance we aspired to? To make sense of his mind required a bigger story: a brilliant intellect, connected families, even divine intervention.

"Make a wish," Dad said.

Cali looked down at the huge carp and back at him doubtfully. Was she wishing for something? Or was she already aware that stories were the stuff of fairytales, meant to foment thinking and art, but never statements of fact?

WHY I BRING THEM

My father answered the door standing naked except for a wet diaper sagging down to his knees. A multicolored DNA helix tattoo I didn't know he had was etched on his sagging chest.

"Oh, you're here," he said offhandedly, as if we had disturbed him. As if he hadn't called us for help. My daughters, eight and ten at the time, stood next to me and averted their eyes.

"We'll wait outside," Cora said.

"What the hell is wrong with you?" I shouted, stepping inside. "You asked us to come! Why would you come to the door looking like a pervert? Put something on for *Chrissake*," I said, pulling a shirt out of his dresser and forcing it over his head. Then yanking the soaked diaper down to his knees, I roughly pushed his feet into a dry Depends, wondering if this punishing act could be considered care.

"Get me my cigarettes, would you, baby?" he asked, sitting dressed now, diffusing my anger with his dependence—acting like every moment offered a cycle of restoration, like we have and will always take care of each other despite his transgressions. I handed him cigarettes and signaled through the window for the girls to come in.

Usually, he was coherent, insightful even, and he loved his grandchildren. Cali was part of a modern dance troupe and she danced like she had lived years beyond her age. Cora played piano concertos without the sheet music because it lived in her once she learned a piece. My father always came to their performances and clapped like he had witnessed greatness, with booming slow claps till everyone else had stopped. But if he wasn't taking his medication or was having a bad day, he might yell at us about the snipers in the yard or show up looking homeless. My daughters came only because I compelled them, because this is how families take care of each other. Also, I wanted them to feel as fortified by his view of them as I did as a child. To see the valiant parts of my father, the way he appreciated the success of loved ones, even in the face of his own dissolution—like the time we sat around the table for his birthday dinner and my balding husband complimented him.

"Frank, I sure wish I had your thick head of hair," my husband had said.

"Well, Ken, I wish I had your life," he'd responded, and we all laughed, grateful for the life we had.

I brought them because, despite his schizophrenia, I wanted them to know their grandfather. I signaled for the girls to come in and they joined me standing in the living room, subjects to his royal highness. A king now, seated by the window, perched on the edge of his recliner, a lit cigarette between his thick nicotine-tarred fingers, my father held court with my daughters, his courtiers.

"Girls, I was hoping you could help me with this predicament I find myself in."

"What's that, Dad?" I asked, putting myself between them.

"You see, I emancipated my goldfish from my fish tank into the church wishing well next door. Then I noticed a great blue heron at the water's edge looking for something to eat." He looked at Cali, mischief in his eyes, cocking his head to the side to convey his sense of irony at the unintended consequences of his good deed. "I'm afraid he may not survive. Do you think you girls could help me rescue him?"

"Why did you put the fish in the well in the first place?" Cora asked.

"I was hoping it would grow big and bring prosperity to the townspeople," he said, like a prophet off his meds.

Happy for a mission, the girls agreed, and we went outside to gather our tools. Since Cali was an avid pond skimmer and net fisher, we had what we needed in our car trunk. Fishing gear in hand, we walked slowly to the church next door to keep pace with his ailing knees.

My daughters and I stood at the wishing well dipping our nets as he found a seat on the bench, watching us as if our efforts were his own.

"That a girl," he encouraged us, our nets empty except for a skim of slimy green algae that covered the well.

After several attempts, ready to give up, I said, "We're never going to find a tiny goldfish in this slime, Dad. Plus, I'm sure it's better off here than in your smoky apartment."

"We can't leave the fish to be eaten!" Cali challenged us.

"I'm sorry, love, we can't see anything below the surface."

Undeterred, she flashed me a look and continued dipping her net into the bright green overgrowth, until finally, our doubt her biggest obstacle, she tossed her net to the side in frustration.

My father watched Cali until she looked him in the eye. He patted the seat next to him. "I'm disappointed too, baby," he said gently, making the connection I loved him for. It's not that he wanted to make it all better, but simply that he recognized her disappointment and was able to join her in a way that made it possible to leave the job undone. She took his hand as he hobbled back to the apartment, leaving the lost fish to work its magic.

FERAL LOVE

When my daughters were younger, my mother complained, "I don't get enough time with the kids alone." That was partly me being protective, but I suggested she come weekly to visit, on their turf and on their terms, which she did when they were elementary school age. She would take Cora out to lunch one week, or loom beads with Cali behind a closed bedroom door another week. When they reached middle and high school age, she visited less, and when she came, she spent more time talking to me. By now she knew I was writing this book and regularly asked to read it. "I want to know what your feelings were as a child." But I didn't trust her with my feelings. I was afraid that she was looking for reassurances about her mothering that I didn't have.

"I'm not ready to share the work yet, but I do have questions."

"Well, I'm not sure I can remember or tell you anything you want to know, but you can ask."

"What made you hate your parents so much?" I asked, trying to understand her alienation from a grandmother who was my saving grace as a child. It is this lineage of estrangement, more than schizophrenia, that I worried about as a parent, afraid that my daughters wouldn't find refuge in my parenting or that I wouldn't love them enough.

"My parents were a *bad fit*," she told me. "They wanted me to keep quiet and behave. I always felt rejected by them. I just didn't trust them."

"Didn't trust them how?"

"When I was young, my mother left me downstairs at my grandma's house while she went shopping. I hated being left and sat in the bay window and whined for my mother the whole time: *Mommy, Mommy, Mommy,* I cried, sure she might not come back. My mother acted like she loved me, but really, she didn't. We argued all the time. I was this *ethical, moral kid* who didn't trust the rest of my family to tell the truth.

"One day my grandma snapped at me, 'Your mother's coming back! Stop acting like you're going to die. You don't think you live forever, do you?'

"Until that moment, I had no idea I was ever going to die. I *never* got over it. They had lied to me by not telling me! My parents had betrayed me, and I had no one to turn to because no one could keep me from dying. My mother was always busy taking care of Grandma. Since her stroke, the whole family had to take care of her. Her children would do anything for her. My grandmother, who I didn't like to begin with, had *traumatized me for life*," she cried.

"Then they sent me to Sunday school because, even though my mother was an atheist, she wanted me to have the comfort of religion. She hoped it would help, and I actually wanted to go and hoped it would too. But the Commandments—*Honor your father and your mother so that you may have a long life*—only made things worse. I didn't like my parents because I was going to die and now, I was going to die because I didn't like them. I started throwing up before every class, then everyone knew something was wrong with me. You don't understand what it was like. At dinnertime I was convinced that my mother forced me to finish my food because she was poisoning me with it!"

"What!"

"*Yes!* I was convinced she wanted to kill me because I didn't behave! It was so important to my mother that I be the way she wanted me to be that I was convinced she was trying to kill me!"

"Are you serious?"

I had never been willing to label my mother as anything other than neglectful, but this sounded insane to me. In *Humanizing the Narcissistic Style*, Stephen Johnson writes, "The feeling of being injured can be incredibly deep, and the narcissist is profoundly motivated to avoid it." My mother's story felt like a confession of *narcissism*, a recounting of a moment that hurt so much she couldn't bear to really care about another person again; she had never gotten over it. If, as Johnson says, "The essential answer for the narcissist is to feel themselves," I wondered, was admitting these feelings to me an act of healing, or a revelation of insanity, or both?

I never understood why she only partnered with men who never would or could meet her needs. It seemed like a combination of low self-esteem and bad taste, but also, she rejected normal healthy people as uninteresting. I was a prime example. I found her choices suspect and dangerous and she found my demand for safety and love confining. Neither of us found satisfaction in the other.

"Do you ever wonder about the fact that Ted was psychotic too?" I asked.

"Both your father and Ted were artists. That was what I was attracted to initially. I wanted to live the artist life, free of the moral hang-ups my parents imposed on me."

Ted *was* a talented painter and potter, but he was antisocial and later became a white nationalist. He never held a job. He lived month to month as a transient hotel guest without a mailing address. He lived off the grid, because he was convinced he was under surveillance, paranoid that the Jewish liberal elite saw him as a threat. He was a man who, rather than handing over his wallet in a street burglary, fought back and was shot in the throat. What was she looking for? Did she recognize something of herself in the other? Something about the way they also felt at odds with the world? Or was she only able to feel worthy in the face of their deviance?

My sister's father occasionally sends Laura Aryan Nation propaganda in the mail from stray post offices across the country. She occasionally talks with him on the phone, and she tells me she worries about him aging alone. But thankfully, this is the extent of her contact with him. These were the first two men my mother chose and then discarded for us to deal with.

* * *

My mother never married our fathers, but she did marry David. David, ten years her junior, was a British man who came to the boarding house around the time I returned home from college. He came in pursuit of Cindy, one of the boarders, whom he'd fallen for when she was visiting London. He had followed her back to America, but within days she broke it off with him, claiming he was too needy. David was the first to make fun of his circumstances. "I'm quite fucked, aren't I? Six thousand miles for a date that isn't working out!" he said, with his charming tendency of a quick intake of breath after he said something, as if caught off guard by his own wit.

So, he lived in our boarding house with his visitor's visa and over time developed an unlikely relationship with my mother. Desperate to get away from England's social constraints, David and my mother had that in common. Otherwise, their relationship never made sense, but she married David so he could stay in the country. They threw a big Halloween wedding party—she dressed as a ghostly bride and he dressed as an Englishman. Friends filled our home in costume and I came dressed as Billie Holiday, the blues singer.

Toward the end of their brief marriage, she became deathly ill with a mysterious infection that lined her intestines. She was convinced it was due to her marriage. David's well-mannered sensibilities were killing her. If he brought her water, it was in too small a glass, or he took too long, or he brought a pitcher that was bound to get warm. She rejected all his attempts at domesticated care. I was living at home after dropping out of school. I checked in on her between work and play to make sure she had what she wanted without too much fuss. "You understand what I need," she told me when I was momentarily at her bedside, and she was right. I spent my childhood figuring out how *not* to be attached. When she recovered after weeks of not eating and serious dehydration, she asked David to leave, explaining that their cohabitation was killing her.

After David left, she took a young man with end stage Lou Gehrig's disease into her home to care for while he was dying. I don't recall why his family wasn't in the picture. She ended up making a career of hospice work, coordinating the volunteer program at Beth Israel Hospital for nearly seven years, drawn again to caring for people who in another way existed on the outskirts of conventions. I never understood my mother's hospice work. She had never been that person who selflessly sat at the bedside. When my grandmother was on her deathbed, it had been my sister and I who held her hand and called our mother, still in New York, to tell her she needed to come if she wanted to see her mother before she died. Maybe it was her illness and near brush with death that motivated her to care for others? When I asked her to read this chapter, she commented that I had gotten her hospice work all wrong. In fact, she was trying to face her fear of dying head-on. That helped make sense of how her hospice work seemed self-motivated.

* * *

In my thirties, my mother found her life-long passion advocating for incarcerated men. She trained to be a chaplain and worked as a one-woman prison advocacy task force. She lobbied for parole reform at the state capital, ministered to incarcerated men in prison, and published a newsletter for inmates and their families.

She also corresponded with several incarcerated men, and that was how she met Donnell, the last love of her life. He was a self-described Black Panther, serving a life sentence.

"What's he in prison for?" I asked, thinking reflexively about my young daughters.

"Half the time they are in prison for something they didn't even do," she answered evasively. He was serving a life sentence in a men's medium-security ward. They had been corresponding for months now. They were deeply in love with each other's ideas. It probably didn't matter to her what he'd done and she had never made decisions about her partners based on things like stability and safety.

"I've met my soulmate, and I want you both to meet him," she told my sister and me. "We're planning to get married," she explained, in large part so they could have conjugal visits. It had been ten years since her annulled marriage with David. My sister Laura and I were both adults, in our twenties, no longer living with her, so I was surprised how agitated I was about her affair.

We drove to the Wallkill Correctional Facility in Upstate New York, just thirty minutes from New Paltz, where my sister was in college and near where I lived with my husband and our two young daughters. My stomach was in knots as we were marshaled into the secured entryway where prison guards documented ID and collected keys, our own liberties relinquished for a time. I made the mistake of wearing overalls and the clips set off all the alarms, but they let me through after a thorough patting down by a female guard.

Already in the visiting area, my mother complained, "If you were African American, they would have sent you home. They never would have let you in." I half wished they hadn't. We sat across from Donnell at the cafeteria-style table, since no touching between inmate and visitor was allowed. There were vending machines against one wall and fluorescent lights flickered above us in the windowless room. He was a tall, dark African American man who appeared to be about my mother's age.

My clothing became the launching point for everything that was wrong with the penal system. "The whole system is predicated on the for-profit incarceration of men, most of whom are African American!" my mother complained, smacking the table with her hand. "They are in the business of taking away the civil liberties of black men," she said, putting her other hand over his. Donnell's eyes, filmy from cataracts, barely made eye contact. My twenty-one-year-old sister, so young, still in the phase of highlighting her hair blonde, looked at me. We watched how my mother paid attention to Donnell, how they held hands across the table, despite the rules, in a show of tenderness and commitment that was wholly unfamiliar in my mother.

Although I knew she was right about the business of disproportionately incarcerating people of color, I didn't begin to understand why she would even consider a relationship with someone who would not get out of prison for a very long time, if ever, someone who seemed to have nothing to say for himself. As if to answer my thoughts, she described what attracted her. "There's a whole set of rules inside, a hierarchy among the prisoners who command respect from the others on the inside, you know? Who gets to use the phone and when is controlled. The guys get to know quickly who's in charge, and they won't even try to use the phone until it's their turn," she explained, energized by these unsanctioned rules of engagement, in admiration of those convicts who took control.

"That's right, woman," Donnell said. "That's what the whole Black Panther movement was about, baby, standing up to the man, making our own rules. I was moving with some pretty heavy cats, but then I got caught up in drugs and made some mistakes! I know I fucked up," he said, like he thought it was what we wanted to hear. He struck me as a smooth talker. There was something about how he wouldn't look at me. The way he talked about that one moment like it was all he was made of that hardened me to him. *Shut the fuck up*, I thought. I came hoping he would have something to offer, maybe he was a deep soul who got caught in the wrong place at the wrong time. Instead, he seemed like another outlaw, another man who had the propensity to be violent, this time a man in prison for life, who she wanted to marry in order to have sex in a trailer.

We said our goodbyes in the parking lot. "Mom, I have to say I have no interest in coming to a ceremony for you two, or whatever marrying in a prison involves. And if a blessing means I'm happy for you, I can't say I am. What could you possibly hope for with a man who will never get out of prison? He seems like a bullshit artist to me."

"He's my soulmate, Natasha! I don't expect you to understand. You do what's right for you," she said, conveying her lifelong approach to being my mother in one phrase. Why had she wanted us to meet him? To get our blessing? It wasn't as if they would allow us into the prison for a ceremony anyway. To reassure herself? Fuck that! My mother's choice in partners had rained chaos on my childhood and this was just a continuation of the same.

"That's what I will do, and if he ever gets out, I don't want him anywhere near me or my family," I said, turning toward the car to leave.

My sister and I sat in silence on the drive.

"That was weird," Laura said,

"What the hell is she thinking?" I said, angry at our mother for shaking up my hard-won sense of security after ten calm years of not having a partner. Years that she showed up to see her new born granddaughter, years when she seemed interested in our family.

"It's so strange how she fawned over him," she said, as if our mother's love hadn't always been unreliable.

That was the last time we spoke of Donnell and her marriage until the following year at a holiday gathering at our house. "How is Donnell?" I asked, assuming he was still locked up.

"Oh, he's in the hospital. They discovered he had an AIDS-related brain tumor."

"Wow! Are you allowed to visit him?" I asked, ignoring the fact that Donnell had AIDS and hoping she had never gotten the conjugal visits they were after.

"He didn't even know who I was the last time I went, so I haven't seen him in months! As his wife, I made sure they didn't experiment on him for research—he was terrified of that, but he didn't even remember me. He asked me how my mother was even though he knows my mother is dead."

"Seriously? I thought he was your soulmate?" I blurted out, offended that her attachment to him, which had so shaken me, had been abandoned that easily.

"He didn't even know who I was. What was the point?"

Later that evening, she and I sat by the fireplace. I fought the desire to close my eyes and sleep as my dog licked my feet in that incessant way dogs take care of their people. "Did I ever tell you about my dogs?" my mother asked, and paused as if picturing her young self.

"I wanted a dog so bad but my parents refused to get one. But then my comportment at school was a problem. My teacher said I talked too much, so she called my mother, and they cooked up a plan. If I talked less, I would get the dog I'd been begging for. I agreed to the bargain even though I resented them both for bribing me into acting a certain way... But the dog we got, Blondie, didn't care about me. It was my mother who fed it, and it attached to her, not me. So, when my mother insisted that I walk the dog, which I really didn't want to do since it didn't love me, I took it outside in the backyard and just stood there. Sometimes, I think I was retarded. I felt guilty about it, and when that dog died, I thought I might have been the cause of it getting sick because I didn't take care of it.

"It wasn't until a feral dog showed up at the cottage one summer that I found the affection I was looking for. I was crazy about that dog. My father coaxed it out of hiding and fed it, and it stuck around all summer. I loved him and played with him all the time. One day, it fell sick and almost died, and I got sick too. It never came back after that summer, but I loved that dog more than anyone."

I wonder now what was it about the undomesticated dog that she loved? Like all the aberrant men she chose, why was she only able to consider the needs of wild things? Sometime after that visit, my mother confided in me one afternoon that she was jealous of how close Laura and I were with our fathers. "You both seem to care for *them* more. I try to be independent, and I've tried not to be needy, but sometimes I wish you cared more about *me*." On the phone that day, standing in the driveway with the heat of the pavement on my feet, I faced the truth of what she said.

"We both missed out on something," I said, the tremor in my voice the only clue that my body was shaking with unacknowledged loss letting loose inside me. Her silence on the other end might have meant she was facing the fact that she had never conveyed the care she now sought for herself. But it was more likely she simply didn't understand the idea of attachment, didn't understand that love flows two ways, or that we even existed outside of her need for us. I identified with the dog that didn't bond with her. I too had failed to be feral enough to capture my mother's attention.

YOU'LL SEE

When my father called that day, I was cleaning out a closet. Cora and Cali, now middle school aged, were home from school.

"Tasha, I've been thinking about something—how's Cali doing?"

"What do you mean?" I asked, standing in dappled shadow as the sun sank below the treetops. I could picture him sitting at his desk, a cigarette burning between his fingers and a thin coating of ash dusting every surface, an enduring trace of the ruin chain smoking and schizophrenia wrought in his life. We had just been out together and he hadn't brought her up then. Instead, he'd been preoccupied.

"Do you hear the snipers in the yard?" he'd asked when we dropped him home.

"No, I don't hear them, Dad, just the kids playing and the birds. I'm gonna call Ken and tell him we're coming home."

"They're bugging my phone, you know?"

"Well, they can listen all they want. I have nothing to hide."

Over time my daughters understood how their grandfather's mental illness was the center that would not hold. "One minute Grandpa thinks the CIA is watching him, but then he carries on a conversation like normal," Cora commented on the drive home. She was right. Beyond the occasional paranoid comment, his delusions seemed more benign and fleeting these days. Maybe it was the sophistication of the psychotropic cocktail or the tempering of schizophrenia that often comes with age, but I felt he was doing better. So, when Dad called that afternoon, I was caught off guard by his questions.

"Is she still dancing?"

"Yes, with the youth company Figures in Flight, and she's painting too," I said, relieved that he was interested in her art.

"Hmm," he said in a ponderous way, as if he were considering a problem. "I've decided I'm going to take her to see the film *Black Swan*."

"Are you kidding, Dad?" I said, remembering the day he took me to see *The Exorcist*. I had never left my children alone with him and on some level, he must have realized that. In fact, his plan seemed designed to test my boundaries. "*Black Swan* is a horror film about a ballet dancer who loses her mind! Absolutely not!" I said.

"I don't know why you won't let me take her," he shot back. "It's an important film."

"I said no!" I responded, feeling less sure than I sounded and confused by his interest in her and this dark film.

As if in a battle over her moral instruction, he pressed on to the heart of his mission, to the core of his intended mentoring.

"*You know she's schizophrenic*," he announced, like a sucker punch jab to the solar plexus that made it hard to catch my breath. It was more of a statement than a question. Like a branding. Like he was admitting her to a club that only he could get her into. His tone suggested that he knew her mind and recognized something, the way my father is able to see through to what is enduring in a person. He offered his unwanted harbinger of schizophrenia's genetic component like a pet offers dead prey. I knew schizophrenia lies in wait until early adulthood. I knew it affected young woman slightly later than males. I knew all this but had never considered my or my children's risk. But who knew better than him the devastation of the diagnosis he bestowed on her?

"I don't know anything of the sort, and neither do you," I whispered coldly, fearful of being overheard by my daughters upstairs, fighting an impulse to hang up. I stayed on the line, like one slows down at a car accident to see what you've narrowly escaped. I lingered in part because, secretly, I was afraid that my father could recognize mental illness, could see it in another person like an animal is attracted to its own kind.

Shaking now with fear and murderous adrenalin, I told him quietly, "If you ever breathe a word of this again, it will be the last time you see us!" Vibrating with anger, I was ready to climb through the receiver and beat this message into his addled mind.

"You'll see," he said. I hung up.

FAR FROM THE TREE

The truth is, until my father's pronouncement about my daughter's sanity, I had never considered the possible fault in our family's genes. I never worried that I could inherit or pass on the voices in my father's head. They were so exclusively his and his alone. If anything, I wanted access to his world and could never manage it.

I recently found correspondence between my two grandmothers. My mother's mother, Annabelle, asked my father's mother, Florrie, if she worried that I might be genetically predisposed to schizophrenia since I was so explosive and prone to taking things to heart. Florrie said she didn't know anything about genetic predisposition; they understood very little about mental illness, but she wrote, "Tash is in every way different from Frank except in their bright minds. Where he is docile and eager to please, she is independently minded. All of this adds up to my belief that there is nothing to worry about for Tash. She will not have an easy life because of her ability to penetrate beyond the surfaces, but it will never be dull. If there's one thing I want to live a long life for, it is to see who she becomes." I cried when I read this—I felt so seen and admired by both my grandmothers, and their belief in me made all the difference when I was a child.

When Cora, at age ten, dressed for Halloween in a white dress and recited Emily Dickinson's "*I'm Nobody! Who are you? Are you—Nobody—too?*" I did worry about her poetic and sensitive nature. Would she suffer in a world that prized extroverted achievers? I worried when she sat in a corner for hours on end reading, or the time she sat at the kitchen table and announced quietly, "Something's wrong," as if intuiting impending catastrophe—I fleetingly recognized the possibility that our children could be contending with an alternate reality. But I never really worried about their sanity and never about Cali. She was strong and surefooted, like her namesake Kali, the goddess of destruction; she could look insanity in the eye and dash it to the ground.

But after my father's pronouncement, I started to inform myself. I read studies and books like Andrew Solomon's *Far from the Tree* and Robert Kolker's *Hidden Valley Road*. Research and anecdotal evidence about the vertical nature of schizophrenia, the frequency with which it travels through family lines, the way it steals identity and alters reality for a loved one and leaves families with a lifetime of coping. I charted the increased genetic propensity from one to ten percent in offspring and siblings of schizophrenics and the epigenetic triggers that put people at risk. Biomolecular mechanisms, like DNA methylation, environmental effects from cannabis use, or hypoxic events such as obstetric complications all factor into schizophrenic breakdowns.

I knew that it usually lies in wait until early adulthood. How did I never consider the risk? Cora was hypoxic at birth and kids experiment with drugs. I spoke lightly with them both about their increased risk and the correlation between cannabis and schizophrenia. But I lay awake at night.

At fifteen, Cora sat across from me at our kitchen table and asked, "Since you don't have schizophrenia, does that mean I won't have it?"

With what I hoped was an imperceptible pause, I responded, "Genetic predispositions can skip a generation, but I'm confident that you are fine."

"I read that schizophrenia has been connected with drug use," she continued, "so I decided I am going to stay away from drugs!" I didn't tell her I had made different choices as an adolescent. Her approach was infinitely better.

As our children reached puberty and did what teens are renowned for: falling apart at the seams or making a case for the world's conspiracy against them— "Everyone hates me!"—I braced myself. At my best, I listened to their anxieties flow uncensored, hoping they felt safe enough to fall apart and come back together with us. Other times, I agonized that their feelings of persecution were early signs of flawed genes waiting to take our daughters' beautiful minds to places we couldn't reach.

When Cora was in college, every intellectual peak made me afraid of her manic potentialities. The depth of sadness she experienced, a depth that seemed ancestral in its weight, frightened me. When Cali regularly smoked pot in high school, I lay in bed at night knitting the connections between cannabis and schizophrenia, risks she dismissed as hyperbole. When she showed brilliant intuition but struggled to process information in school, I worried it was early signs of disjointed thinking. As she raged at the pressures of college life, I worried that her fury was madness! *Don't you wish I was a normal fucking kid?*" she roared, shouting my fears out loud.

In the end, all I could do was stay vigilant and believe we had done our best. It was easy to see their strengths. Their empathy and courage would carry them safely into adulthood.

Cora walked into my room one night with the book, *The Fault in Our Stars*. "Mom, it's time for me to read this book to you," she said as she slid into the bed next to me and started reading about a young woman her age navigating love and cancer.

"*When you go into the ER, one of the first things they ask you to do is rate your pain on a scale of one to ten ... I'd been asked this question hundreds of times over the years... When the nurse asked me about the pain, I couldn't even speak, so I held up nine fingers. Later, after they'd given me something, the nurse came in and she was kind of stroking my head while she took my blood pressure and said, 'You know how I know you're a fighter? You called a ten a nine.' But that wasn't quite right. I called it a nine because I was saving my ten."*

I'm moved by the empathy and feeling with which she breathes identity into the characters. In years to come, I will watch her champion environmental causes and fight social injustice, with more courage than a honey badger.

When Cali, our then nineteen-year-old, traveled to Europe and South America between high school and college, I spent many sleepless nights agonizing about her traveling on her own.

Towards the end of her trip, she mentioned wanting to travel together. I jumped at the opportunity. We adventured to untraveled parts of Albania, a country whose language neither of us spoke. A now experienced traveler, she often took charge and easily found the way to our inn or restaurant. We watched *Forrest Gump* because Tom Hanks's wife was of Albanian descent, and they played back-to-back reruns of anything he was in. On a rainy day, as storm clouds rolled over the mountains that surrounded the city of Gjirokaster, we walked through the ruins of Southern Albania and sat on the rocky beach as a herd of goats marched past us at the shoreline, their young shepherd urging them on.

When it was time for me to head home, as she continued on the last leg of her trip to Greece, we stood at the bus stop surrounded by loitering young men, waiting for what? Selling something? Looking for work? Scoping out vulnerable tourists? I pulled her shawl over her braless top and bare shoulders, and kissed her goodbye.

"What was that for?" she asked, letting the shawl fall open.

"Look around you, love," I said. From my seat on the bus, I watched as she drew the shawl back over her shoulders, and stood waving until I was out of sight, our roles momentarily reversed.

I think the kids are all right and that I have loved them enough. But, like my father, I imagine bad actors in their midst; I fancy I can protect them even in my sleep and would go to any length to do just that. This is my ten: this question of my daughters' well-being, their company is what I most look forward to, their suffering, the thing that keeps me up at night. As Valeria Luiselli says in her gorgeous novel, *Lost Children Archive,* "Having children has compelled me to embrace life fully and understand it on their behalf... to go out looking for a specific pulse, a gaze, a rhythm, the right way of telling the story, knowing that stories don't fix anything or save anyone but maybe make the world both more complex and more tolerable."

SYMBOLS IN THE MORNING

I hadn't talked with my father since his incursion into my daughter's psyche. My children came first; it was an easy choice. French toast was sizzling in the pan, and the kitchen smelled of cinnamon and hot oil. Cora and Cali were moving in the kitchen getting their lunches together, and feeding our dog, when the phone rang.

"Tasha, I need your help."

"What is it, Dad?" I asked, trying to keep the impatience from my voice.

"Well, Tasha," he repeated, "I, I need your help getting on the computer."

"For what?" I asked, determined not to be taken in by his drama.

"I... I... I... um... I," he faltered for what seemed like forever. He couldn't get out the words. There was something about his confusion that compelled me to pay attention, to stay with the moment, even though the morning clock was ticking.

"Dad," I said, trying to get him to focus. "What is it you need the computer for?"

"I can't seem to put it into words."

"Well, maybe if you describe what you want to do."

"I... there are these... these places that I can go for help," he managed.

"Help for what? If you need help, Dad, you should call Tony"—his psychiatric nurse. "What places are you talking about?"

"Three places on my comforter that I can go." I signaled to the kids to get the syrup out of the fridge and start on their French toast.

"Places on your comforter?" I asked, confused.

"Yes," he says, relieved that I finally understood. "There are these messages on my comforter that I can go to for help, but I don't know how to decipher them and I want to get on the Internet to find their meaning."

"Oh," I said, stopped by the poignancy of his quest. "I don't think you're going to find the meaning on the Internet. It's not like it offers insights, Dad, just information. Maybe if you write down what you see, we can figure out what they mean."

"But I don't know how to write them."

"What about drawing what you see?"

"I guess you're right," he said with some resignation in his voice, as if all my pragmatism had taken the magic out of his quest.

"I really have to go and drive the kids to school. We can talk later if you want." And just like that, I was back to helping him make sense of his disjointed world. I was relieved I didn't hassle him off the phone.

IS IT TRUE?

Soon after his first hospitalization, before my parents met, my twenty-three-year-old father traveled to Mexico in search of God. My grandmother gave him money for the trip against Grandpa's better judgment. When I asked about the discord, Dad said, "She gave me the money, didn't she?"

My uncle said, "Grandma was always funding Frank's crazy schemes, like a gambler always betting on the same horse."

On a hot afternoon, with the clothes on his back and cash in his pocket, my father landed in San Miguel de Allende, a small historic city, then and now an artist mecca nestled in the mountainous central region of Guanajuato. He went for art and adventure, and an interest in magic mushroom ceremonies.

"Tell me again about the time you did psychotropic mushrooms with the Indians in Mexico, Dad," I asked one afternoon, wondering to what extent his early drug use contributed to a permanent break with reality. I put him on speakerphone while I made dinner; the girls were home from school in the other room.

"I was painting at that time, baby. Mostly I was painting this prostitute who was living with me and who had just had a child. She was beautiful nursing that infant, like the Madonna. One day I went to La Cucaracha, a big dark bar everyone went to. There were these Nordic filmmakers who were traveling south to film the mushroom ceremonies of the Mazatec."

"How did you meet them?" I asked.

"I may have struck up a conversation with the gentlemen. Those psilocybin mushroom ceremonies were powerful, and I was interested in finding God at the time," he said.

The next day my father headed south with them on dusty blond roads to the Sierra Mazateca, where a shaman-like curandera was known for sharing the mushroom ceremonies with foreigners. "We brought gifts of fishing hooks and a mirror and asked to be taken to where the ceremonies were held." I imagine three or four tall, strapping Scandinavian filmmakers and my father, a five-foot-eleven-inch New Yorker with a jaunt to his step, marching through the jungle growth. He would have been in his glory, his sense of purpose galvanized by this larger-than-life quest. They emerged from the dense growth of broad spiked agave and flowering jacaranda trees to a village in the high valley, overlooking the majestic Mazateca Mountain range.

"Once we found the chief, we gave him a transistor radio, and in return, I was given a female companion," he tells me. This sounded like a white man's fantasy, but in papers I've read, other visitors to indigenous groups reported being gifted a companion. I'm affronted that a woman's attention could be gifted by anyone but herself and that as a white man he felt entitled to her companionship, but she was important to the story he had to tell.

Sitting around the campfire, the guests shared a pile of mushrooms, which made them throw up on the outskirts of the fire pit. In the words of the shaman Maria Sabina, the mushrooms open doors to "a world beyond ours, a world that is far away, nearby, and invisible. There is where God lives, where the dead live, the spirits and the saints, a world where everything has already happened and everything is known. That world talks." I wonder, was my father delusional at the time? Was he in search of the healing shown in studies of depressed or terminally ill patients who benefitted from a single dose of psilocybin?

"We tripped through the night, and at sunrise, I stood on the ledge of a mountain. An eagle swooped through the air, wings outstretched, and I was convinced that I could fly. I spread my arms out and headed toward the ledge. My woman friend had to knock me down to keep me from running off the cliff. She kept me from killing myself, Tasha."

"Were you trying to kill yourself, Dad?"

"No, I thought I could fly!" he hollered.

At this point Cali, walked into the kitchen and mouthed the words, "Is this true?"

"I don't know," I mouthed back, shrugging my shoulders, but her question started a tremor that I hoped couldn't be seen in my hands below the counter, a vibration from something unhinged inside of me. Was it the trauma of my father's unraveling? Was it the way his illness took everything but wasn't talked about openly? Was it the vacillation between the way I loved my father and then doubted him, the way something simultaneously doubted and desired became something to be protected, never questioned? My daughter is asking. My body is answering.

When I tell you I felt safe in my father's care, it is true, but in writing this story, the other undeniable truth is there were times when my father's unbounded approach to parenting stuck in my memory as something that needed to be examined in the light of day. My recollection of our adventures is often sketchy and illusory, like the vague memory of my father and me in Manhattan, an unusual outing that probably signaled that he was manic at the time. My father decided to "show" me another movie, this time along the Broadway strip of Times Square, which at the time was a mix of peep shows and porn movies. I was prepubescent. I remember the ticket window on the street, a bald white man selling tickets, a dark entryway, walking into a nearly empty theater in the middle of the day, sticky floors, and the light of the film bouncing off the faces of stray men around the theater. I don't have a memory of my father in the theater with me, or the film itself. But I remember feeling like I was trespassing in a corrupt world. I can't fathom what my father's state of mind was at the time, but I have this memory.

According to a review by clinical psychologist Dr. Mathew Boland, the act of forgetting or denying memory in order to move on and cope is a common adaptation to system overload or a reality collapse; my father's reality was in constant collapse. I didn't talk about the things I couldn't make sense of—instead, it was easier to dissociate or forget—and they become less real in the service of a daughter making her father more substantial than he was.

PART 3

REDWOOD

2011

Time was not kind to my father. In his seventies, his knees were bone on bone. There have been studies involving mice hung from their tails, which proved SSRIs (selective serotonin re-uptake inhibitors) decrease humeral bone formation. He was a human testament to the effects of psychotropic drugs over the course of a lifetime. His doctor recommended knee replacement surgery, but his weight and COPD (chronic obstructive pulmonary disease) from a lifetime of smoking made him a bad candidate. Also, he periodically refused to take the Seroquel, Depakote, and Prolixin cocktail that kept him sane. His aides, who by law weren't allowed to administer his meds, couldn't convince him otherwise. But it was incontinence that made it hardest to care for him in his own home. He regularly refused to shower and change his clothes. "I don't need a shower; I've been baptized by the Lord," he half joked. His home smelled of cigarettes, piss, and food gone bad.

After a lifetime of my father being institutionalized, I found the prospect of finding assisted living for him heart-wrenching to face. But Dad was lonely and feeling isolated, and he actually wanted to live with others.

But diagnosed schizophrenics are not altogether welcome in the places where we put well-behaved grandmas and grandpas for safekeeping. Even in old age, when dementia and Alzheimer's put everyone in an altered reality, his options were limited. We visited a few residences where wheelchairs lined the halls of the home, and sedated seniors sat vacantly staring. Dad's opinion was, "Everyone's so old." Plus, he wouldn't fit in with a well-mannered senior crowd with small talk at schedule meal times. My father was an artist and a philosopher who felt rules and schedules were a poor substitute for living.

It was at Redwood, more of a halfway house than an old folk's residence, that he felt most at home.

On Cora's thirteenth birthday, I moved him in.

Redwood, in Beacon, New York, was not the Old-World institution its name conjured in my mind—not a grand estate on a hill with a gated entrance and long driveway. Instead, it was a dilapidated, rectangular three-storied building with a flat roof. The building was made of beige and brown faux cement siding that went out of fashion like the needs of the poor it was built for before the Reagan era. Resident smokers loitered outside, stooped against the breeze to catch a light. It was a gathering that reminded me of so many street corners of the New York City of my youth—public spaces where disappointment and addiction were shared, with cigarettes and liquor bottles secreted away in brown paper bags.

At the far end of the parking lot, a tall, light-skinned, middle-aged African American man was cruising the perimeter with a transistor radio on his shoulder playing Donna Summer's "Love to Love You Baby." He wore skintight jeans, women's clogs, and a cut-off belly shirt. He had fake eyelashes and a stocking headband as if in preparation for a wig he's not wearing yet. I wondered if he was a resident out for some air, or a visitor turning tricks.

"Is this the main entrance?" I asked, leaning out the car window.

He ignored my question.

"Excuse me, we're moving my father in today. Is this the main entrance?"

No answer.

"What's the matter with him?" I ask, turning to my dad and driving on.

"He's probably a snob," says Dad.

"You think so?"

"A snob is someone who doesn't value human interaction," he added, and I realized I had a prejudice that a cross-dressing prostitute wouldn't be snobby. My father's assessment seemed truer. There was no manic arrogance in him today; instead, his insightfulness moved me as it always has. A father, who has spent a lifetime committed to insane asylums. A father I was institutionalizing once again.

We arrived with Dad's essential belongings: one suitcase of clothes, a marble chess set, a few paintings, CDs, and a portable radio, as well as three big boxes of absorbent undergarments.

Nisa, in the business office, shook my hand and officiously seated us in front of her desk, armed with the pile of paperwork to put the finances in order. She wore a pantsuit with a girdle, and stockings that swished when she walked. Her gold chains and bracelets signaled her role as *money keeper*.

"Sign here and his check comes directly to us, and then there's the matter of the balance owed." I hadn't given real thought to the costs of the place, only that people more desperate than my father reside here, and the facility makes do with their funds. Nisa explained there were overlapping days between check-in day and when his benefits will kick in. "How do you want to pay that balance? Check or credit card?" she asked. I write her a check, knowing it won't be the last time we're asked to pay out of pocket. I feel stupid not having asked more questions in advance. We get through signing the papers that transfer all his benefits to the facility and we head upstairs to settle him in.

By now he has urinated through his not so dependable undergarment and needs a change of clothes. I leave him in his new room to take off his wet pants while I bring up his suitcase and boxes of diapers. When I walk back into his new room, he sits bare-assed with a puddle of pee under his chair.

"How's it going, Dad?" I ask, wondering what we'll wipe up the puddle of pee with.

"I could use those diapers," he says, looking exposed.

I pull out a Depends and turn the other way, so he can put it on. My father weighs nearly three hundred pounds, and clearly, he's not the person they had in mind when they created the first pull on diapers. I wipe up the pee. Then I place Dad's clothes in the laminate armoire; his radio and chess set I put on the desk. His roommate, who isn't there, has shoes lined up neatly on the floor and a large screen TV on the wall at the foot of his bed. I wonder how his new roommate will manage living with my incontinent father. After just a few minutes of me unpacking while he lies on the bed exhausted, the loudspeaker intones, "Frank Williams, please report to the medical facility." I continue to unpack and he continues to lie there. The message repeats, and in an unusual act of compliance, he pushes himself up from bed.

"I better head down there."

"You do that, Dad. I'll finish unpacking."

When I go to find him, an older man shuffling down the hall winks at me in a wizardly way, as if he knows me, as if we were meant to be there. "Hi," I say, grateful for his familiarity in this institutional poorhouse.

In the elevator a younger male resident asks if I'm moving in. I smile. "No, it's my dad," I say, a little concerned that I was mistaken for a prospective resident.

"Are you his mother?" he asks nonsensibly, but he was right, I felt the anxiety of a caregiver abandoning her charge.

It was getting late for me to get home to my daughter and her birthday celebration, but I was determined to find my father and say goodbye. I find him sitting against the hallway wall with six other residents, waiting to be seen by the doctor. He sits with his hands loosely at his side, compliantly waiting for his turn. I'm not sure whether to be reassured or worried by how quickly they've gotten him in line to see the doctor. Sitting next to him is a heavy-set lady with a few teeth missing and a warm smile. "Hi, I'm Natasha," I say, extending my hand. "This is my dad. He's new here. Have you been here for a while?" I ask, trying to make a connection.

"Oh yeah. Seven years!" she says reassuringly. She launches into the where and when of getting a cup of coffee or a haircut, and I ask if she will help my dad get back to his room. "Oh sure," she says, "I'll help him get around."

Leaving feels like a neglectful act, like abandoning a child on his first day of school. I have no idea if his new friend will help him get back to his room or how he will know it's mealtime. I have a pit in my stomach as I imagine the stories the rude cross-dresser could tell about life at Redwood, stories that I'm sure would keep me awake at night.

I stop in at the office on my way out. Dolores, the intake manager we met on our first visit, takes in my anxiety over her bifocal glasses and with a penetrating look says, "Don't worry, we'll take care of him."

Yeah right, I think, imagining all the ways this could go wrong. I rush to my car through torrents of rain that make it hard to see the road.

When I arrive at the school to pick up my daughter, the sky has started to clear, the sun is warming the damp spring air, ready for something to take root. Cora, a smidge taller than five feet, with long amber hair and a soft touch, comes over to me and whispers tremulously into my ear, "I got my period." Her breath catches with emotion.

"On your birthday, how timely!" I look into her hazel eyes and hold her close. "Let's take a walk on the nature trail," I say, grateful that I was there in time to receive her news, the way it knit me into her life in a way I never dared expect. As we walked, she told me how the day went.

"Maya showed me where the pads were and stood outside guarding the bathroom door," she said, grateful for the care of a close friend. I tucked my arm in hers and teased,

"We'll have to get you some red panties now." She smiled and we walked in silence. "What kinds of supplies do we need from the pharmacy: pads or tampons?" I finally asked, aware of the fine line between saying too much and not knowing enough.

When I got my first period, I was driving north to Canada with my mom's parents for the summer. I was quietly relieved to have this coming-of-age moment in the safety of my grandmother's care. If my mom had been there, somehow it would have been about her, about having to stop to get supplies, about not having money to afford them, about the imposition of another's needs. Instead, my grandmother and I went into the gas station and she stood nervously outside the restroom door, happy to be needed.

DON'T LET GO

"Don't let go of that apartment!" Dad said, one week into his new digs at Redwood. He knew I was still paying the rent to hold on to a one-bedroom apartment in Kingston.

"I tripped and fell walking to the elevator and my one knee is killing me. I can hardly get around."

"Yes, they called me about the fall."

"And my roommate is terrible!" he continued, not finished making his case.

"What's so bad?" I ask, thinking about the neat room with a large screen TV his roommate had. I had expected it would be my dad who would be the difficult one.

"All the guys come to watch TV at night," he says cryptically.

"Why is that a problem?"

"They're watching porn," he says, dropping what feels like a dirty secret in my lap.

"Do you have to watch?"

"It's the sounds they make—" he says in his New Yorkese.

"Okay, Dad," I interrupt, trying not to picture my dad caught up in group ejaculation, men here and there, in various corners of the room unceremoniously jerking off to the television scene. I picture my father lying with his back to them. Nothing about his Irish Catholic upbringing would encourage such a public sexual display.

"I'll ask at the office about getting you a room change."

"Yeah, that would be good, 'cause I have a new friend and she doesn't like to come to my room. I want you to say hi to Susan," he says without further introduction, and he hands the phone to his new friend who apparently has been standing at the foyer pay-phone listening this whole time.

"Hello?" she says in a very quiet voice, and waits for an answer.

"Nice to meet you, Susan," I say but she doesn't respond. "How long have you been at Redwood?"

"Oh just a few weeks," she answers lightly.

"How do you like it there?"

"I don't."

"How did you get there?"

"My daughter brought me."

"Oh, what does your daughter think of the place?"

"She's very busy," she tells me, and I wonder, has her daughter has ever been to visit? I picture Susan as a petite woman, to match the gentleness of her voice, and I wonder why she's befriended my obese, urine-soaked father? How did they strike up a conversation? Over shared cigarettes, I'm guessing.

"Well, it's nice to talk with you, Susan."

When she puts my dad back on the phone, he asks brightly, "What do you think?"

"She sounds intelligent."

"Susan and I were thinking that maybe she could come back to the apartment with me since neither of us is happy here," he says, as if he had been happy living independently at his apartment in Kingston.

"What's her diagnosis?" I ask because, although this home is for the elderly, it also houses an indigent mentally ill population.

"I don't know." He then calls out, "Hey Susan, what's your diagnosis?"

I can picture them standing in the front foyer where the pay phone hangs on the wall. I hear her quiet, thin, voice say matter-of-factly, "schizoid personality disorder," and then she clarifies, "It's basically one step from paranoid schizophrenic." My father's diagnosis. Does she know this, I wonder?

I like the idea that he found companionship, but the reality of taking someone like Susan back to his old apartment is another story. "Schizoid personality sounds like maybe the Susan you know today has other sides. I think you need to get to know her better before you make plans for her to move in." He agrees to stay through the month to give Redwood a chance and the relationship some time to grow.

* * *

Over the next several weeks, the urgency of his calling increases. "This place is hell. It's not what it appears. These people are subnormal, and I can't carry on a decent conversation with anyone but Susan, that is. Here, she wants to tell you how bad it is in here."

Susan gets on the phone, and says, "Frank's right. These people are subnormal and idiotic!" I hear a twinge of venom in her voice that hints at one of those other Susans we were bound to meet.

"You have to get me outta here!" he insists, taking the phone back from her.

I wait and hope that things get better. I bring him the cigarettes he asked for. I briefly meet Susan standing outside smoking a cigarette with Dad. She has shoulder length hair and as I imagined she's petite and well mannered. I decide to join him for a meal, to try the food he's complained so bitterly about and ask Susan, "Will you be at dinner?"

"Probably not," she says, offering no further explanation and that's the last I see of her. We sit at table #12, designated with a playing card in a clipped holder, and I sit just behind him. Dad introduces me to his table mates. "This is Mr. Welcome." An older brown-skinned man with missing teeth and a scraggly gray beard is wearing a woman's Lord and Taylor sun hat with a rounded brim, the kind of hat you would expect at a garden party.

"This is Anthony," he says of a quiet older gentleman with a cropped and graying afro, who gently touches his silverware as he waits for the food to arrive.

"I'm Natasha, and who are you?" I say to the man across the table whom Dad doesn't introduce.

"Manny," he says with a gentle nod in my direction. He looks out of place in his white blazer, light blue golf cap. He has a paperback book and spectacles resting on top, neatly placed next to his plate as if he's pretending to be somewhere other than here. I feel an instant affinity with Manny. I, too, have spent a lifetime imagining myself elsewhere: in better schools, in well-appointed homes. I too have tried to order my life in the face of my parents' chaos.

Residents sit waiting while pills are delivered in little paper cups, and trays of food follow. A few women rebuke the staff for letting others take food before they are served. "You can't let them take that food off those trays," a woman says, ready for a fight with the next taker. Conversation is sparse, and then without ceremony, dinner is finished: empty trays are pushed forward and residents stand and wander away. An older woman sits at the upright piano playing a hauntingly out of tune "On the Sunny Side of the Street," while others sit and listen or move toward their rooms. People walk around, scavenging food that's left uneaten. My dad reaches over and takes the food Manny left on his plate. I sit enough behind him that he can't see me crying now, tears streaming silently down my face, at my father fending for himself in this poorhouse. This is his future and his past, but it's where he fits, and he needs more care than I can manage. I find myself indulging romantic fantasies about how he and Susan will continue to deepen their friendship and hoping that he will make friends with other residents, who like him, have lived on the fringe of society.

* * *

But he hates it! He calls me, sometimes multiple times a day, an onslaught of messages:

"Tash, it's your father, call me when you get this message."

"Tasha, I'm trying to reach you about the terrible conditions here. Call me as soon as possible!"

"Where are you, I've been trying to reach you all day!" he calls five minutes later. Some days I ignore the calls, find comfort in a solitary bowl of cereal, or yell at my daughters for leaving clothes on the floor. They know to give me a wide berth. Other days his insistence is unavoidable.

"He's called six times since we've gotten home from school!" my kids shout from the other room, never even considering answering the call themselves, which I'm glad for.

Although Ken is supportive, he didn't have much to do with making arrangements or decisions about Dad's care. My mother, who moved to Albany to be closer to our family years ago, also has little to do with him. She lives independently in an apartment near the capital. At seventy-five, she's able bodied, continues to run a one-woman prison advocacy operation out of her apartment, and spends most of her time alone. She comes to recitals and occasionally for dinner, but she long ago divorced herself from caring for my father, as did the rest of his family, uninvolved except for occasional cards and rare visits.

I talked with his social workers about bringing Frank back to his apartment. No one thought it was a good idea, but I put him on a list for a ground floor studio in his old apartment complex which would allow him to get in and out easier. I wasn't prepared to leave him someplace he hated. I hoped that maybe he would appreciate his liberties and privacy more, having recently lived without them. I hoped we could buy him a few more months or even years at home. If I were in his position, this is what I would want.

An apartment becomes available and his checkbook in hand to pay Redwood the balance owed, I discover he's spent all but $200 of the $1200 he had when he first got there. In just three short weeks he has spent over a thousand dollars—on what?

"Cigarettes and snacks from the vending machines for my new friends," he tells me proudly. It doesn't matter on what; he'd spent everything he had. This hits me with the force of a tractor-trailer that had been veering off the road for months now. What was I thinking? My father is not able to care for himself and I can't do this! I *can* pay the bill, but I can't manage the mounting pressures of schizophrenia, incontinence, and daily caregiving.

I stand up, slam the keys to his new apartment in front of him, and tell him, "You're staying! Spending all your money makes it impossible to do anything else!" And I walk out.

Nisa the office manager calls after me nervously, "Natasha, what are you doing?"

"I don't know, but I'm not taking him home," I yell back as I walk out the door. "You keep him. I can't take care of him!"

"Don't drive mad," she warned me, her now not so impressive bracelets clanging on her wrists, as I march out the door toward my car. I feel unfit to be his guardian. First, I'm taking him home, then I'm leaving him.

I call Ken and turn on the GPS, as if it could tell me where to go from here. "Turn left at the bereft father, drive out of the parking lot, and don't look back," I imagine the annoyingly calm GPS voice intoning. I take a deep breath. How do I leave a father who can't care for himself, in an institution he hates, which will never advocate for him like a family member? There's no one else to help him, and I am not the daughter who walks away. I get out of the car and go back inside.

I'm taken to the psychiatrist's office in the basement of Redwood. The psychiatrist, the social worker, and I sit in the small office piled high with patient files. We talk while we wait for them to find my father.

"I just can't leave him here. He hates it. Doesn't he have the right to grow old in a place where he's happy?" I say, rationalizing why it's my job to take him home even when I won't. "I can't stand the phone calls anymore!" I say, keeping an eye on the closed door, worried about the notes they are writing about the unreliable daughter who indulged and now wants to abandon her charge. Will they decide that I, too, am unfit to live on the outside? Because, I think irrationally, it's my behavior that's in question here.

Instead, they assure me, "We know how hard this is for you. But we can help you if you leave him with us. Frank returning home would be a mistake," the social worker offers gently. "You can't take care of him yourself!" she says. I bristle because, what does she think I've been doing my whole life? I start to cry. It's their acknowledgment of what it takes to care for him that moves me. Since my grandmother died, I have leaned on social services as a partner in the care of my father, but never before has anyone suggested it wasn't my job. Tears irrepressibly stream down my face.

Finally, they find my father and bring him into the office. They do all the talking. He listens, looking at me crying in the corner chair. The social worker who initially seemed patronizing feels more like an ally now.

"Frank, your daughter can't take care of you at home. You should stay and give this place a chance. Stay another month and you'll see it will get better," they coax him.

"Is that what you want me to do, Tasha?" he asks, watching me, tears still streaming down my face. Unable to speak, I nod my head yes. He wordlessly reaches into his back pocket, takes out his wallet, and hands me his ATM card.

"Here," he says, relinquishing his ties to life outside, his money, and his autonomy. I find this gesture heartbreaking, and the tears that have no sense of place or privacy flow like a baptism from the inside. It's another cycle of restoration; like always, he has given me the only thing he has, and I, in turn, will never abandon him.

But for now he will stay at Redwood. Although I suspect nothing has changed, except my father's immediate desire to placate my sadness, I feel lighter knowing that he will try to make it work. We walk to his room and he sits heavily on the edge of his bed, facing the window, his back to me like a heartbroken dog.

"Bye, Dad," I say, and leave without looking him in the eye.

THE SECOND LEAVING

During the next week, Dad took matters into his own hands. He smoked in his room, which was strictly forbidden, and didn't show up for medication. "I just want to leave this hell hole!" he yelled with no thought of his agreement to stay. They called for a psychiatric consult and my father was sent to the ER from Redwood.

"He's not delusional," I tell them. "He's just doing what he knows will get him kicked out." The social worker at the hospital determined Dad should go to a rehabilitation center, since he refused to return to Redwood. They sent him to a special unit for "oppositional seniors" in Connecticut to be evaluated. *Would he carry the label of schizophrenic and oppositional now?* I worried. But it was out of my hands, which in a way was a relief.

He ultimately landed at the Pawling Rehabilitation Center, where they were evaluating him for independent living. When a ground floor apartment became available where he had previously lived in Kingston, I felt I had no option but to bring him home again. I arranged for home nursing care and went to pick him up.

He was waiting in bed when I arrived. "I lost twenty pounds," he told me proudly like a child, and I was struck by how institutional care often benefitted him.

The last time I talked with him, he had told me that his friend Susan had also been transferred to Pawling for rehabilitation. Did they coordinate this? Had this all been part of a clandestine plan to steal away with each other? The idea of her managing to be in the same place as him seemed fantastic. I had the impression that she had by the end rejected being his companion, even though I didn't really ever know what their relationship amounted to. I found myself irrationally fantasizing that when I got there we would swoop her up and bring her to his Kingston apartment to live out their days together.

"Dad, let's go say goodbye to Susan and see about getting your stereo back from her room at Redwood," I say, curious to see her. We found Susan shuffling down the hall in slip-free socks and mismatched clothing. Her shoulder length chestnut colored hair had been cut short to her head, leaving mostly grey. She looked like a woman who had nothing left. Standing in front of us, she kept pulling on her stained shirt as if she wanted to hide her sagging breasts, and I wanted to cover her up; her humanity, her fragility was so palpable. I wondered how my father found this woman and why she was so compelling to me.

"Hi Susan, it's nice to see you again," I said.

She looked me in the eye with humbling recognition and said kindly, "I know you are," her change of pronoun shifting the focus from her to me in a disarming way.

"We wanted to see you and also thought we would try to get Frank's stereo that he left in your room. Would you be willing to call Redwood on my phone and get them to let us in?" I asked.

Sitting next to me hunched over with her head in her hands, she agreed, "That's fine," but she's counting to herself: two, three, four, five... as if she is counting the moments she has to bear contact with us. Was she dreading him leaving again, or was our presence disturbing to her? Dad leaned in to see her face; maybe searching for some clue about the moment she is lost in. His head is cocked to see her face, between her hands; his thick grey hair and gentle eyes remind me of a silverback ape tending to one of his own. Does he understand where she's gone? He doesn't say anything or touch her, only bears witness to the abyss she seems to be battling. I am reminded of the moments in my childhood when my father tried to comfort me at the end of the weekend. It was his desire to help without knowing how, the way neither of us knew what I needed that joined us.

"Dad, do you want to give Susan your phone number?" I asked.

He leaned in to her and repeated the question, "Susan, do you want my phone number?"

"No, I don't," she mumbled into her hands. I felt like we had betrayed her by coming, and again by leaving. I touched her shoulder and said goodbye. I felt nauseous with the act of going. I wanted to fill our shared well of sadness by staying. I was not so different from this woman. I recognized her dissociated fragments, her gentle vehemence, her grace in the face of her unreasonable loss, as my own abandoned parts.

Headed for the exit, I marched ahead of my father, angry over leaving her and all the ways it felt like being left. We passed the rooms where senior residents were watching out of time cartoons, past the limbless denizens in wheelchairs gathered next to the elevator who called out to us "See you later, alligator," as if they knew I was really a child on the run from my own pain. The exit door wouldn't open on its own. I had to bang on the blue handicapped button with my fist to get out.

LIKE JOHN WAYNE

Back in his new apartment, my father took a few bad falls, a combination of chronic oxygen deprivation (CPOD) from years of smoking and bad knees. He landed in the hospital with a CPAP machine breathing for him and it took me a whole day to get to see him; at this point, more clearly than ever, my children's lives came first. Lying in the hospital bed, his breathing was labored even with the CPAP clamped on his face. The nurses told me that he had been very unresponsive, that his electrolytes and respiration had been failing, and they had been worried about his pulling through the night. Why hadn't they called me to let me know?

He acknowledged my presence minimally, and I wondered if he could be dying. I pulled the mask off his face so we could communicate, ignoring the recurring chime, *ding, ding, ding*, which alerts the nurses' station that his mask is unattached. They ignored it too.

"Dad?" I asked loudly, as if his hearing were going rather than his will to live. "I want to know what your wishes are. How do you want this end game to look?" I said awkwardly, as if we were playing a game of chess.

He looked at me, with sad and faded eyes, and with a touch of largess, said, "Like John Wayne."

"Maybe more like the Marlboro man?" I joked, and he chuckled. I smiled too, and the older gentleman in the next bed looked over appreciatively. I had the feeling we were all relieved to be talking about what was at stake at the end of life—death. But also, I felt like a bad daughter for acknowledging that at this point, maybe his dying wishes were more important than keeping him alive? I rubbed his swollen crusty feet and asked him what he needed.

"I could use something to eat."

I got him what they would allow: broth and ginger ale, and he responded remarkably to the touch and sustenance, as if all he needed was care and a good laugh, which I hadn't been giving him much of lately.

"It's a good thing this CPAP alarm isn't a matter of life and death," I said about the alarm still chiming, and he laughed again.

"You know they're trying to kill me?" he said, seriously now. "You gotta get me out of here!"

WHEN YOU'RE HERE

With the help of the hospital social worker, I found Dad a bed at Mountain View Rehabilitation and Nursing Home in New Paltz, New York. It was a small, privately-run home that would provide psychiatric oversight and nursing care, all paid for by Dad's Medicaid and Medicare benefits. It used to be called *Blue's* because the original owners were named Mr. and Mrs. Blue, a fitting name for a man who loves jazz. It was a homey-feeling place, as nursing homes go, with small units, and residents who had family members that visited. This was key.

In his room, I found my father sitting at his desk looking in the mirror as if he didn't recognize himself in this old man's face, sunken in from a lack of teeth and slackening skin. I pulled out the groceries I'd brought for late night snacking. I arranged dates, bananas, and barbeque potato chips on his desk. Dad took the bag of chips, opened it, and began fisting chips into his mouth while half looking at himself in the mirror. Like a child, he lifted more chips than he could possibly hold and shoved them open-handed into his toothless mouth, dropping chips on the floor, licking his fingers after a few mouthfuls, unaware of anything but the chips and his appetite. I sat watching, embarrassed by his lack of decorum. After a few minutes, I folded up the bag and put it away.

"We should go to our intake meeting with the staff now," I reminded him. He seemed overmedicated, and I asked them if they could titrate back some. As his health care proxy, I told them there were certain medical interventions we didn't want, in particular, the emergency room visits for the battery of tests they perform as a matter of course, even though there was really nothing to be done to help him at this stage. At one point, they made it clear that I was actively advocating for palliative care only and had to sign papers to that effect.

"Dad, you understand what we're asking for, right?" I said, signing the papers that would limit his care. In his overmedicated stupor he didn't answer me, and I was struck by how vulnerable he was to my influence by making these decisions. I wanted to keep him comfortable, and avoid all the treatments that would prolong his life beyond his ability to enjoy it, but I felt guilty.

"Also, could we please take him off the low sugar and mashed food restrictions? Let the man eat what he wants at this stage of his life," I joked, to seem less bossy, hoping they could tell I loved this man I was relinquishing to death.

Quality of life, nonintervention, comfort, end-of-life care. I had to repeat this mantra to myself to drown out the voice inside that was wondering why I wouldn't do everything possible to extend my father's life. But also, I knew this was how we die with dignity: by not prolonging life to the point that you become a stranger to your loved ones and your own memories. I couldn't bear the thought of his joining the ranks of contorted bodies and unresponsive stares I saw in so many resident faces. It would be better to die while he still knows himself.

* * *

A few days later I showed up at the nursing home and Dad, whose medication seemed better now, reacted as if manna from heaven had just showered down. "Ahhh, Tasha you came! This is wonderful," he exclaimed, as he tried unsuccessfully to engage his belly muscles to sit up in bed. The unfettered love and appreciation he still had to share astounded me. This is life with my father, either there is danger afoot or I'm awash in his adoration.

The nursing home is small, friendly, and heartbreaking with room after room of blaring televisions and waiting seniors. "Let's sit outside," I suggested to get away from the loneliness and smell of shit that reaches out of each room into the halls. We head outside to the courtyard to play a game of chess. The garden is surrounded by the wings of the building on all sides. I set my dog, Theo, free to chew on sticks in the yard, relieved for the fresh air, and we set up the board.

"What a beautiful day," I said.

"It's always a beautiful day when you're here."

I paused to consider what, at first, seems like enthusiasm for Mountain View. "It's always a beautiful day when you're *here*." But I quickly realized the emphasis was on when *I'm there*. I tried to accept the sweetness of it. I was his link to the outside world, and yet I can't shake the implication that I am his significant other, a role I'm both attached to and have resented.

I gratefully turned my attention back to the chess game. Despite over fifty years of medication and drug use, his mind was still sharp. I saw how he positioned himself to protect his pieces while he moved in for my king. He typically won the game within five or six moves. Today, he coached me. "Get more of your power out on the board," he said, and the metaphor was not lost to me. I needed this kind of coaching in life, playing to win rather than trying to anticipate my opponent's next move. During this particular game, something clicked for me; I was able to think a few moves ahead, and with his army thinned and his king at risk, he remarked, "You're playing a fabulous game, baby!" I felt the familiar sensation of being lifted to my potential by my father's admiration. I relished that I was about to put him in check, even though he might be letting me win.

After the game, I wheeled him back to his room and noticed an open pad on his desk. In his childish handwriting he wrote:

I have waited on piles of materials. Disjointed thoughts...

Francis Williams owes twenty dollars to self for betting on sleep.

2 pairs of shoes for 2 pairs of shoes for two pairs of shoes; an excess of shoes in bed.

Dear Sir, The announcements of the baseball game as of yesterday. I have three strikes against me...

VISITING HOURS

"Ante up," said Aunt Irene, the great orchestrator of our gatherings. She came with poker chips, cards, and art supplies. Cora and Cali also made a rare appearance. "I can't stand the smell," they usually said and begged off visiting their grandfather. But today, I was grateful they were with us.

My Aunt Irene and her new wife, Claske from the Netherlands, and my Uncle Sticks had come to visit Dad at Mountain View. The family was headed to my cousin's house in Maine, and I felt the familiar sting of my father and I not being included in extended family gatherings. Still, it mattered to both of us that they came.

"Oh, great!" Dad exclaimed, sitting up in bed when they arrived.

We moved outside, ready to pick up where we had left off thirty years before sitting around Aunt Margie's dining room table playing a Penny Ante game of poker. Recently, I found a picture of myself as a baby, sitting at the table in a highchair holding a hand of cards with a shot of whisky placed at my elbow. I can imagine all the adults around the table laughing till they cried at how well I held a poker hand. This afternoon, we sat in the garden to play a game of five-card draw, chips clanging on the metal table and cards swiping the surface as we drew. All of us felt relieved for the way the game united us. You can tell a lot about a family by how they bet in poker, and this family bets low, underplays their hand, and anticipants lose.

"Come on," someone urged the next bet, "we don't have all day!"

"Hey, look at Frankie, he's winning!" Irene said, and we reveled in his victory, even if it amounted to a pile of plastic poker chips.

* * *

After a couple of hours of play, we started rehashing old stories like we always did. Uncle Sticks recounted how Frank convinced him, the younger brother, to help deliver telephone books. Dad insisted they put all the phone books in the trunk at once, weighing Frank's old Kaiser to the ground. Frank sat at the wheel as a driver, for a pittance of the pay; Sticks ran door to door and delivered all the books. Or the time Frank started to change the oil in the Kaiser but didn't get around to putting the new oil in. He and Grandpa fought in the driveway, about how Frank hadn't finished the job on the car he shared with Grandma, until Grandma, tired of the battle between them, got in the car and drove down the street until the engine seized. We laughed and laughed about all the ways my father's schemes shaped our lives, gave us comic relief from the larger impact of his illness. It was always all about Frankie, until it wasn't, and the special company packed up to leave.

* * *

Another day, my cousin David, Irene's son, a viola player, arrived for a visit. David came to see his uncle each August when the Philadelphia Orchestra took up residency at Saratoga Performing Arts Center. David had always been close with his uncle and even in the darkest times of my father's life, David made time to see him. Dad was never happier.

"Ah, David," my father said, thrilled to see him, and David

laughed at his uncle's pleasure in his company. The three of us sat in the solarium sipping red wine.

They talked about music, and David shared stories of his motorcycle adventures in Mexico, which my father simultaneously admired and worried about. Shaking his head in consternation, Dad scolded him, "You've got to protect those hands," and David smiled widely in the face of his uncle's concern. I was more concerned with David's reclusiveness.

"What's a handsome professional musician like you doing, still unmarried at almost fifty?" I asked David.

"I guess I haven't found the right woman," he said, and then admitted, "Maybe I'm not the right man. I've found the best way to live is without expectations." The lines on his handsome face showed vulnerability.

"You hold people at arm's length," my father said, looking deeply into David's eyes. "That's just who you are," he offered restoratively.

On the way back to his room, we passed the run-down piano sitting in the solarium that no one plays, not even my daughter, who can play beautifully, or my father, who hasn't played in years. Back in the day he played well, better than he played saxophone, his instrument of choice.

"Play something for us, Frankie," David asked.

"Nah," my father declined, sitting lethargically in his wheelchair with no hint of moving. David persisted, rolled the wheelchair in front of the piano, and lifted the key lid.

"Please, do it for me," the young musician urged.

Dad placed his big blocky fingers on the broken ivory keys and waited until the music moved him. I sat behind him, and David stood, leaning on the upright piano facing him. After a long delay, Dad started to clunk out a gentle but somehow grand jazz riff, awkwardly at first but the music gained momentum as he played. Like Charles Mingus, Dad's musicality is lyrical and deep with feeling. The melody resonated like the ground under a horse's hooves galloping back to the barn, surefooted, determined, going home. There is something familiar, deep, and primal about how these phrases communicate his connection with something that transcends his life, something even bigger than his delusions of grandeur or the reality of his losses.

When he finished, he brought his hands wordlessly to his lap and sat looking at the keys as if they might come back to life without his effort. David and I clapped loudly in the empty room, and Dad sat back from the piano as if it had taken something out of him to play. Like Chief in *One Flew Over the Cuckoo's Nest*, you want to follow my father. You root for him knowing there's a certain amount of danger for one whose power is so close to the heart. Together we wheeled Dad back to his room, and said our goodbyes to David.

I sat with Dad a few more minutes, wanting to be the one who stayed a little longer when out of the silence he announced:

"Tasha, I have a problem."

"What is it?" I said grudgingly, not wanting to solve his problems just then.

"Well, I need to get these chips together."

"What chips?" I ask.

"Well... " he pauses awkwardly. "I need to gather up bingo chips."

"Are you playing bingo, Dad?"

"No, not really."

"I'm confused."

"Yeah, so am I," he admits.

THE PHOENIX RISES

Bracing against his three-hundred-pound body pitching down the ramp into the yard, I wheeled my father into the sheltered garden of the home. Caring for him had become a weekly pilgrimage, not an identity worn like a battle shield, but an act of allegiance to a father whose love I still depended on. Overlooking the garden was a hallway with chairs and a large free-standing cage with two lovebirds that I usually wheeled outside when the weather was warm. But today there was someone sitting inside with them.

With a blanket on his lap, he sat waiting like a child with his hands at his side for me to finish taking food out of the bag. He still had a thick head of hair and grey whiskers that spiked unevenly out of his chin. The cloudy sadness in his eyes reminded me of a dejected alpha ape, powerful but lost to his troop. Down the hill from where we sat, there was another woman my age tucking a blanket around her father's legs. "Look, she loves her father too," he said, and it was true—of my parents, it was still my father I preferred.

I came planning to read a childhood scene I remembered but didn't know why; it would give us something to talk about. "Dad, can I read you something I'm working on?"

"Sure," he said, the autumn sunlight at our backs and pollen floating like sea animals in the still air. He lifted the roast beef sandwich on a hard roll with onions and tomatoes to his toothless mouth and began tearing off bites and gumming the food. Most people would have found it impossible to eat that sandwich without teeth, but my father was uncommonly strong and had always defied social conventions, like wearing dentures. His mouth full of sandwich and mayonnaise dripping down his chin, he took the pile of napkins I handed him and I opened my computer to read:

My father wasn't a churchgoer, but it was Easter time, and he identified with the resurrection of Christ, having delusions of being the Messiah himself. I looked to see if he reacted to my characterization of him, but he was busy eating. I continued, *We were headed to the local Catholic Church, on Long Island, a parish we had been to before whenever Dad was called by God to worship. On this day we arrived in Grandma's maroon 1948 Oldsmobile to an empty parking lot...*

"You don't remember what we were at the church for?" my father asked.

"No," I said. "It's just a shadowy scene I recall."

"Well, Tasha," he paused momentarily with a trace of both apology and thrill. "I took you because... I was in search of a priest to perform an exorcism on you, my dear," he said loud enough for anyone to hear. I felt a familiar tightening of my insides and looked around relieved to find that we were alone.

"What? No. I don't remember that. An exorcism?" I repeated quietly, vibrating now, as my cells let loose something long guarded. I recently read a neurobiologist explanation for how the stress cycle needs to be completed, like when an animal, felled in the hunt, will lie, twitching, releasing the neurological stress of the chase before dying.

"You see," he said, with a touch of manic importance, "after taking you to see *The Exorcist* the night before, it was clear to me that you were possessed by the devil! As my daughter, you were at risk, you know?" Of course, I remembered seeing the film, but I

265

hadn't connected that night with going to the church. That's why we weren't there for a service, I realized. That's why the church was empty.

"What did the priest say to you when you asked him to perform an exorcism?" I asked, incredulous.

"He probably told me to seek psychiatric help," he said, and I can feel my anger rise at the priest who sent us away, a delusional father and his eight-year-old daughter.

"Why did you take me to the film in the first place?"

"It was a good movie, Tasha, and I wanted to show you the devil in his works."

"But I was so young."

"I was losing my mind and building a case that I was the Messiah, and since you never mentioned it, I was convinced that Satan had possessed you. He would strike at my weakness, which was you, baby; that's why I took you."

The afternoon wind picked up; a flock of geese squawked in formation overhead, as I absorbed this revelation. Dad turned his attention back to tearing off chunks of sandwich with his phantom teeth. My father was trying to make sense of his world, turning the voices in his head into prophecies. In the same way that Brothers Grimm tales were meant to preserve hard-won lessons from generation to generation, my father took me to *The Exorcist* to teach me how to contend with the monsters in *his* head. He told stories of a princess who woke a sleeping dragon and convinced him to take her for a ride into the night sky. He wanted to make me royalty, to prepare me for the risks of being his daughter, for the dangers of wanting things we didn't have, but also to consider that flying closer to the astral plane was where the real action was. Maybe this was part of my fascination with birds; like my father, they weren't tethered to this planet.

I stepped inside the home and brought the lovebirds' cage outdoors. Their bird feet moved sideways on their perches into the sun. I regularly fantasized about liberating those birds.

"What if I opened the cage and let them fly free?"

"Well, Tasha, you could," he said, admiring my audacity, but knowing I wouldn't do it.

"If I could choose an animal to be, I would be a bird," I said. "Some people have flying dreams—I don't. That always seemed fanciful, but if I could *be* a bird and soar on an air current... that's what I would be." He sat unresponsive, distracted by something bigger than my transfiguration.

"What kind of animal would you be, Dad?"

"Hmm," he said, opening and closing his mouth as if chewing on the question. "I'd be an elephant," he said definitively.

"Why an elephant, Dad?"

"Because they protect their young and they remember."

* * *

As I'm shaping this story, Public Radio broadcasts the thirtieth anniversary of the making of *The Exorcist*. I'm thunderstruck to realize Cali is dancing to the theme song of the film. The modern dance piece *Welcome to the World* showcases her youth company dancing with a brother company of recently released convicts. Every time I watch the dance, the juxtaposition of the adult and youth bodies as they reach for the hope and redemption the piece offers, moves me to tears. Every arch of my daughter's back and lift of her chin offers renewal. Her grace moves like a response to the quiet trauma of my father's mental illness in our family. Even the improvement my mother sought in the eyes of incarcerated men is in the room as Cali's young body is lifted into the air by the muscled arms of convicts. I feel my grandmother's legacy of care, my father's calling, and my hunger for family all embodied in the dance.

What I also learned was that the film had been a national phenomenon. My father wasn't the only one taken hold of. Released in 1973 at twenty-four select theaters in the United States, *The Exorcist* sold out hourly to huge crowds. They stood on line in record numbers for the chance to see what a modern-day possession might mean. Many of those same audience members threw up, walked out, and even fainted from watching the film. People were perversely fascinated by the movie based on the true story of a modern-day possession. Medical and religious leaders in the US and Europe speculated about the fervor the film evoked—it was a cultural and psychological reckoning with broken homes, bad seeds, and a lack of faith. The film's argument for believing in God was its gory depiction of the existence of evil. For my father, the Messiah, it resonated with his spiritual calling and spoke directly to him about the prehistoric forces of evil that would target his children—an exorcism was the best way to protect me in his mind.

As I sit at my desk writing, Cora is playing the *Moonlight Sonata* in the other room. It's a piece my father's mother taught herself to play when she was an aspiring pianist, and her son Greg taught himself later in life. At my father's seventieth birthday party, we rented a backroom in a Parisian bistro and all of his siblings and my family came together to memorialize the man whose pain and triumphs indelibly changed us. We ate escargot, drank red wine, and I sang a difficult jazz tune, Abbey Lincoln's "Down Here Below"—"*You made me just the way to be... a heart with feeling eyes to see, a spirit free that says I can... I am here because there's you*"—which in hindsight, is an ode to God, the significance of which was lost on me until now. Afterwards, my uncle played the *Moonlight Sonata*. This may be where she heard it first. Cora plays it beautifully, and each note, every pause, her choosing to learn the piece offers me the possibility of release. That song reverberates through the initial conditions of my forbears, like the flutter of a butterfly impossibly traveling the continents. Similarly, the act of possession in our family has carried through the generations. When my father was ill, he seemed to lose custody of who he was. In this same way, his biggest fear was that his children and grandchildren would be vulnerable to a possession, either by the devil or by his same illness. As his daughter and as a mother, his fears seem so human, so paternal to me, and although it was confusing to be his daughter, he never stopped feeling responsible for the ones he loved, and that is the part of our story that really matters.

As my children repurpose the art that shaped our family, the melancholy of the sonata, and the redemption of the dance, bear witness to the lives that came before us, *lives possessed by misfortune* that shaped us even as we cast them off. My chain-smoking ancestors provided the ashes for the rising of the Phoenix I witness every day in my children.

IN MY DREAMS

I had never had a dream before where my safety depended on my husband. I always fought off bad guys alone, often naked and unable to cover myself in a public place. I often dream I am unprepared for work and can't make copies or get to meetings on time. I ramble around the houses of my grandparents, my mother, and occasionally the apartments of my past; sometimes my kids are there and even my parents, but for the twenty years I've been married, my unconscious registered my autonomy like an unfaithful wife. I have felt guilty or in some way disloyal never depending on Ken in my dreams.

But then one day, there he was in my dream, catching me from a free fall off a cliff. When I woke up, I felt so relieved, not only about being saved but because Ken was finally showing up in my dreams. Ken has been a constant partner, self-reflective and loving, he never begrudged my caring for my father. In fact, in the end, it was Ken whom my father was willing to let wipe his ass; it was Ken who entered the bathroom with rubber gloves and came out with a cinched bag for me to dispose of. It has been Ken who reminded me that my father was lucky to have me. But why did I feel responsible for his not being in my dreams in the first place?

Why this feeling of infidelity? Is it a remnant of the guilt I felt at separating from my father? Was it my difficulty trusting the people I love to remain who I think they are? Is it guilt I'm still carrying from the high stakes of fealty in our family?

THE PARTS OF HIM I LOST

My father's approach to dying was as chaotic as his living. One day he was alert and conversational, and the next he couldn't breathe. His last week was no exception. Early in the week, he was in the hospital, then he was filled with a resurgence of energy that, I've heard from hospital staff, often accompanies the end.

Dad wanted me to get a shower gift for Lamiya. Lamiya, who the staff referred to as "Frankie's wife," was assigned as his aide at Mountain View. She was thirtyish with dark brown skin, a variety of fabulous wigs, and Asian letters tattooed along the side of her neck. Dad loved her toughness, and she relished being able to be herself as his caregiver. She was pregnant and about to have a baby. Between them, they joked that the child was theirs.

"Do you want me to get something for the baby?" I asked.

"I was thinking you could get Lamiya a dress," he said, making a characteristically untraditional gift choice. Then he shook his head from side to side in mock consternation. "I don't know how I got hoodwinked into this whole baby thing!"

"What do you mean?" I asked, pretending not to understand.

"You know about this baby being mine," he said, smiling like a Cheshire cat. "The baby looks just like me, you know," he said, making eye contact now, since we'd gotten to what was really at stake—that his love for Lamiya had in some way resulted in her pregnancy, an immaculate conception! I consider the features of the little boy from the picture on the corner of Dad's mirror, who bears no resemblance to my father. Plus, I'm pretty sure Dad's been impotent for some time.

"Do you still think you're the Messiah after all these years?"

"Nah," he said, with a half-hearted dismissal.

Lamiya left her coat and shoes in his room when she came to work, and towards the end he was prone to calling out to her at night.

"Help, help, help!" he shouted.

"What you yelling about?" she demanded, standing with her hands on her hips, at his door.

"It's a matter of survival, baby."

Two days later, Ken and I got to the nursing home and Dad was passed out; he had torn off the CPAP mask in his sleep and gone unconscious. I instinctively yelled out, "No, no, I haven't said goodbye!" and Ken knuckled my father's chest and brought my father back to consciousness. They sent him back to the hospital.

By the time I got there, a shot of prednisone had breathed new life into him. I found him sitting up, half-naked, his faded DNA tattoo the same pastel tones as the hospital gown that had fallen off his shoulders. He was energized and shouted at me, "Where have you been? You know you have to stay close now," as if he knew these were his last days.

"Yes, I know, Dad," But it was the fourth time he'd gone unconscious from oxygen deprivation in recent months. I'd felt on the verge of losing him before.

Back at Mountain View, the staff finally agreed to abide by our decision for palliative care only.

* * *

I called my family, including my mother, to let them know it was time to say goodbye. I did some research, not for the first time, to see if I could find Barbara, and found an obituary from the previous December at a funeral parlor in Baldwin, Long Island, where her family lived. There were no surviving family members named or contacts listed. I could only assume this was Dad's Barbara and that she had died.

My cousin David and Katharine, his partner at the time, were the first to arrive. We gathered around my father's bedside to Skype with David's mother, Irene, in Holland.

"Frankie, I love you," she said, crying, a disembodied head on the phone screen. "Is there anything you want to say to me?"

"Nah," he said, and we all laughed.

Even though I knew it was necessary, arranging hospice care felt like another betrayal. I called in the hospice worker. David and Katharine sat in on the family meeting. With the hospice worker as witness, I confirmed the decision with Dad.

"Because you don't want to be on a ventilator and your oxygen is tanking without the CPAP, I've called in hospice, Dad, which means we are going to stop giving you medicine and focus on keeping you comfortable. Is that what you want?"

"That sounds reasonable," he answered.

The hospice worker looked at me and said, "Well, that's a gift."

I wondered why it felt so wrong.

A little later, sitting alone with him, I reluctantly asked, "Dad, I know you've said you want to be buried, but I would find it comforting to have your ashes. When the time comes, what do you want me to do?"

"When the time comes, you'll bury me," he said simply. I realize now that the Messiah needed to keep his body intact.

* * *

The next day my mother, Ken, Cali and Cora, my two uncles, their spouses and adult children arrived. The ten of us squeezed around the edges of his room, our conversation accented by the *psha, psha* of his CPAP mask. Silently he began looking at each of us, and the room fell quiet as he acknowledged the family who stood by him. Wordlessly he made space for each of us in that moment to face his love.

Ken encouraged our dog to jump onto the bed to sit between Dad's legs, which made him smile for the second to last time. We reminisced. John Paul's wife Nancy recounted, "The first time Gus, at six years old, met his Uncle Frank, I was in the kitchen and overheard Gus asking Frank, 'Why don't you have any teeth?'"

"'Well, that's a long story, young man, but I will tell you, by all means avoid state-paid dentists,' Frank advised."

We all laughed and cried at the injustices my father had shouldered and tried to warn against. That Medicaid dentist had pulled every tooth out of his mouth for dentures well before his strong teeth had given up the ghost.

When it was time to leave, everyone stood up to say their goodbyes. My mother patted Dad's chest and said, "It's been a good ride, Frank."

Uncle Sticks said, "Don't try to steal home," which made my father grin from ear to ear even behind the oxygen mask.

I took Dad's advice and stayed close. I slept at the nursing home on a recliner in his room and advocated for morphine to make him comfortable. The second night, he woke up disoriented and bent on climbing out of bed.

"Dad, please, you can't walk. You'll fall down."

"Why can't I get out of bed?" he raged at me with his last words, his eyes full of the determination with which he lived his life.

In the morning, shallow inhalations rattled in his chest. As I looked through his clothes in his armoire to find him a clean shirt, he stopped breathing. He took his last breath while I wasn't looking. I've heard that happens, that it's easier to go without anyone to pull you back.

* * *

My father died on February 26th, 2017, six days after my birthday. That weekend we buried him in the woods, in the green section of our local cemetery. Wrapped in a canvass shroud befitting the Messiah, he was laid out on a pine board with handles. Our three family dogs ran circles around the graveside as we stood together on a freezing cold gray afternoon and memorialized him.

When I went to my father's graveside for the first time to plant tulip and daffodil bulbs, the soft ground above his grave had sunk down, and I felt drawn into the space where he used to be.

> *It wasn't until your body was gone,*
> *that I felt the space that was you leaving.*
> *Missing was the large belly that cushioned our losses,*
> *and eyes that saw through to me,*
> *and those hands, those tar-stained, steady hands,*
> *which sheltered mine, even when you didn't feel sound,*
> *especially then.*
>
> ~
>
> *We have a lifetime of devotion to each other:*
> *Me, the daughter, who found refuge in your love*
> *You, who found redemption in your children,*
>
> ~
>
> *I once asked what kind of animal you would be,*
> *you told me, "An elephant"*
> *"Why an elephant?" I asked,*
> *"Because they protect their young, and they remember"*

Epilogue

On the anniversary of my father's death as the Covid pandemic swept into the United States, I did three things I swore I would never do.

First, I went looking on the Internet for the four missing children my father had with Barbara. In writing this story, it seemed cowardly not to investigate. How could I take a measure of our life without knowing what became of his other children? I knew Barbara's sister and brother had adopted at least three of the four remaining children, but I wasn't sure where they were living. More importantly, I didn't know if they were okay. The last time I saw the two oldest kids was over thirty years ago at the funeral of my half sister, their youngest sibling at the time; I was twenty-one and they were ten and six. I had never met the other two.

Even though I had long ago decided against caring what became of them, even though they might choose to have nothing to do with me, I wanted to know how their lives had turned out. I also wanted them to know how much their father had loved them from afar. "They took all my children, baby," he would complain when the conversation lagged and he had time to consider his losses. Not *all*, but I had long ago stopped being a child to him.

I found a family with the right last names that lived in the state I knew they had lived in at one time. Then I did the second thing I never thought I would do. I paid a stealth online search engine for their full names and contact information so I could search for them.

When I found Katarina on Facebook, it was like looking back in time at a photo of her mother. She looked so much like Barbara it was undeniable I had found one of them. There were pictures of two sisters and two brothers who looked remarkably like Frank in different ways. In the pictures, they stood arm in arm on the beach with tan faces and big smiles. They appeared to have successful lives, and they had each other—and in that moment I felt alone. I had been the only one left with him.

I was sure I had found them but increasingly less sure that they would want to hear from me. Years ago, they had lost contact with our father. Plus, I wasn't sure what they knew or didn't know about who their birth parents were. I ruminated for days, unsure if I should reach out, sitting with a familiar longing for something that wasn't mine to have. They had their own family.

In the end, I decided they could ignore me if they chose to. I would try not to take it personally.

Good morning, I'm not sure of the best way to introduce myself- I'm the daughter of Frank Williams. He had a long-term relationship with Barbara B., who you may or may not know as a member of your extended family? I sent you a message via Facebook, and would welcome a chance to connect- Natasha

Her reply popped up on messenger the next day:

Natasha! Oh my gosh! I would love to! This is so exciting. I've been wondering how to get a hold of you. Do you have time tomorrow to talk? Say around noon EST? Or this afternoon even! I don't have to catch a flight until 4pm. If that doesn't work let me know what times work for you. Can't wait! Here's my number: 9*********. Also, can you let me know what your number is so I don't ignore it thinking *it's a robo call :)- Katarina*

We spoke that afternoon for over an hour. She told me her older brother, Elias, and the next youngest sister, Kayla, were raised by Barbara's sister, Elsie, and her husband. They had moved to Atlanta for her adoptive dad's work; this is part of why they lost touch with Frank and Barbara. The youngest brother, Joshua, was adopted by Barbara's brother and lived on Long Island. He was 10 years old before he learned that his cousins were in fact his siblings.

She asked about Frank, and I told her he had died in 2017. I had tried to contact the family, had looked for Barbara at the time and found an obituary in Hempstead with no surviving relatives.

No, Katarina told me, Barbara was alive and well in an assisted living facility. *Amazing.* We made a plan to meet in person a week later when I was in New York City for work.

In the meanwhile, I received a voicemail: "Hi, this is Elias, your half brother. Katarina told me she spoke with you and I would like to talk with you too," he said in a way that seemed both inviting and demanding. I had spent my life avoiding these siblings and now they were making it clear they wanted contact. As it happened, I was going to Philadelphia that weekend with my husband, which was thirty minutes from Elias. We made a plan to meet for dinner while Ken was at a work function.

I got to the restaurant early and sat nervously waiting. When he arrived, we hugged and sat down. I was looking into the face of a young blond version of my father. He had Frank's square jaw and engaging eyes, and he moved like Frank—deliberate movements that felt like shared cellular DNA. I ordered a drink. He doesn't drink, he said, ordering seltzer. He was upfront about his positions from the start. "I'll tell you—I don't consider Frank and Barbara my parents. I call Barbara periodically for birthdays, but it's not easy for me."

"That makes sense," I said. Katarina had reminded me that he lived with Frank and Barbara on and off in the first two years of his life and it had affected his verbal and emotional development as a child. Their adoptive parents had done a lot of early intervention to get him talking. He said he was glad when their family moved to Atlanta and the contact with Frank and Barbara stopped. "We had a normal childhood during those years."

"What was your mother like?" he asked as we traded stories, maybe wondering if she was the reason I came out okay.

"Well, she was complicated, but she made sure I went to school and had a place to go when Frank got crazy."

He asked about other members of the Williams family: aunts, uncles, and cousins. We discovered, like my uncles and cousins, Elias liked motorcycles. I texted David, who lived in Philly and had been invited to join us but wasn't able. "He has a Suzuki Hayabusa."

"Oh, he likes speed." David texted back. Elias wanted to meet more of the family when Covid allowed. I said they wanted to meet him, and Philly would be a good meeting spot since we have family in DC and Maryland too.

Sitting with Elias, I imagined this was what it would have been like to meet my young father when he was handsome and sane with a promising future. Elias was a successful lawyer with a full-time practice and a wife and children. I pictured my mother having just met Frank at that party and how she went back, compelled to find out more. There was something self-contained and mysterious about this second offspring of my father. Something inscrutable. He was direct and curious, but I had the sense there was a lot more going on with him than he would tell. Maybe more than he cared to know himself? I thought my father's wordless companionship was a product of his schizophrenia and the effects of the medication, but sitting with Elias, I had the revelation that our father's economy of words and ponderousness was something essential about him—not a symptom of his schizophrenia—part of something fundamental to the person he was.

When we finished our meal, I walked Elias to the central train station near my hotel and wondered about his wife and children. Who were they? What were they like? "What did your wife think about our meeting?" I asked.

"I didn't tell her," he answered.

My meeting with Katarina the next week was March 12, 2020, the day after the CDC declared Covid a pandemic and the day before NYC was essentially shutdown with the first Covid outbreak on Friday the 13th. We met near Grand Central Station in Manhattan at a large Mexican restaurant I knew of. I waited for her outside the restaurant at the corner of 40th and Lexington Avenue and recognized her in the crowd of people walking toward the restaurant, a petite 5'3, like all the women in our family. Her confident stride stirred a mix of admiration and insecurity. Would we like each other? How was this going to go?

Even though the pandemic was at our doorstep, we looked at each other, arms outstretched, and hugged. She wore a sophisticated knit dress and knee-high boots, and her blonde hair was pulled on top of her head. She took charge and suggested we should sit at a table and eat something even though she wasn't "exactly hungry." I love people who aren't afraid to take charge. Her eyes were dark blue, and some hair fell around her face in tufts she curled and played with as we talked. She told me how open Elsie had been about who their parents were, how their father had adopted all three of the kids, and how she lost him to cancer around the same year Frank died in 2017. Her response to me was open and welcoming, but she said, "I keep to myself most of the time," which I remember about Barbara.

After a close call with cancer, she started her own business to develop a mobile app, which she was developing and acquiring a patent for. It would help consumers identify food and personal care products on a color scale—green was good, or yellow and red not so good—for people with cancer and other chronic diseases like diabetes and heart disease. (It's officially patented now, btw. She's officially a US inventor.) Frank, the inventor, would have been so proud—not to compare his imagined powers with her innovation, but our father would have been proud.

She told me she definitely worried about her own sanity at times, knowing she had two schizophrenic parents. "We all knew our father and mother were both schizophrenic. Schizophrenia is a continuum," she said with the straightforward courage I've come to recognize in her, more concerned with how to articulate her ideas than with my reaction. "It's really all the same. When my phone went off, played music, or I heard disembodied talking, I was sure I was hearing voices. My mind was all over the place. You should see my wall. With my business—it's like *A Beautiful Mind*. People walk in and wonder how I contain the chaos!" She mentioned being diagnosed with something—was it attention deficit disorder (ADD)? My mind leaps—maybe why I missed what she said or maybe she never clearly said.

"I remember when Jackie died. We were trying to get her, you know? The week before the accident, we went to visit and took Jackie out to take family pictures. I was two. Elsie was going to use them to try to get custody." She tears up, propping up her hair with her hands again. I want to reach across the table and put my hand on hers, but it feels too soon for that.

"What I want to know is what happened when Frank and Barbara split up for good?" she asks directly about the last time they saw each other, not unlike Elias trying to understand the parent they only knew through their aunts and uncles' opinion of him.

"Frank called me for help because he said a dirty cop was trying to frame him for drugs. He said Barbara, who may have been street walking for him, had disappeared," I said cautiously.

"Barbara didn't disappear. She went back to LI to check herself into the hospital. She was pregnant, went off her meds to protect the baby, and was afraid of Frank," Katarina tells me, not responding to the potential trafficking.

"The other children came after Jackie's death? I didn't know. I thought they were born earlier than Jackie when they still lived on LI." God, it was hard to imagine them having two more children in the condition they were in.

"What kind of man was Frank?" Katarina asks more pointedly. "My uncle said he was violent toward Barbara. He doesn't want us to talk about Frank—worries it will upset her."

"It's a side of him I have never seen," I respond, "but my mother told me that once when Frank was losing his mind, he punched her in the belly when she was nine months pregnant with me. I was shocked—honestly, I didn't believe her. It's something I've been trying to reconcile because when I ask family and friends about this side of him, they all say he was never violent, passive even. But when I press his siblings on the topic, more than one person in the family confirmed that he pushed Barbara down the stairs once when she was pregnant with one of the other children."

"This is what Elsie and my uncle said happened," says Katarina. "According to Barbara she purposely fell down the stairs to hide the fact that freak punched her when she was pregnant."

"Irene, his sister, has stories of how cruel Frank was when he was crazy, but again, I never saw that." *Did something flip when he was losing his mind? Was there pent-up anger at his mother? Was he afraid of the responsibility of a baby despite how much he wanted it?*

How did his illness change him? I wanted to know. Even after growing up with him and caring for him into old age, I wasn't sure.

I was struck by how we were both asking the same question. Trying to understand who our father was—beyond his schizophrenia, what kind of man was he? I was searching for an adult understanding, separate from my idealized version of my father. Was he a good man whose life was informed by empathy? Did he really teach me about love, or was his passivity a perfect palette for me to imbue with the love I wanted? I paused and considered what to say to this beautiful young woman he brought into the world

"What I can tell you about him is that he had tremendous empathy and understanding. Those who knew him and even those who just met him felt he could see what was essential about them. He would have made you feel seen and loved."

She had tears in her eyes and scrunched her hair again and said, "People say that about me. That I have empathy. Maybe that's where I get it? Barbara still says he's the love of her life."

I love Katarina's drive to understand and show herself. She reminds me of a series of strong women in our family; even though we hardly know each other, we have traits in common.

We left each other with promises to arrange a meeting between the two families, sure we would see each other again once the pandemic passed.

Over time I spoke with the two youngest siblings by phone and Facetime. Kayla lived in San Diego, where my sister Laura lives, and the other son, Joshua, who was adopted by Barbara's brother, lived at home with his parents on LI. He was just over thirty years old and in school getting a master's in music composition. Our father would have been impressed.

Since the pandemic persisted longer than any of us imagined, we scheduled a couple of group virtual meetups where my aunts and uncles got to meet the new nieces and nephews. Like in Hollywood Squares, we viewed each other in boxes, for a game of figuring out what is enduring about a family you've only imagined over the years.

Between them, Frank and Barbara had five children. Statistically, those kids were twenty percent more likely to inherit the schizophrenia. One in five could have the disease... but that's a story for someone else to tell. Our father brought six children into the word despite his mental illness. There are five remaining who wouldn't have it any other way. All of us with the same blueprint for body parts and height, the same proteins that fold and combine to form our curiosities and fears. We took his depth, his features, and a certain way our hands are animated by ideas that can't be touched or seen.

* * *

REFERENCES

BOOKS

Damasio, Antonio. *Feeling & Knowing: Making Minds Conscious.* Pantheon, 2021.
Greenberg, Michael. *Hurry Down Sunshine: A Father's Journey Through Love and Madness.* Other Press, 2009.
Kolker, Robert. *Hidden Valley Road: Inside the Mind of an American Family.* Doubleday, 2020.
Kuhn, Harold W., and Sylvia Nasar. *The Essential John Nash.* Princeton University Press, 2007.
May, Rollo. *The Courage to Create.* W.W. Norton and Co., 1994.
Saks, Elyn. *The Center Cannot Hold: My Journey Through Madness.* Hachette Books, 2008.
Solomon, Andrew. *Far From the Tree: Parents, Children and the Search for Identity.* Scribner, 2012.

ARTICLES

Bortolon, Catherine, and Stéphane Raffard. "Dissociation Mediates the Relationship Between Childhood Trauma and Experiences of Seeing Visions in a French Sample." *The Journal of Nervous and Mental Disease*, vol. 206, no. 11, Nov. 2018, pp. 850-858. doi: 10.1097/NMD.0000000000000885.
Boström, P.K., and J. Strand. "Children and Parents with Psychosis—Balancing Between Relational Attunement and Protection from Parental Illness." *Journal of Child and Adolescent Psychiatric Nursing*, vol. 34, no. 1, Feb. 2021, pp. 68-76. doi: 10.1111/jcap.12302. Epub 7 Dec. 2020. PMID: 33285033; PMCID: PMC7898685.
Cepelewicz, Jordana. "The Brain Doesn't Think the Way You Think It Does." *Quanta Magazine*, Aug. 2021.
"Divers Save Drowned Tot." *New York Post*, Apr. 1986.
Elbogen, E. B., et al. "Beyond Mental Illness: Targeting Stronger and More Direct Pathways to Violence." *Clinical Psychological Science*, vol. 4, no. 5, 2016, pp. 747-759.
https://doi.org/10.1177/2167702615619363.
Engels, Mary, and Stuart Marques. "Back from a Watery Grave." *Daily News*, 11 Apr.

1986.

---. "'Miracle' Girl Breathing on Her Own." *Daily News*, 12 Apr. 1986.

Murray, Evan D., et al. "The Role of Psychotic Disorders in Religious History Considered." *Journal of Neuropsychiatry and Clinical Neurosciences*, vol. 24, no. 4, Fall 2012. http://neuro.psychiatryonline.org.

Junginger, John. "Psychosis and Violence: The Case for a Content Analysis of Psychotic Experience." *Schizophrenia Bulletin*, vol. 22, no. 1, 1996, pp. 91-103.

Lacan, Jacques. *The Seminar of Jacques Lacan: The Four Fundamental Concepts of Psychoanalysis, Revised Edition*. Edited by J. Alain Miller, translated by Alan Sheridan, W.W. Norton, 1981.

Longden, Eleanor. "The Voices in My Head." *YouTube*, uploaded by TED, 8 Aug. 2013, https://www.youtube.com/watch?v=DjD6_mW7CUc.

Marcolin, M.A. "The Prognosis of Schizophrenia Across Cultures." *Ethnicity and Disease*, vol. 1, no. 1, Winter 1991, pp. 99-104. PMID: 1842526.

O'Reagan, Kirsten. "11 John Nash Quotes to Make You Think." *Bustle*, 24 May 2015, https://www.bustle.com/articles/85470-11-thought-provoking-john-nash-quotes-that-are-as-offbeat-wonderful-as-he-was. July 2024.

Ritunnano, Rosa, et al. "Subjective Experience and Meaning of Delusions in Psychosis: A Systematic Review and Qualitative Evidence Synthesis." *The Lancet Psychiatry*, vol. 9, Jun. 2022. www.thelancet.com/psychiatry.

Sartorius, N., et al. "Two-Year Follow-Up of the Patients Included in the WHO International Pilot Study of Schizophrenia." *Psychological Medicine*, vol. 7, no. 3, Aug. 1977, pp. 529-541. doi: 10.1017/s0033291700004517. PMID: 905470.

Silverman, M.J. "The Influence of Music on the Symptoms of Psychosis: A Meta-Analysis." *Journal of Music Therapy*, vol. 40, no. 1, Spring 2003, pp. 27-40. doi: 10.1093/jmt/40.1.27. PMID: 17590966.

Skeem, J., et al. "Psychosis Uncommonly and Inconsistently Precedes Violence Among High-Risk Individuals." *Clinical Psychological Science*, vol. 4, no. 1, 2016, pp. 40-49. https://doi.org/10.1177/2167702615575879.

Spiel, Shira, et al. "Intergenerational Trauma, Dependency, and Detachment." *The Journal of Nervous and Mental Disease*, vol. 211, no. 9, Sep. 2023, pp. 679-685. doi: 10.1097/NMD.000000000000168.

Swain, Frederick, et al. "Four Psilocybin Experiences." *The Psychedelic Review*, vol. 1, no. 2, Fall 1963, https://maps.org/2007/11/13/psychedelic-review-archive/.

Taylor, Pamela J. "In Review: Psychosis and Violence: Stories, Fears, and Reality." *The Canadian Journal of Psychiatry*, vol. 53, no. 10, Oct. 2008, pp. 647-659. doi:10.1177/070674370805301004.

Tesli, Natalia, et al. "White Matter Matters: Unraveling Violence in Psychosis and Psychopathy." *Schizophrenia Bulletin Open*, vol. 2, no. 1, Jan. 2021, sgab026, https://doi.org/10.1093/schizbullopen/sgab026.

Acknowledgments

Thank you to the writer and professor James Lasdun, who read my essay "The Second Coming" about finding assisted living for my aging schizophrenic father and encouraged me to write the whole story. To Marlene Adelstein, who edited my early draft and kept asking, "Where's the mother in all this?" To my mother, who asked, "Don't you think I should read the book?" and who fostered the independence it took to say, "Not yet." To my aunt Irene who read, edited and encouraged this book into being over many years. Thank you, New York State Writers Institute and the Fine Arts Work Center, where this work started and continued. To our library writing group, who helped me believe in the writing when I didn't. To the posse of six writers who met working with Alison Williams and Dinty Moore and continue to meet virtually. We launched essays and books and continue to support each other. To my dear friends and beta readers, Tracey Dewart, Daisy Foote, Darcey Smith, Kristin Flynn, Dee Pitcock, Amy Weiss, Jackie Somas, and Tom Nussbaum for reading earlier drafts and helping me shape the story. And for Tom's generous and invaluable coaching in pitching the book at the Bread Loaf Writers Conference. To James Baldwin, Toni Morrison, Ocean Vuong, Leslie Jamison, Justin Torres, Alex Marzano-Lesnevich, and the many other writers who have been my refuge and inspiration. And . . . to the mental health organizations that support families standing by loved ones with mental illness.

About the Author

The Parts of Him I Kept is Natasha Williams debut book. She has an MA from the University of Pennsylvania and attended the Bread Loaf School of English and the Bread Loaf Writers Conference. Excerpts and essays have been published in the *Bread Loaf Journal, Change Seven, LIT, Memoir Magazine, Onion River Review, Writers Digest, Writers Read, Post Road,* and *South Dakota Review*.

Apprentice House Press
Loyola University Maryland

Apprentice House is the country's only campus-based, student-staffed book publishing company. Directed by professors and industry professionals, it is a nonprofit activity of the Communication Department at Loyola University Maryland.

Using state-of-the-art technology and an experiential learning model of education, Apprentice House publishes books in untraditional ways. This dual responsibility as publishers and educators creates an unprecedented collaborative environment among faculty and students, while teaching tomorrow's editors, designers, and marketers.

Eclectic and provocative, Apprentice House titles intend to entertain as well as spark dialogue on a variety of topics. Financial contributions to sustain the press's work are welcomed. Contributions are tax deductible to the fullest extent allowed by the IRS.

To learn more about Apprentice House books or to obtain submission guidelines, please visit www.apprenticehouse.com.

Apprentice House Press
Communication Department
Loyola University Maryland
4501 N. Charles Street
Baltimore, MD 21210
Ph: 410-617-5265
info@apprenticehouse.com • www.apprenticehouse.com

www.ingramcontent.com/pod-product-compliance
Lightning Source LLC
Chambersburg PA
CBHW031422150426
43191CB00006B/361